D0801015

797.14

# TEAM SPIRIT

# TEAM SPIRIT

## LIFE AND LEADERSHIP ON ONE OF THE WORLD'S TOUGHEST YACHT RACES

**BRENDAN HALL** FOREWORD BY
**SIR ROBIN KNOX-JOHNSTON**

MAIDENHEAD LIBRARY
13 APR 2013
01 628 796 969

This adventure is a gripping read for the armchair sailor, non-sailor, any skipper and for that matter business leader.

Honest, insightful, informative and underlined by the fact that as a team they won.

Bravo.

**Pete Goss, British yachtsman, Vendée Globe competitor and author of *Close to the Wind***

A really great read for anyone interested in team performance at the very highest level, coupled with a fascinating insight into human endeavour in a pressure cooker environment.

**Paul Bennett, Director, Henley Business School**

*Team Spirit* is an insightful and honest story of the real ingredients of success. In most aspects of life, success derives from a focused team acting in harmony with clear and decisive leadership. These skills are invariably prerequisite in the crucible of offshore ocean racing, and never so brilliantly demonstrated as in Brendan Hall's book.

**Chris Masterson, Chairman, Montagu Private Equity**

My personal exposure to extreme challenges and an unforgiving, competitive environment is limited to dry land and motor racing; building the Formula One team that became Honda GP, Brawn GP and now Mercedes GP, so I was exposed to the meticulous planning, the careful people management, pure hard work and the extreme stresses involved in trying to accomplish big tasks.

Brendan forced himself through an incredible adventure that tested him as both skipper and leader. When the pressure increased, his instincts, training, attitude and clear thought kicked in. It doesn't surprise me that he was able to keep his crew motivated and bring his yacht home in first place.

In this book, Brendan demonstrates that he is not just able to learn wisdom from others, but also pioneer many solutions that can readily be applied to business scenarios, and he has been able to record these in a compelling and exciting manner.

**Adrian Reynard, Founder of Reynard Racing Cars**

This book is as much a team management manual as it is an exciting and well-written account of a great ocean adventure. Brendan Hall's lessons about preparation, people skills and persistence make it required reading for budding CEOs and team leaders, as well as anyone putting a crew together to sail a boat.

**Roger McMillan, Editor, *Australian Sailing + Yachting* magazine**

Published by Adlard Coles Nautical
an imprint of Bloomsbury Publishing Plc
50 Bedford Square, London WC1B 3DP
www.adlardcoles.com

Copyright © Brendan Hall 2012, 2013

First published by Adlard Coles Nautical in 2012
This paperback edition published 2013
Reprinted 2018, 2019

Hardback: 978-1-4081-5750-3
Paperback: 978-1-4081-8799-9
ePub: 978-1-4081-5865-4
ePDF: 978-1-4081-5864-7

All rights reserved. No part of this publication may be reproduced in any form
or by any means – graphic, electronic or mechanical, including photocopying,
recording, taping or information storage and retrieval systems – without the
prior permission in writing of the publishers.

The right of the author to be identified as the author of this work has been
asserted by her in accordance with the Copyright, Designs and Patents Act,
1988.

A CIP catalogue record for this book is available from the British Library.

This book is produced using paper that is made from wood grown in managed,
sustainable forests. It is natural, renewable and recyclable. The logging and
manufacturing processes conform to the environmental regulations of the
country of origin.

Photos courtesy of the author and Clipper Ventures
Typeset in 10 pt HaarlemmerMT by Saxon Graphics Ltd, Derby
Printed and bound in Great Britain by CPI Group (UK) Ltd, Croydon CR0 4YY

**Note**: while all reasonable care has been taken in the publication of this book,
the publisher takes no responsibility for the use of the methods or products
described in the book.

FSC
www.fsc.org
MIX
Paper from
responsible sources
FSC® C020471

# CONTENTS

# ROUTE MAP OF THE 2009–2010 CLIPPER ROUND THE WORLD YACHT RACE

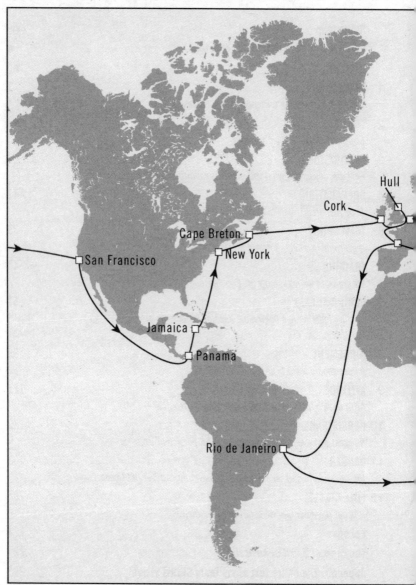

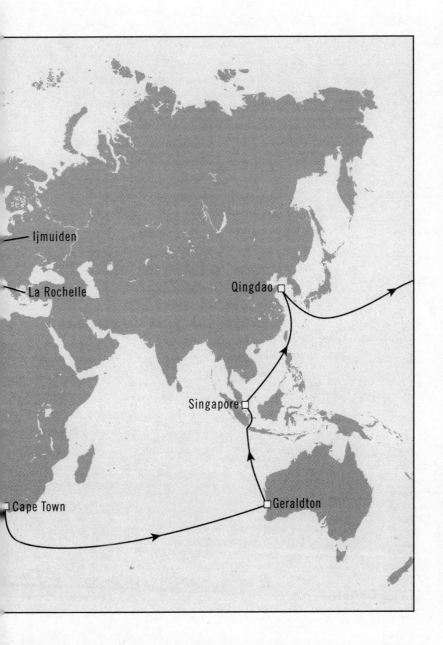

Ijmuiden

La Rochelle

Qingdao

Singapore

Cape Town

Geraldton

# FOREWORD

Don't we all like to win? Competition, whether against other humans or the environment, is an integral part of human nature and one of the reasons we humans have developed into the prime animal on this planet. We can compete on our own or in teams, but the moment we have more than one person in a competitive unit we have to find methods to overcome the inherent instinct for people to behave as individuals, and work instead as one. But how to create an effective, harmonious and competitive crew from a group of disparate characters? This is a question asked by chief executives of businesses and skippers of yachts all over the world. We know that the more we can create a well-motivated and harmonious team, in whatever field, the better the results we will achieve.

But how to achieve this?

The crew of a yacht comes from diverse backgrounds, and often different countries. Their attitudes, formed by their upbringing, work and experience, do not provide homogeneous raw material. Bringing them all together successfully so they pull in the same direction, and are motivated to put all their efforts into achieving the one objective of winning as an effective team, is an art that is almost as elusive as the Holy Grail.

Living in a small boat is like being in a pressure cooker. Everyone is packed together in a confined space, with limited privacy. The crew works unsociable hours and shares the risks that are an inevitable part of crossing any ocean. There is no escape when living cheek by jowl for prolonged periods. You are as isolated from the world as if you were in space. It can take only one member of the crew to be out of step, not pull their weight, be overly opinionated or criticise everyone else, to turn what should be a thoroughly enjoyable experience into a nightmare. It is for the skipper to prevent this from happening.

People think that the skipper's task is just barking orders and supervising the crew. There is far more to it than that. At Clipper we choose our skippers very carefully, being far more impressed by their experience than their pieces of paper denoting marine qualifications. We know that most of the skipper's time is taken up with personnel management and we do our best to prepare them for the challenges they will face over long months racing around the world. They have to be slightly distant to avoid any signs of favouritism; they have to be technically capable; they have to be good planners; and they have to watch the individual members to prevent small worries turning into major issues. People will handle this differently but it is not an easy job, and anyone who has successfully skippered a Clipper yacht around the world has shown the sort of qualities that businesses cry out for.

Brendan shows how he dealt with it all, and brought in his boat and crew as winners. This is a thoughtful read for anyone contemplating a long ocean voyage, whether as crew or skipper. It has many lessons for how to get the best out of a group of people. Brendan did his research, worked out what he thought would be best, and then put it into practice. As the story of *Spirit of Australia*'s odyssey unfolds, we share the successes and failures as he and his crew worked together to achieve their final, well-deserved victory.

Sir Robin Knox-Johnston

# PREFACE

I was so worried, I was physically sick.

I've skippered a lot of boats in heavy weather, but I'd never felt like this before. The only thought in my mind was that people die in conditions like this.

The boat lurched sideways as it was struck by another massive North Pacific wave and I was thrown against the wall of the boat toilet. I caught a glimpse of myself in the small mirror and the fear was written on my face.

*Come on! Be strong, Brendan. We'll get through this. You'll keep them safe. Man up. Be strong.*

Outside, up on the deck of our 68ft racing yacht, the crew struggled to turn the wheel as we were struck side-on by that 50ft wave. The impact was like being T-boned by a lorry. The boat jolted sideways and lay over on its side. A 3-ton wall of white, frothing water flooded over the deck. The helmsman was thrown off balance and fell backwards towards the ocean below, brought to a jarring halt when his safety tether went taut. The backup helmsman, who was braced when the wave struck, grabbed the wheel and forced it over as the boat struggled upright again. 'Are you ok, guys?' shouted a scared voice from the hatch. The backup helm gave the thumbs up.

It was pitch black, the hurricane-force storm was reaching its violent crescendo, the crew were frightened and we were smack in the middle of the North Pacific Ocean, thousands of miles from the safety of land. We had already taken a pounding and the next 12 hours were going to be some of the longest of our lives.

I had to be a strong leader, keep a strong, calm face and tell the crew that we were going to be fine. That's what they needed to hear. But we weren't fine – the waves outside were enormous and every 20 minutes or so we would get smashed by one from an unusual angle, like the one that just got us. Fatalistic as it sounds, I knew that if there was a massive one out there with our name on it, it would get us, roll us over, snap our mast off and possibly drown the crew up on deck. We couldn't see it and we certainly couldn't avoid it.

I gave reassurance, I put on a calm face and I stayed strong. We were as safe as we could be in the conditions and we were prepared for the worst. But the nightmare thought remained.

People die in conditions like this.

# 1

# LEADERSHIP

*The only real training for leadership is leadership*
*ANTONY JAY*

My name is Brendan Hall and this book is the story of my race around the world as the skipper of the racing yacht *Spirit of Australia* in the 2009–10 edition of the Clipper Round the World Yacht Race.

Being a sailing yacht skipper is a big undertaking. You are the one person responsible for the safety of the boat and the safety and well-being of the crew, for planning the voyage and navigating across the ocean. If you're in a yacht race then you're usually the one in charge of plotting the best course to win, interpreting the weather patterns and positioning the yacht in the best place to take advantage of the wind. It's a large burden to bear, but ask most yacht skippers and they'll tell you they have the best job in the world and they wouldn't swap it for anything. I'm definitely one of these people.

After ten months and 35,000 nautical miles of ocean racing, my crew and I won the Clipper Round the World Yacht Race, beating our nearest rivals *Team Finland* by 22 points. To have circumnavigated the world and to have won a highly competitive race was an amazing achievement for all of us. We struggled through the lows of defeat, the setback of damage, the tension of being 18 people cooped up together on a small yacht – and came out the other side, a victorious team.

Our success was not because we had a secret weapon or were more skilled sailors than the other nine teams competing; it came down to factors that were entirely human: teamwork, motivation, persistence and courage – things that are at the heart of any great endeavour.

This is the story of my journey as the skipper of a winning yacht, interwoven with some of the lessons I learned along the way about leadership under pressure, which I think will benefit everyone, because we are all leaders in our own way. We all feel responsible for people in our lives, be they family members, friends or work colleagues. We want to do our best for them, look after them and help them reach their potential. We want their respect and cooperation. Sometimes we have to tell them things they don't want to hear.

Being a good leader all the time can be difficult and sometimes we struggle with it, but that just goes with the territory. I was 27 when I began the race and I'll be the first to admit that I wasn't always the perfect skipper. As much as I wish I was, I'm not always the hero of the story. Like all leaders, I made my mistakes and I learned valuable lessons from them. In fact, some of my most memorable leadership achievements were a direct result of learning from a mistake I made or from not being the good leader I should have been. In sharing these negative experiences too, I hope you can learn from them the same way I did.

As Mark Twain humorously remarks: '*If you hold a cat by the tail you learn things you cannot learn any other way.*'

# 2

# THE RACE

*Every artist was first an amateur*
*RALPH WALDO EMERSON*

The Clipper Round the World Race is a unique thing in the sailing world. There are many round the world races. Some of them are singlehanded races, like the famous Vendée Globe race, which runs every four years, where the elite of the singlehanded sailing world race their powerful high-tech boats to the limit on a non-stop lap of the planet. Their challenge is managing the boat, their sleep, doing *everything* by themselves, and improvising solutions when things break. They cannot stop until the finish. These races give us harrowing stories of individual courage, bravery and determination, a lone sailor triumphing over the elements.

The Clipper race is not like this.

Other races are team races, like the renowned Volvo Ocean Race, which runs every three years, where the world's best veteran ocean racers compete in shorter race 'legs' from continent to continent, with a cumulative points tally. The boats are some of the most powerful sailing yachts ever built. The budgets of the competing teams are in the order of tens of millions of pounds, with international sponsors like Ericsson, Puma and Telefonica pouring enormous resources into having the fastest, most advanced boat constructed and recruiting the rock stars of the sailing world for their teams. If there were a Formula One of ocean sailing, this would be it.

The Clipper race is not like this, either.

The Clipper race runs every two years and is unique because the people racing the boats are not professional sailors. Except for the skipper, they are all amateurs and about 40 per cent of them have never sailed in their life before signing up to the race. They go through a selection process to get on the race and, if accepted, they pay a fee to the organising company, Clipper Ventures, for their berth. They pay depending on how much of the race they want to do. The race is similar to the Volvo Ocean Race in that it is raced as a series of 'legs'. Some crew choose to sail the whole way around the world, others just want to do a leg or two.

The Clipper race is not as extreme as the Volvo Ocean Race. The boats are made from tough fibreglass, rather than lightweight carbon fibre, and they cost only a fraction of the price. If the Volvo boats were the Formula One cars of ocean racing, then the Clipper boats would be the Land Rovers. They're strong, durable and safe and the crew don't need to be experts to drive one.

Clipper Ventures wanted their race to be a true test of amateur sailing skill, without the expensive yacht design arms race that characterises the upper echelons of the yacht-racing world. To ensure absolute fairness, all ten Clipper yachts were built at the same time, in the same factory from the same mould. They weigh the same; they all have the same sails and the same equipment.

It's called a 'matched fleet' in the sailing world, and it means that any race result out on the water is down to the skill and grit of the team sailing the boat, and not because the boat itself is superior.

The matched fleet ensures an incredibly close race where the pressure is always on. On the leg of the race from Cape Town, South Africa to Geraldton, Western Australia, my boat, *Spirit of Australia*, finished a creditable second place, finishing 33 minutes after the winning boat, *Team Finland*. That was after 4,900 nautical miles and 25 days of non-stop ocean racing.

Clipper Ventures don't send people out onto the oceans unprepared. All crew members have to undertake an intensive four-week training programme at Clipper HQ in Gosport, on the south coast of England. In that time, experienced sailing instructors train the amateurs to become safe, competent crew members who can look after themselves on board and are well drilled in all the procedures and manoeuvres involved in handling a 68ft racing yacht.

Clipper Ventures also recruit the skippers to lead their teams of amateur sailors. In every race, they recruit ten exceptional sailors from a pool of about 160 serious applicants from all over the world. Racing around the world is a huge challenge and the dream of many professional sailors, so there is no shortage of talent applying. The selection process is intensive and the skippers' sailing skills are tested to the limit.

As a race skipper, the Clipper race is a formula you won't find anywhere else. Your crew are not volunteers or professionals; they are customers who are paying for an experience – an experience skilfully marketed to them as a life-changing one. You don't get to choose your team, either – the race organisers do that. They spend a lot of time dividing the total crew pool of 450 people into the ten teams. They have certain criteria to fulfil, like making sure each boat has a good mix of men and women, a mix of ages, and a mix of sailing experience. Some people who come to do the Clipper race are already skilled sailors, so care is taken to divide them equally between the teams. The crew who are doing the entire race are known as the 'core crew' and the people who are only doing a leg are 'leggers'.

As you can imagine, with the race open to everybody, you get people signing up for a lot of very different reasons. Some apply because they love sailing and want to cross an ocean, others because they fiercely want to win an ocean race. Some want to do the race to escape a humdrum life and other people are doing it to get back on their feet after a messy divorce. I even met one crew member who said she was doing the race to meet a husband! Some are competitive, others aren't. Clipper Ventures cast the marketing net very wide, so the people who sign up are an incredibly diverse bunch. This is one of the great strengths of the race, but it's also the single biggest challenge for the skippers – managing all those expectations.

That's the Clipper Round the World Race. Amateur crews. Professional skippers. Tough boats. Racing hard across the world's oceans every two years.

# 3

# INSPIRATION

*First say to yourself what you would be;*
*and then do what you have to do*

*EPICTETUS*

## LIVERPOOL, JULY 2008

As the boats appeared on the horizon, a cheer went up from the crowd of 10,000 people lining the banks of the River Mersey. The Clipper race fleet was coming home. Ten months earlier, the fleet began their circumnavigation in this very river, to the boom of the starting cannon. Within minutes, the ten-strong fleet sailed away over that same horizon we were all expectantly looking at now. In ten months, they had sailed all the way around the globe: 35,000 nautical miles. Today, we would witness the final mile of a truly epic voyage.

When the fleet left the dock all those months ago, the boats looked immaculate. Shining stainless steel, polished alloy and sponsors' logos colourfully emblazoned on the side of the hulls. The boats' battle flags were flying proudly and the sails lying on deck were white as morning snow, having been delivered brand new from the sail loft only a few weeks earlier. It was a formidable and impressive sight to behold.

The crews of the yachts had a shiny new look to them as well.

Wearing brand-new red oilskin waterproof suits and shiny brown waterproof boots, they looked fresh and ready to go. The looks on their faces told the story, though. Some were taking a final moment to say goodbye to family, embraced in their loved ones' arms. Some were sitting quietly by themselves, swallowing the enormity of the challenge they were about to embark upon. Others busied themselves with jobs on the decks of the yachts – all under the watchful gaze of the thousands of spectators who had come to see them off.

And now they were coming back.

As the fleet approached the finish line, it was clear to see the boats were no longer as shiny as they were before the start. The sails were a dull grey, many of them covered in stitching and patches from the numerous repairs they had received over the course of the race. The branding on the hulls was scuffed in places and peeling in the corners. The stainless steel fittings were caked in salt, which masked their lustre. These were boats that had seen some battles and had the scars to prove it. Two of the boats had new masts, replaced in Hawaii when they were both dismasted in the treacherous North Pacific.

The crews looked different as well. Even from the shore, there was a different look to them, compared to the start of the race. The frantic, nervous energy that we saw before was replaced with a slower, but more confident approach to manoeuvring the boats up the river. Well-practised drills were executed with skill as the boats tacked their way up the river towards the line that would signal the end of the race.

The cannon fired, the crowd's cheering reached a crescendo, and it was over. Ten boats, ten skippers and 180 crew, back where they started, having just sailed a lap of the planet. Amazing.

But there was only one winner.

The boat named *New York* won the overall race by two points, narrowly beating their main rivals *Hull & Humber* in the final race from Ireland to Liverpool. It was an amazingly close race and the two leading boats were less than 200 metres apart for much of it. One mistake, one line-handling error or one misjudged tack and the goal they had been striving towards would be lost. The pressure was at maximum. *New*

*York* held on by the skin of their teeth and won the close contest, securing the team achievement of a lifetime – winning a Round the World Yacht Race.

They were inspirational.

Inspiration is hard to come by. Genuine inspiration, that is – when you feel it down to your core. You know that something has shifted inside you and the trajectory of your life is going to be different because of it.

Seeing the crew of *New York* being presented with the huge glass Clipper trophy in front of a crowd of thousands was my moment of inspiration. Their skipper, Duggie Gillespie, stood there, raised arms holding the trophy aloft, while his crew cheered and celebrated their success. His smile was from ear to ear and I knew only too well the blood, sweat and tears that he and his team had shed to earn that victory. The 2007–08 Clipper race was theirs.

His achievement was inspirational to me. To have led a team of amateur sailors around the world was an amazing feat in itself, but to win the race – legendary. I knew in that moment that the trajectory of my life was shifting.

I had to win this race too. There was no other option. The 2009–10 Clipper race was going to be mine.

You might think it a naive thought, a false bravado whipped up in the noise and emotion of the moment, but you couldn't tell me that at the time. My mind was made up and I was going to dedicate everything I could to making sure I was as prepared as possible, to give me and my future team the best fighting chance of that same success.

Reflecting on it later that evening, I began to feel uncertain. The interview for potential 09–10 race skippers was still eight months away. If I botched the interview or the sailing trial and didn't get selected, then all my preparation would have been for nothing. Doubts began to creep in. Was I seriously capable of skippering one of those boats? Was I good enough? Why would a crew follow me? I was a good sailing instructor and a good leader, but was I really on the same level as those skippers who led their teams around the world and back into Liverpool?

*Yes, Brendan, damn it. You can do it and you are good enough. Stop doubting yourself. If you really set your mind to this and work your arse off, you'll do it!*

*Get busy.*

# 4

# PREPARATION

*To be prepared is half the victory*
MIGUEL DE CERVANTES

My preparation for the race was extensive. I can say I was definitely the best prepared of all ten race skippers – meaning I had done the most work beforehand.

My campaign began the week after arriving back from the 07–08 race finish in Liverpool. My first step was to seek out and talk to as many of the previous race skippers as possible. I got contact details for as many of them as I could and arranged meetings. Some of them seemed perplexed that I was contacting them so soon after their own race had finished to talk about how I should go about building my campaign for the next one. Nevertheless, I arranged dinners with many of them and got my notepad ready.

This step was so critical to the direction of my preparation. Seeking out those skippers and getting as much information from them as I could helped me focus my energy on the things that really matter in a race campaign. And the things that really matter in a race campaign were not what I was expecting.

I quickly learned from all the skippers I spoke to that the secret of winning a yacht race is down to people management. A happy, motivated and informed crew race the boat hard. A disheartened, browbeaten and lazy crew don't.

I should have known this. It seems self-evident looking back at it now, but I was convinced at the time that the secret of performance was down to their skill at choosing the right sail combinations or their canny judgement when analysing weather systems.

In my thirst for technical details, I was overlooking the critical factor. As the pages in my notepad filled up, one thing became crystal clear to me: being a race-winning skipper was going to be about 20 per cent sailing skills and 80 per cent people-management skills.

This holds true in the world ashore and I'm certain that any successful CEO would agree with the above statement. A leader has to have technical skills, no question, but once you are in charge of that department, or leading that project team, leadership and people skills become far more important. It's easy for people to focus on honing and sharpening their technical skills, becoming the best they can be at what they do, to the detriment of their people-management skills, which become more and more important as their career progresses.

The *New York* skipper Duggie summed it up best when he said he would rather have a clueless amateur crew member who was a good team player and had a willingness to learn over a technically great sailor who had a bad attitude and couldn't get along with others.

I wasn't sure I agreed with him at the time, but I dutifully wrote it down. Looking back now, I am in absolute agreement with him on this point. People skills count for more than technical skills.

Attitude over aptitude. Always.

From speaking to those skippers, it seemed that there was a multitude of ways to manage the crew. Obviously, the boats were ranked in position from first to tenth, and logic says that I could have saved myself a lot of time and just spoken to the top three skippers to see how they did things. I didn't, though. I decided I needed to get a full appreciation for how all the skippers managed their boats and, in hindsight, this was the most enlightening part of my research.

I was asking them some tough questions, like what is your biggest regret about the race? What would you do differently if you could have your race again? Why didn't you do so well in the race?

Again, I was expecting to hear answers about poor tactical decisions, gear failures, bad sail settings, wind holes and crew mistakes. These questions were hard to ask, and some of the skippers found them hard to answer, but the answers were all related to how they managed the people on their boat.

Some of them confessed to having a short temper with their crew or getting frustrated by having to explain things over and over to a new crew member. One described how the tension between two crew members became so bad that they got into a physical fight. One of them wished he'd been harder on a certain crew member who was too pushy with others, but let it slide because the crew member was a great sailor. One admitted very frankly that he did too much work himself and the crew felt he didn't trust them. I think many of them welcomed the chance to get it off their chest and I was a very intent listener.

The notepad was nearly full to the brim by this point – I was writing in the margins and on the inside back cover, but it was all so worthwhile. The answers to those hard questions were gold.

Back at Campaign HQ (my bedroom in a shared house in Portsmouth) I began planning, taking the best bits from what the past skippers had told me, making sure to avoid some of the crew problems they stumbled into, and turning it into the foundation of my race campaign.

Over the course of the next five months, I created a spreadsheet with every factor I could think of that would affect the speed of the boat, the team's performance and my own performance. It came to over 500 points.

I needed to give myself a clear objective for all this, so at the top of each page I wrote, 'My Objective: To win the 09–10 Clipper race through belief, teamwork, performance focus and continuous improvement.' Those were the key things that I thought were going to win the race for us.

I had a page where I wrote down everything we could do to the boat to make it faster, more comfortable or safer. My hands were a blur and I had hundreds of ideas to write down, such as:

> - *Sandpaper and smooth inner part of spinnaker pole beak to reduce chafe.*
> - *Numbers on mast for main luff tension – indicator marks on sail luff.*
> - *Have spare lines already spliced with shackles.*
> - *Wall-mounted hooks in wet locker.*
> - *Eat from dog bowls and use plastic cutlery.*
> - *Draft markings along the foot or periodically up the sail, 40%, 50%, 60%.*
> - *Take only required spares, not too much 'just in case'.*
> - *Limit crew to 20kg personal kit (excluding oilskins + boots).*
> - *Plot boat polar data and best speed data into Seapro navigation software, using weather routing tool to help plan passage.*

I realise that to anybody who isn't a sailor the above statements might as well be in a different language, but the point is that I had very, VERY clear ideas on how to set up the boat, the physical environment, to increase performance. I felt things were progressing well, though I was about to discover I had only touched the tip of the iceberg.

The next step was to decide on how I wanted to tackle the main challenges on the race. On a page simply called 'Challenges', I began to write.

> *The biggest challenges to achieving my objective will be:*
> - *Crew management – crew coming on board with greatly differing expectations.*
> - *Integrating the leggers into the core crew as smoothly and quickly as possible.*

- *Keeping up morale and a sense of fun.*
- *Effective conflict management.*
- *Creating a culture of knowledge sharing, openness and team solidarity – a great place to be.*

*Some ideas to overcome these challenges:*

*Crew management – crew coming on board with greatly differing expectations:*

- *Agree on team objectives from the outset – lean towards performance focus.*
- *Give all crew tasks at crew allocation, stress that the success of this campaign is going to be the result of 44 intelligent, creative people putting their heads together.*
- *Be very clear about how hard we want to push – it's not just enough to say 'we want to win'.*
- *Outline what will be expected if we want to live that objective.*
- *Be totally upfront about what to expect, but encouraging about the rewards of effort.*
- *Stress the challenge of the event, tell the crew to visualise themselves as winners of the Clipper trophy.*

*Integrating the leggers into the core crew as smoothly and quickly as possible:*

- *A comprehensive set of joining instructions for leggers before they join the boat (a CD or DVD posted to them maybe).*
- *A training guide to each role on the boat (helm, trimmer, bowman).*
- *An online space where the whole team can get together and share thoughts.*
- *Previous leggers to contact upcoming leggers by phone and tell them about what to expect.*
- *Create a culture in the core crew that the leggers need to be brought up to speed ASAP.*

- *Get leggers to 'shadow' a core crew member when joining the boat. All crew are encouraged and incentives are given for training others.*
- *Get all crew – leggers and core crew – to write an application to join the boat, so they emphasise their own positive qualities.*
- *Get a crew member to write a comprehensive joining brief for new leggers joining the boat.*

*Keeping up morale and a sense of fun:*
- *Pre-race – team-building and training sessions with fun stuff afterwards.*
- *Celebrate success as much as possible, crossing lines of longitude, equator crossing, birthdays, etc.*
- *Read inspiring quotes, passages to the crew during daily meetings.*
- *Morale officer as a job for crew maybe? Let them come up with some ideas to keep things light.*

*Effective conflict management:*
- *Avoid common sources of conflict:*
  - *Unclear goals, roles and allocation of roles.*
  - *Lack of fairness.*
  - *Differing standards of performance.*
  - *A lack of crew involvement in decision-making.*
  - *Individual insensitivity to others' needs.*
- *Make sure everyone pulls their weight equally, no special dispensation.*
- *Use the daily meeting to bring thoughts out into the open and discuss different methods of doing things – encourage positive conflict and discussion.*
- *Big source of conflict is differing standards of tidiness below deck – make crib sheet with 'the rules' on it so everyone is aware.*
- *Mediate between two people who are at odds with each other.*

- *Keep a respectable distance between self and crew, to take a detached standpoint on crew issues.*
- *Keep aware of the personalities on board and the issues that are arising – keep an ear to the ground, or rely on somebody who is very good at sensing to help me out.*
- *Agree on a set of agreed values before the race and stick to them, everyone pulls their weight, never step over a job.*
- *Lead by example in these values, otherwise it becomes hypocritical to impose these on others.*

*Creating a culture of knowledge sharing, openness and team solidarity – a great place to be:*
- *Award a prize on every leg for the best trainer.*
- *Daily briefings to be used as a forum, where the team can discuss what is going well, what is not going so well and how we can improve performance.*
- *Much comes down to my own personal manner and that of the two watch leaders – never to stifle a new idea.*
- *If something new is suggested – 'love the idea' for 10 minutes and then make a decision. Dismissing it out of hand will offend crew member.*
- *Be aware of the 'what's in it for me?' mentality. Encourage everyone to share knowledge so we can all benefit from it.*

I referred back to that page often on the race, making sure I was doing what I set out to do, and it kept me honest in a sense. It was an incredibly valuable exercise and I would strongly recommend that any leader take a few hours to make their own list of challenges and how to overcome them.

I smiled. The campaign was taking shape, but I still hadn't touched the hardest bit.

The next page of my spreadsheet was called 'Personal' and on it I wrote two questions:

What is going to make me a winning skipper?

What is going to stop me from being a winning skipper?

And there I sat, staring at the blinking cursor. It would be easy to ask those questions of somebody else, but it's far harder to turn the telescope of human observation around and look at yourself. It took me a long time and a lot of soul searching and brutal honesty to answer those questions.

---

*Things that are going to make me a winning skipper:*
- *I'm patient.*
- *I like having clear and constant communication with crew to keep them in the loop.*
- *I'm very organised.*
- *I understand the effect my mood and behaviour has on crew, self-awareness.*
- *I'm competitive when racing.*
- *I prepare and plan thoroughly.*
- *I'm quite enthusiastic when motivated.*
- *I'm cool and calm in a crisis.*

*Things that are going to stop me being a winning skipper:*
- *Poor crew management, trying to avoid conflict and letting issues fester.*
- *Emotional resilience, taking negative feedback, sarcastic comments or criticism personally and dwelling on it.*
- *Not maintaining enough distance between self and crew, wanting to be liked.*
- *I stress easily when many things are dividing my attention.*
- *Behaving inconsistently towards crew I dislike or who irritate me.*
- *Thinking 'aloud' in front of crew about problems or concerns.*
- *I can get emotionally attached to decisions I make, seeing any question or criticism as a threat to my authority. Need to work on this.*

---

- *I can become temporarily despondent when things aren't going my way.*
- *I am irritable when tired.*
- *I am not an experienced weather router and I am afraid of making poor tactical decisions.*
- *I'm not a joker or a funny man, I can seem a bit too serious at times I think.*

These were things I knew I did. Not all the time, but often enough that they came into my mind when asking myself the question. Others were things people had told me – my girlfriend, parents, friends and past crew.

Looking at that list on paper, it didn't look like the list of a good leader. It doesn't even look like the list of a normal friendly, outgoing person. Would *anybody* want a person with those behaviours in their workplace?

On balance, I think everybody can look down that list and identify with a few of the points. I'm sure most of us can remember a time when we snapped at somebody who didn't deserve it when we were tired.

At some point we have all probably taken an honest criticism too personally and dwelt on it or let it shape our opinion of the person who gave it to us.

I knew I wasn't going to change my personality just by writing down my negative behaviours, but I knew then that if I wanted the best fighting chance of winning this race – a race that came down to 80 per cent people management – then I needed to try to improve. My fingers began typing again.

*Ideas to try to overcome and improve on these things:*
*Poor crew management, trying to avoid conflict and letting issues fester:*
- *Not being afraid to bring up an issue, perhaps in a vague way in a daily meeting.*

- *Talk to people one-on-one regularly. Show empathy if they are feeling upset.*
- *Go away and think about things before coming to a decision that might cause an issue.*
- *Avoid making decisions based on emotion in the heat of the moment.*
- *Encourage positive conflict, debate or discussion during open group meetings.*
- *Explain to crew at leg starts that personal conflict is going to be unavoidable.*
- *Get crew to research the Tuckman team-building model and the forming, storming, norming, performing stages we will experience.*
- *Talk to the crew openly about potential sources of conflict and that we need to be adult enough to bring it up in a civil manner and sort it out.*
- *Explain the dangers of letting conflict fester. Let people give examples of when it has happened to them in a workplace or something. Really stress the importance of keeping it under control.*

*Catchphrase: PROBLEMS ARE SOLUBLE. PROBLEMS ARE INEVITABLE.*

*Formal means of conflict resolution:*
- *Try to sort it out yourself first, either privately or at a daily meeting. Be mindful not to embarrass or humiliate somebody in front of the team.*
- *Take it to your watch leader first, see if they can sort it out.*
- *If they cannot sort it out, come and see me.*
- *If you have a problem with the watch leader, come and talk to me directly.*
- *If you have a problem with me, talk to the watch leader and they can bring it to me – anonymously.*

*Emotional resilience, taking negative feedback, sarcastic comments or criticism personally and dwelling on it:*

- *I think I am quite resilient on the face of things, I accept criticism openly and concede points if I feel they are valid.*
- *The problem is that I go away and think about these things and it brings me down, or I take it personally and start to dislike the person who brought the criticism.*
- *How to overcome this?*
- *Firstly, understand that criticism is going to be aimed at me, more than usual if I want to run a performance-driven crew. Some crew are going to be unhappy and will blame me for it.*
- *Know that some crew are probably just venting. I am a very obvious and convenient foil for them when things aren't going well.*
- *Remain a step removed from it. Ask myself, 'Why are they saying this, what is their motivation?'*
- *Remain detached and don't let my own emotions into it.*

*Not maintaining enough distance between self and crew, wanting to be liked:*

- *Crew need to understand that I'm doing this race for myself and my own reasons.*
- *I will be liked by the crew and respected by them if I behave as a skipper should.*
- *I'm not on the race to make best friends with the crew. Distance is necessary to differentiate me from them.*
- *I like getting positive feedback . Remember that the skipper's job is fairly thankless – people complain if you mess up, and say nothing if you do well.*
- *Get watch leaders to read a leadership book. This will give them a level of empathy for my position and the difficulty of it sometimes.*

*I stress easily when many things are dividing my attention:*

- *Make lists. Break things down into smaller, more manageable chunks and prioritise.*
- *I need to delegate jobs and try not to do everything myself.*
- *Have a 'don't bring me problems, bring me solutions' policy with little jobs, encourage people to be proactive.*

*Behaving inconsistently towards crew I dislike or who are irritating me:*

- *When confronting somebody about a problem, do it in an empathetic way, seeking to understand rather than criticise.*
- *Do not blame somebody for a mistake they made. This will guarantee they will take it personally.*
- *General communication with crew – keep them informed and up to speed to avoid chatter and speculation.*

*Thinking aloud in front of crew about problems or concerns:*

- *Remember who could be listening when talking with somebody.*
- *Use the watch leaders as sounding boards for things that are bothering me.*
- *The exception to this will be crew issues where the watch leader could be a part of it and telling them could aggravate the problem further.*
- *Most of the decision-making will be around navigation and weather issues, which can be openly thrown around and discussed with the crew. Just got to make it seem like I am not giving up my authority by being negotiative.*

*I can get emotionally attached to decisions I make, and see any question or criticism as a threat to my authority:*

- *I think I started out like this when I first started skippering courses. I would actively disagree with people when they made a suggestion just because I wanted to seem more knowledgeable.*

- *I have largely overcome this habit, I think. I assess ideas on their merits and if they are better than my original suggestion, then I will accept them.*
- *I think a lot of people want to make suggestions to the skipper as a way of showing off their own knowledge, wanting me to be impressed and praise them.*
- *I can do this anyway, giving them a compliment and satisfying that desire, but not really using their suggestion, unless it's a good one.*
- *I need to be able to change my mind and not be afraid to say I don't know the answer to every question.*
- *I need to make the crew understand that I have to be able to change my mind at short notice, especially when it comes to things like sail changes.*

*I can become temporarily despondent when things aren't going my way:*
- *I'm just going to have to find a way to get over this. Try turning a negative into a positive.*
- *I think it will be important to readjust our short- or long-term goals to avoid crew (and my own) despondency.*
- *If it becomes obvious that we won't win a leg, then we need to adjust the goal to coming in the top five or something.*
- *Having personal goals will be important, kept secret from the crew.*

*I am irritable when tired:*
- *Most people are, just be aware of it and try not to snap at anyone.*
- *Make sure I'm getting sufficient sleep. I think a lot of skippers drive themselves into the ground and their performance suffers.*

*I am not an experienced weather router and I am afraid of making poor tactical decisions:*
- *I think the key will be to make conservative decisions and keep as close as possible to the rhumb line.*

- *Bringing some other core crew members into the weather routing team would be very beneficial, or at least getting input from other crew before making a decision.*
- *I think getting some specialist help in this area would be a huge benefit.*

*I'm not a joker or a funny man, I can seem a bit too serious at times I think:*
- *That's just my style, I guess. I think I can be quite funny and entertaining, but only when the conditions are right for it and I feel comfortable in the presence of the crew.*
- *When I get annoyed, my sense of humour is the first thing to go.*
- *This could be a real issue – being able to lighten the mood when the chips are down is a huge asset.*

So that was it, my poor leadership behaviours and character flaws laid bare. I had nowhere to hide and certainly no excuse not to try to improve. For better or for worse, that was me and I knew what I needed to do.

Like they say in Alcoholics Anonymous meetings, the first stage of getting sober is admitting that you have a problem. There was certainly room for improvement in this area and without this step of honest introspection, I wouldn't have known. It was a hard step to take, a bitter pill to swallow, but in the end I became a better and more mature leader because of it and now urge others to do the same.

My next stop on the campaign development train was to go to a friend of mine who administers psychometric tests. These are tests designed to measure knowledge, abilities, attitudes and personality traits. They are done on a computer and usually revolve around a long series of questions with multiple-choice answers.

I've always been sceptical of these sorts of tests. You can test somebody's knowledge with a questionnaire, sure, but their personality traits? Surely they cannot be reduced to a series of agree/disagree questions. Still, it was certainly worth a try, so I sat at his computer and did a 150-question test. After completing its calculations, the software generated a report that told me everything about my personality traits and leadership style, which it summed up as 'Negotiative'. It gave the following neat description:

> Negotiative Leaders motivate subordinates by encouraging them, through incentives etc, to work towards common objectives. Hence, through a process of negotiation, attempts will be made to arrive at some mutually equitable arrangement with the other members of the team so as to motivate them to work in a particular way. Negotiative Leaders tend to rely on their skills of persuasion to achieve their stated goals.

Wow. Spot on! My scepticism grudgingly evaporated. That description was pretty much how I went about being the skipper of a boat and how I related to my crews up to that point. The report expanded on this for about five pages and it was uncannily accurate on almost everything. I was amazed at how it could derive the statements in the report, many of them quite personal, from the 150 questions it asked me, but whatever it did clearly worked. There are a myriad of tests out there and I know they are used in corporate recruitment, but I think they are also a hugely valuable tool for any aspiring leader to use on themselves.

The test didn't reveal anything new to me, but – like my spreadsheet – seeing it written on paper made me more conscious of it and how I could play to the strengths of my leadership style.

It's important to play to your own strengths. As alluring as it is to want to emulate the strengths and the style of leaders you admire, you should stay true to yourself and your own strengths. The leaders you admire didn't reach those lofty heights by trying to emulate others. They knew their own strengths (and weaknesses) and led with them. It is called strengths-based leadership theory and there is a raft of research on it, carried out over the last 20 years. It's fairly conclusively proved that the best leaders are the ones who play to their strengths. This may sound like common sense, but the tricky part is in *knowing* what your strengths are in the first place, in order to capitalise on them. This is another area where psychometric testing can help.

All the time I had been doing this preparation, I had been working full-time as a sailing instructor and yacht delivery skipper, taking yachts from country to country. My schedule had been punishing and the hours I put in every day equated to having two full-time jobs. As well as the campaign preparation, I was getting ready for my interview with Clipper Ventures, which was looming.

I was a bag of nerves the night before my interview and didn't sleep a wink. I'd always done well in interviews in the past, but this was the most important one I had ever done. I hoped that my hard work in preparation would impress the race director and was also conscious of the fact that if I messed up the interview, then I could flush it all down the toilet and go home knowing that I'd been working myself to the bone for *nothing*.

I stood, patiently, outside the office of the race director, waiting my turn. My dream and my ambition were on the line here and it all hung on the words I said and the attitude I conveyed in the next hour.

*Relax.*

It wasn't just that. I knew from the grapevine that there were some great sailors applying for this race. There was a massive pool of international talent for Clipper to choose from and most of the applicants were older and more experienced than me. There could well be ten better candidates than me and I simply wouldn't get selected, no matter how well I did in there. The office door opened.

*It's now or never.*

I had the interview and thought it went well. The race director, Joff Bailey, acknowledged my preparation and seemed to be generally happy with my answers to the questions he fired at me, most of which were about how I would deal with difficult crew members and the pressure of competition. We talked for an hour and a half, then, with a firm handshake and look in the eye, I was told to come back in two months for a skipper sailing trial.

On a cold February morning, I turned up at the marina and set off on my race skipper trial sail. It was an intensive three-day sail with the race director and a few other skipper candidates. We were put through our paces, tested relentlessly, and were deliberately put into simulated disaster situations to see how we would cope with the pressure and how quickly we could improvise and think on our feet. It was a tough test, but I expected no less. At the post trial debrief, the race director, Joff, gave me some positive feedback and told me to hold tight and wait for the announcement in *another* two months' time.

The two-month wait was agonising, but my preparations continued at full speed.

The day of the announcement came. True to form, I hadn't slept a wink all night. Mid-morning, I was called into the office of the race director. I was sitting on the edge of my seat and my heart was beating like a bass drum. When he told me I'd got the job I suppressed my urge to cheer and high-five him. We shook hands and with a serious look he told me that getting the job is one thing, keeping the job is another.

*YEE-HA!!*

I was the skipper of boat number nine. It didn't have a sponsor yet, so it was just called 'boat nine'. The first thing I did was go down to the marina and say hello to her, where I got a very pleasant surprise. Guess what her name was in the previous race? *New York*. This was a race-winning boat, and although she was identical to her nine stablemates, I felt this was definitely a good omen.

Over the next few days, I got to know the other nine skippers who were selected. Some of them I knew already, others I had never met. It quickly became clear that I was the youngest and least experienced of the group. Some of these guys had *seriously* impressive racing CVs. Eero Lehtinen ('pronounced Aero – like the chocolate bar,' he tells people), the skipper of *Team Finland*, had already circumnavigated twice and skippered a boat around the world in a race called the BT Global Challenge. Chris Stanmore-Major, skipper of *Qingdao*, had been involved with the America's Cup. Pete Stirling, skipper of *Jamaica Lightning Bolt*, had done 27 transatlantic crossings. I had done four. Piers Dudin, skipper of *Hull & Humber*, was an experienced solo sailor who had sailed by himself from South Africa to England in a tiny 21ft racing yacht. These guys were some serious competitors and there was bravado aplenty as we all chatted together and shared our saltiest stories.

I wasn't about to let on, but suddenly the prospect of winning the race seemed a hell of a lot harder. These guys were here to win, too – and they were older, wiser and had sailed many thousands more miles than I had.

But no, this race wasn't about who had sailed the most miles or how impressive our CVs were, it wasn't even *really* about who the best sailor was. The skipper who managed and motivated his crew the best was going to win this thing. I had to keep my focus on that one simple fact: 20 per cent sailing, 80 per cent people management.

We were all great sailors and the other guys were prepared.

But not like me – I was *really* prepared.

## LEADERSHIP LESSONS

### Stand on the shoulders of giants

The key to my preparation for the race was the interviews I conducted with the past race skippers. I learned a long time ago that people love talking about their experiences, so an opportunity to speak, without constraint, to a willing and eager listener is rarely turned down, particularly when people are talking about something they're passionate about.

The information I gained from those interviews steered me in a very different direction to the one in which I'd been heading. Without their input, I would have approached the race focused on the technicalities of sailing, rather than concentrating on the human element.

Not only did their input pave the way for our success, but it significantly reduced my own anxiety about the race. Mounting a winning round the world race campaign was a huge and daunting task. At the beginning, I felt as though I was taking the first steps up a very steep mountain. By hearing the stories of those who had done it before and listening to them relate their own pre-race anxieties, it gave me confidence that I could do it as well.

After some interviews, I received emails with more information, extra notes and stories that people had remembered after I left. They went out of their way to help me out and stayed in touch throughout the race, offering further advice and support. It was a huge confidence boost, knowing I had some trusted advisors of whom I could ask questions and who would give reliable advice, based on real world experience.

I would urge any leader beginning a new project or setting out on a new voyage to seek out subject experts or people who have done it before. It doesn't matter if you don't know them. Look them up and send an email. Tell them you want to learn as much as you can from them and suggest a meeting. Engage their passion for their area of expertise.

Take a notepad and write down their thoughts and answers. Oh, and remember to pick up the bill.

The small investment of time and energy spent at this stage will return ten times over down the line, when the time comes to lay the foundations of the project.

## Learn from their mistakes

The most revealing question I asked those past skippers was: 'What's your biggest regret about the race?'

It might have seemed like bad manners, asking them to detail their failures and mistakes. The first few times, I asked the question in a clumsy, roundabout way. What surprised me was the openness and honesty of their answers. There was no offence taken to the question and I felt amateurish for not asking it more directly. I got the sense from some of them that this was something they had wanted to talk about, but never had the opportunity. The ensuing conversation was some of the most enlightening for me and, I think, cathartic for them. In a world where mistakes are often stigmatised, the chance to share mistakes and failures with a non-judgemental, confidential listener is usually welcomed.

I can think of at least a dozen scenarios on the race when I was confronted with the exact same situations as the past skippers. If it wasn't for them giving me an example of how *not* to handle the situation, then I'm sure I would have made the same mistake they did. If I hadn't asked those tough questions, I would never have known.

### Know yourself; know your strengths

I was having dinner with the 07–08 Clipper race winning skipper, Duggie. I was enthusiastically making notes and sponging as much information as I could off him. I wanted to emulate his success and I thought through emulating his style of leadership, I would be on the right track. Duggie must have picked up on this and he gave me the most valuable piece of advice all night when he said, 'Brendan, you can't run your campaign like I did mine, because you're not me. You have your own personality and your own style. You need to stay true to yourself.'

He was absolutely right. I needed to be true to myself and to my own style of leadership. I needed to be an authentic leader, not one striving to emulate the style of another. In retrospect, I think that if I had continued down this path, it wouldn't have taken long for my crew to see through the imitation. The trouble was that I didn't really know what my leadership style was and I had only thought about my leadership strengths and weaknesses in a vague, non-verbal way.

The process of drawing up that spreadsheet and looking in detail at the behaviours that I thought were my strengths ('What is going to make me a winning skipper?') and weaknesses ('What is going to stop me being a winning skipper?') gave me a clarity of insight I hadn't felt before. I took some input from others, people who knew me well like close friends and family, but most of it came from my own reflection on my leadership to date. I had been a professional yacht skipper for several years, so there was plenty of experience to analyse. The process of facing my shortcomings and leadership flaws was a difficult one, even a depressing one at times, but I knew it was a necessary step to becoming a better leader and achieving my goal.

The psychometric testing helped greatly as well. It didn't tell me anything I didn't already know, it just articulated it in a more refined manner. To know that the set of behaviours I used as a leader put me in the category of being a negotiative leader was helpful and made me more aware of what I could do to play to my strength of negotiation.

Afterwards, I spent a lot of time researching strengths-based leadership models. These were incredibly helpful and began to solidify in my mind the leadership style I required in my two watch leaders, in order for us to work well together and be an effective management team. Three negotiative-style leaders would be less effective than a negotiative leader, a supportive leader and a directive leader working together. We would have to complement each others' styles to be as effective as possible.

I believe any leader should invest time in undertaking these two exercises – honest self-reflection and introspection, and a simple psychometric leadership profile (there are many to choose from). These two things started me down a track that led to my greatest success and I think it's doubtful I would have achieved my goal if I hadn't done them.

# 5

# TEAM SPIRIT

*If everyone is moving forward together,*
*then success takes care of itself*

HENRY FORD

Even though my workload was huge, I redoubled my efforts and stepped my preparation up a notch. The 'crew allocation' day was coming up. This was the first time I would meet the people I was going to lead around the world. I had one chance to make a first impression and let my team know I meant business.

I worked like a demon, preparing a briefing pack I could give my crew on the day, spelling out what I wanted our campaign to be about. It ran to over 30 pages in the end and I felt the crew would see it as a sign that I was professional, had done my homework, and was worthy of their respect from the start.

So the day rolled around. Clipper Ventures had assembled all the crew in Portsmouth. The announcement took place in an enormous auditorium and the excitement among the crew was almost tangible. This was where they would find out which boat they were on and which skipper would be leading their team around the world.

The skippers, all ten of us dressed up in smart suits with gold-buttoned blazers, were lined up at the front of the auditorium, looking up at the 450 excited, chatting faces. After an introduction by Sir Robin Knox-Johnston, the legendary solo sailor and founder of Clipper Ventures, it was time to allocate the ten teams.

At this time, my boat still didn't have a sponsor. Clipper Ventures were working hard to find one, but things move slowly in these circles and it was taking time. I'd heard rumours that a potential Australian sponsor was on the cards, but nothing was confirmed. I decided that our team needed a temporary name, because 'crew of boat nine' didn't sound particularly exciting. The other boats had names already, which gave their crew a natural identity and a banner to rally around. Proud names of cities, regions and countries like *Hull & Humber*, *Uniquely Singapore*, *Cape Breton Island*, *Qingdao*, *California* and *Edinburgh Inspiring Capital*.

Our sponsor and boat name would come soon, but I decided that for now we would call ourselves 'Team SPIRIT'. A catchy name that I felt summed up what I wanted to achieve. The fact that our boat ended up being named *Spirit of Australia* was a truly serendipitous convergence.

One by one, we skippers went to the podium and read the list of names in the envelope we had each been given. I was ninth in line, so had to stand there as the crew names of the first eight boats were called. I shifted restlessly from foot to foot, fingering the envelope nervously in my hands.

In that envelope were the names of my crew, my team. The people for whom I would be personally responsible over the next ten months. I would be keeping them safe, keeping them healthy, keeping them motivated and making them believe we could win this race together. Would they make a good team? Would they respect me? Would they live up to my expectations?

*Breathe. Stay calm.*

In truth, they were more than just people's names on a list, they were 44 life stories, now intersecting and running together for the next ten months. Some would be old, some would be young, some would sail well and others wouldn't. Some would focus under pressure, others would fold. But for better or worse, they were about to become my team and I had to do the best I could for them.

*Stand tall, shoulders back.*

In three short months, we were going to set to sea together. We would see the very best and the very worst of each other's characters. Together, we were going to feel the joyous highs of victory and the crushing lows of defeat. Together, we were going to suffer setbacks that would test our physical endurance and mental strength. Together, we would have to stand united against the power of the ocean, that ancient, implacable force of nature, which all sailors must respect and fear. The experience of the race was going to be life-changing for all of us in ways we couldn't possibly fathom at the time, assembled in that buzzing auditorium. Nearly my turn.

*Keep calm, deep breaths.*

Time seemed to slow down as I walked to the podium, cleared my throat and read the 44 names I would remember for the rest of my life.

After the selection was over, each team went away into a separate room to get to know each other and begin the long task of laying the foundations of their campaigns. This was where I got to meet my team properly for the first time. The nervous energy was evident as we got together in a circle of chairs and made our introductions.

All eyes were on me now. This was where I had to show these guys I was here to win and that I meant business. I had to set out my stall in a persuasive way, conscious that I would only get one shot at this. I introduced them to my concept for Team SPIRIT and gave everybody a gift I had prepared – a blue rubber wristband with *Team SPIRIT 09–10 Pride. Energy. Support.* printed on it. It was a nice way of breaking the ice and I know some of my crew still wear their Team SPIRIT wristbands to this day.

From my well-prepared notes, I read what I wanted from them in the lead-up to the race.

---

*I want Team SPIRIT, in the lead-up to this race, to be characterised by three qualities:*

**Pride**
- *Pride in our team and the goals and values we agree upon.*

---

- *Pride in our boat, which we will clean, maintain and prepare to the highest standard.*
- *Pride in each other, as we learn, develop and improve together.*

**Energy**
- *Individual energy to put as much effort as possible into helping with the campaign in any way you can.*
- *Team energy to cooperate, organise, communicate and build the foundation of our race, using creativity and hard skills.*
- *Energy to learn as much as possible about ocean racing and performance sailing.*

**Support**
- *Support for each other, helping and offering advice and time willingly.*
- *Support for the boat, helping to prepare her for our race.*
- *Support from your family, friends and loved ones. Get them excited about the team and what we're doing and get them involved however you can. This is so important!*

**Team SPIRIT**
*Pride. Energy. Support.*

So far, so good. Nodding heads and a murmur of general approval. Was this the first stage of genuine buy-in?

I pressed on. Next up was my Team SPIRIT 'vision', which I had spent months writing and rewriting. This was my opus, my manifesto, my constitution. I felt strangely nervous to be reading it out loud to anybody besides myself.

Let's see how this goes down...

## The Team SPIRIT Vision

*I want this team to become an outstanding sailing team, an enthusiastic and energetic team, where everyone works their hardest, receives respect, strives to improve and is recognised publicly for their contribution.*

*There are five key elements to my vision:*

**Communication** *I want good communication to become the defining characteristic of this team. I will put in place systems to ensure communication is open, honest and moves in all directions.*

**Crew integration** *Team SPIRIT is a team of 44 people of whom 18 are sailing at any one time. Everybody plays an important part in our team and the success we have will be as a result of the combined energy and support from everybody, whether you're sailing or ashore.*

**Continuous improvement** *I want everyone to be thinking about ways to do things better. In short, if you can see or think of a better way of doing something, then I want you to share it.*

**A culture of knowledge sharing** *In an environment of free and open communication, a real culture of knowledge sharing can grow.*

**Effective conflict management** *Conflict is unavoidable on a race like this. Every boat has its problems and I expect ours will be no exception. What will make our boat exceptional is how we deal with that conflict.*

*Conflict isn't something to be shied away from. In fact, issue-based conflict can be a very positive thing. A debate (provided it stays civil) over the best way to hoist the spinnaker is a constructive thing, making everyone consider the issue, identifying all the alternatives and concluding upon the best practice.*

> *So there you have it, my vision for our team. It's by no means an exhaustive list, but I want those five points – crew integration, continuous improvement, knowledge sharing, conflict management, and above all COMMUNICATION – to be the foundation upon which everything we do is built.*

[The above is a precis of the Team SPIRIT vision. The full version can be found in the Appendix].

More nodding, more smiles and more looks of approval. This was going very well indeed and so I continued.

Over the next few hours, we discussed a lot of issues and topics as a group. From our uniform, to pre-race team-building days, to having a crew fund where everyone chips in some money to buy things we want for the boat. The drive was building. This great, lumbering machine was gathering speed, pushed by the energy and enthusiasm of 44 people whose lives were now intertwined. It was my job to keep that momentum building and keep it aimed at the ultimate goal: winning this race.

At the end of the day, after the party had died down and the crew had gone home, I went back to my yacht – boat nine. This sturdy vessel was going to be our home and keep us safe around the world, as it had done with crews on the previous two races. I sat on the deck, listening to the sound of the water lapping against the hull, and reflected on the day and what I had told my team.

*Remember, Brendan, words are cheap. Now you've got to follow up on all that stuff.*

The next day I emailed out a survey to my crew, asking them questions like:

What is your motivation for doing the race?

What do you hope to gain from the race?

What would you describe as your best and worst personality trait(s)?

From your past experiences/current careers, what qualities and skills do you feel you can bring to the team?

The answers I got were hugely varied and gave me a detailed insight into the crew and their motivations. I knew I needed this information as somebody with a 'negotiative leadership' style. I could only negotiate successfully with somebody if I truly understood what they wanted and their reasons for wanting it.

Here is a small, but fairly representative sample of answers to the question I considered the most important.

What do you hope to gain from the race?

- 'I am looking forward to the challenge of living in close quarters with many different personalities.'
- 'Having nearly drowned three times, I have a fear of the sea, and I want to face that fear.'
- 'Winning. Learning a lot more about all aspects of sailing. Having some fun, along with all the hard work.'
- 'Learn to sail, well. See the world, meet new people, and learn something new about myself. Hopefully win.'
- 'No.1 podium finish. I am very competitive.'

There were 44 sets of answers to consider – 44 sets of expectations and 44 opinions on how we should run the boat. Not every crew member was going to get exactly what they wanted out of the experience, that much was clear. I had to come up with an ethos that would satisfy the majority of needs for the majority of crew. The crew were hugely invested in the race, with the core round the world crew paying £32,000 for their place on the race and sacrificing their earning potential for ten months. Many had put successful careers on hold and were leaving their loved ones to pursue their dream of doing the race. They had high expectations and they were the stakeholders. As their skipper, I was accountable to them and responsible for them. If they collectively became unhappy with my leadership and took their case to the race management, I would eventually be sacked and replaced. It had happened before. Managing those expectations was going to be key to winning the race, but also to keeping my job.

# LEADERSHIP LESSONS

### Create a team identity

I was concerned about my fledgling team beginning our adventure without a name or identity. The only rallying point we had was the boat itself, and the name team number nine didn't exactly evoke a strong feeling of association or unity. I wanted a strong identity, right from the outset, and the name Team SPIRIT came to me very easily. It wasn't the most original name, but I felt it would give a feeling of unity and boldness.

By the end of that first meeting on crew allocation day, the Team SPIRIT identity was heartily embraced by the crew, who wore their blue wristbands proudly.

Over the following months, until our sponsor came along, we became known as Team SPIRIT throughout the fleet. After a while, I reflected that beginning our campaign without a sponsor was actually a blessing in disguise. It shifted the focus of our identity away from the boat and onto the crew as a distinct group. In an email to the crew, I expressed this in the following way:

> In the end, though, the name on the side of the boat won't make any difference to the experience we have or the performance of our team. When we're beating up through the Luzon Straits at night in 40 knots of wind and rough seas, we won't see the sponsor's name on the side of the boat and it won't matter to us.
>
> What we will see, though, is each other, our teammates.
>
> It's us, *as a team*, that will keep each other safe in rough weather.
>
> It's us, *as a team*, that will give the boat its character.
>
> It's our hard work, cooperation and effort that will see us standing on the podium.

Giving our team a positive, distinct identity from the beginning was a good idea of mine. When our Australian sponsor came along, we were thrilled that they decided on the name *Spirit of Australia*, allowing us to keep our Team SPIRIT identity as a crew, alongside the name of the boat itself.

## Have a vision

First impressions last, as the saying goes. At our initial crew meeting on crew allocation day, I only had one shot at creating that first impression. I had to set out my stall, tell the crew what I was about, and show them I meant business. I wanted the crew to see how much preparation I had already put into this campaign and that I had carefully considered how I saw it moving forward. Key to this was setting out my Team SPIRIT vision.

It had taken me months to write, pulling together ideas from the many leadership books I had studied and from the interviews I did with the past race skippers. It went through many revisions before I was finally happy with it. It was a bold statement, possibly idealistic, but it laid out what we would aspire to. Many of the things in my vision were just common sense, like wanting good communication and effective conflict management, but the act of explicitly stating what my vision was made a good impression on the crew and gave them a lot of confidence in me, something I needed in order to build momentum and get the campaign moving quickly.

The content of my Team SPIRIT vision formed the foundation of the rules we had on board and what we considered acceptable and unacceptable behaviour. As long-winded as it was, it was the embryo that developed into the ethos we had on board and was a small but important component of our overall success.

## Understand your team members' motivations

The survey I sent out to the crew, following our meeting, helped me to understand their individual motivations, which helped me a lot in shaping the direction of the campaign and my subsequent interactions with them. As a negotiative leader, I was particularly conscious of this – my style relied upon negotiating with them towards a common goal in the context of their own motivating factors. Trying to spur a non-competitive crew member with words of hard racing, competition and victory wouldn't work. I knew I would have to take a more individual look at each character and see what made them tick – hence the survey.

Upon reflection, I am glad I did it in this format. I emailed it out and gave them a week to return it to me. Their answers would be confidential. Rather than discussing this as a group, where people can often give answers based on what they think the leader or group want to hear, I wanted to give them time and privacy to consider their answers.

The answers were very revealing, in some cases. Some detailed the break-up of their relationships or the feeling that they hadn't done anything of importance with their life thus far. The race was a way of turning their lives around by doing something extraordinary. Their motivation was changing the direction of their life. At the other end of the spectrum, there were crew whose sole motivation was to win an ocean race.

There was clearly a wide and divergent range of responses. I wasn't going to be able to make sure everybody got *exactly* what they wanted from the experience, but I felt I could satisfy most of the motivations the crew had with the aims of the campaign. It would be difficult and I knew there would be personal issues down the line, particularly from the crew who weren't that interested in racing, but knowing this in advance helped me to defuse any issues with them before they turned into problems.

Understanding my crew's individual motivations helped me know what tools to use to motivate them. Not all people respond to the same motivation, whether on a sailing boat or ashore. In my experience, the best way of figuring out their motivation is also the simplest. Ask.

# 6

# TRAINING

*We are what we repeatedly do. Excellence, then, is not an act, but a habit*

*ARISTOTLE*

The enthusiasm and energy of the team was fantastic. Our online space was buzzing with people doing research into weather patterns, ocean currents, sleep deprivation, nutrition and exercise. Everybody had bought into this plan of mine and the communication among the crew was genuine and open. I had recommended to all the crew that they should get a copy of Dale Carnegie's classic book *How to win friends and influence people*, which I had read many times. For anybody who hasn't read it, please do. It's a little dated, written in 1930s America, but the lessons on human interaction contained within its pages are timeless. I could have recommended a technical book, a sail trim manual or heavy tome on racing tactics, but I thought *How to win friends and influence people* would ultimately bring more benefit to the campaign and each crew member's individual experience.

Having spoken to most of my crew one-to-one by this point, their biggest anxiety was being on board a yacht for weeks with people they didn't get along with. They had been through many trials and outlaid substantial money to get on this race and they were afraid that it could be ruined if they were part of an unhappy crew. I could certainly relate to this anxiety. I had been a part of some great crews in my career, crews where everyone got on well and the atmosphere was positive and happy. For my money, there is no better place in the world than on a sailing yacht with a great group of people. I had also sailed with bad crews, where difficult, strongly opinionated characters got on everyone's nerves and made the whole experience an endurance test rather than an enjoyable passage. Interpersonal relations can become quite strained on boats because of the uncomfortable, confined space the crew have to occupy together and the fact that there is no escape from somebody they don't get along with. From the moment they leave the dock, the crew have no option of going home at the end of the day and venting their frustrations to a sympathetic ear over a glass of red wine.

My Team SPIRIT crew would have to cope with minimal sleep, exhaustion, very limited contact with friends and family, zero luxuries, and being cold, wet and homesick for up to five weeks at a time. Every condition that makes most people generally grumpy and miserable would be present and there could be no escape. On top of all that, the pressure would be huge. The pressure of being responsible for the safety of their teammates. The pressure of performing their job well in every sailing manoeuvre. The pressure of racing harder than our rivals would be the greatest. Every six hours we would get an email from the race office called a sched (pronounced 'sked', short for 'schedule'), telling us if we had gained or lost miles on our competitors, so the results of our labours were immediately apparent.

I knew we would have our problems and crew fallings-out. Every boat would. Any randomly selected group of 44 people are not going to get along perfectly at the best of times, let alone on a racing yacht with all the conditions and pressures mentioned. In getting the crew to read *How to win friends and influence people*, I thought I would arm people with the mental tools to defuse at least some of the crew problems the past skippers had told me about.

We were at the stage of preparation for the race where the ten boats went out racing with their race crews on four week-long training races. This would give the crews and skippers the opportunity to bond properly as a team and get into the routines that would become their daily existence for ten months of ocean racing. This would be the first real contest, then, between the ten teams. The races counted for nothing points-wise and were done as part of the training syllabus, but nobody was treating them as anything other than serious competition.

Already there was talk on the dockside about the favourite teams to win the race. The talk naturally focused on the abilities and experience of the skippers leading the teams, as all the teams were even in terms of the crews' sailing ability. Not surprisingly, the young Brendan and his unassuming crew on boat nine weren't thought to be near the front of the pack.

There was plenty of bravado among the crews and plenty of competitive banter. Jokes, jibes and boat nicknames were being thrown about in good humour. It was good fun, but there was a serious undercurrent of competition. Every team had to prove themselves up to the task and wanted to win these early races.

I made a rule for my crew that we wouldn't 'trash talk' any other teams or get cocky at this early stage. I have a humble attitude to life and I believe sailing is a sport that deserves humility, so that was the attitude I expected of my crew as well. We maintained this attitude all the way around the world, even once it was mathematically assured that we would win the overall race. We stayed humble, accepted praise warmly, and shared gladly in the success of other teams.

The racing was fierce during those four weeks. The starts were aggressive, with all boats jockeying hard for the best position on the line. The races went up and down the English Channel, around buoys and navigational markers. For most of the crew on every boat, it was their first experience of long-distance racing. We practised our manoeuvres, set our spinnaker, changed our headsails and I sharpened my weather routing and racing navigation skills. We experienced the whole spectrum of weather conditions, from rough 40-knot winds and heavy seas breaking over the bow of the boat to being absolutely becalmed with zero wind and the boat drifting in lazy circles on the tide.

When the wind began to build, the power of these 68ft yachts was quite intimidating, and the loads on the lines pulling our sails into shape were huge. The powerful winches could exert over 5 metric tons of load onto a line very easily. The lines themselves had the diameter of a bottle cap and were made from the very latest high-tech synthetic fibres. They had a breaking strain of more than 8 tons. With that amount of load in the lines, mistakes could lead to serious injury. One wrong move by a tired or distracted crew member could see their hands get pulled into the winch and fingers crushed, literally in the blink of an eye. If a line was pulling out of their hands and they didn't let go quickly, then the resulting rope burn could put them in hospital for surgery. We had to respect the yacht and its potential to hurt us if we weren't meticulous and careful with our winch drills. Safety was our number one priority on board. A serious injury would leave us, at best, one crew member down; at worst it would mean abandoning the race to get them to shore-side medical help.

As the days wore on, the crew slipped into the routine of offshore yacht racing. Since the early days of seafaring, life at sea has been governed by routines and the most important one is the watch system. As we were racing 24 hours a day with 18 crew, I decided that we would opt for a two-watch system. This means that one watch of nine people would be up on deck sailing the boat and keeping a vigilant eye for approaching ships while the other nine slept in their bunks. Then, at a fixed time, the watches would change and the nine that were sailing would get their turn to rest. I decided we would do six hours on watch, six hours off watch during the daytime and four hours on, four off at night. On long ocean crossings, days of the week and even the date become irrelevant, it's either light or dark and you have a job to do regardless. The distance to the finish is the only number that matters.

In addition to this master watch system, we operated a rolling 'mother' watch. Every day, two people (one from each watch) would drop out of the watch system to become 'mothers'. That day, their job would be to bake the bread, prepare breakfast, lunch and dinner, wash up, clean the boat, make tea and coffee for everybody. It was a full-on day that usually turned out to be more exhausting than being in the normal watch system. At the end of a day on mother watch, the two mothers got to have a shower and a 12-hour period of unbroken sleep – the epitome of luxury to an exhausted sailor. As you have probably deduced, this meant people only got to shower once every eight days. Ocean racing is a horrible-smelling sport.

There were more duties that needed to be shared around, like pumping out the water that collects in the bilge of the boat (the space below the floorboards and bunks). This had to be done manually, using a bucket and manual pump. Every boat collects water in the bilge. Some of it leaks in around the bolts holding the keel on, some of it comes down the inside of the hollow mast, but it all finds its way into the bilges.

The boat has electric bilge pumps, which can get most of the water out, but not all of it. The rest we had to get rid of ourselves and I made it a rule that it needed to be done every hour. It wasn't that the water was dangerous or the boat was slowly sinking, far from it, but the water sitting in the bilge was extra weight that we were carrying around with us, needlessly. Every hour, whoever was on bilge duty that day went below with the trusty black bucket, sponge and manual pump and cleaned out the bilges, checking under every bunk and making sure the bilge was dry. In truth, the 5 or 10 litres of water they brought out every hour weren't going to make a huge amount of difference to our speed on a 32-ton yacht, but it produced a mindset that we would leave no stone unturned in looking for that competitive edge.

That mindset, that performance-driven attitude saw us alter the weight distribution of the things we had on board. Heavy stores and tins of food had to be stored low down, beneath the floorboards, rather than on the shelves in the galley. Our heavy spare ropes were stored under the floor in the centre of the boat, rather than in the dedicated rope-locker in the bow. We did all we could to move as much weight as possible towards the centre of the boat and away from the ends. We used two of the most comfortable bunks on board to store our three spinnakers, because they were directly above the keel and that was the best place to put that weight. Small changes that probably made a 0.5 per cent difference to our speed, but 0.5 per cent difference and the competitive mindset that comes with it adds up to a lot of miles over a four-week ocean race.

I worked out that every extra kilo of weight we carried was an extra kilo of water that the boat had to displace as it moved its own length through the water. Over the 35,000nm of the race, that one, single extra kilo of weight meant our boat had to shoulder aside another 282 tons of seawater.

I set some very strict guidelines on the amount of gear people were allowed to bring with them. I made the rule that each crew member could bring no more than 20kg of kit on board, excluding their essential Gore-tex sailing oilskins and boots. We bought communal things like sunscreen and shampoo from the crew fund, so we didn't end up with 20 individual bottles. Every kilo counted.

My crew, in their enthusiasm, were coming to me with ideas of how we could improve life on board. One suggested a spice rack for the galley. Another suggested a rice-cooker. The idea of individual fans for the crew bunks came up, as did the suggestion that we should buy a crew laptop, so people could email family in port. My response was always the same: 'Does it make the boat go faster?' If the answer was no, then it wasn't going to happen.

'Does it make the boat go faster?'

That one powerful question summed up our whole approach to the race. It wasn't the only question we asked, of course. If an extra piece of equipment would make something safer or help keep up crew morale, then it would certainly be considered, but asking the question made sure everyone kept our goal of winning the race in the forefront of their minds. After a while, the crew bought into this ethos, too, and were coming to me with ideas on how we could reduce weight, including removing fire extinguishers, floor panels and heavy spares. All very unseamanlike ideas and I rejected them with a disapproving frown, but inside I was very pleased to see them thinking in such a performance-driven way.

Sleep was a problem for me during those early training races. The conditions were rough and the boat thumped and crashed through a short, sharp English Channel swell. I couldn't stay on deck all day and night, and I needed the crew to become comfortable sailing the boat without me standing at the back reminding them what to do.

I tried sleeping in the navigation station of the boat, sitting on a thick cushion with my back against the wall, which was very uncomfortable, but it meant I could keep an eye on the boat's navigation computer and I was dressed and ready in case I was needed on deck in a hurry. The act of undressing from my oilskins, climbing into my sleeping bag and closing my eyes seemed irresponsible. Anything could happen when I was asleep. My mind just wouldn't relax and let sleep come. The cogs kept churning over a constant stream of 'what if?' questions.

*What if the guys on deck aren't looking out for ships and we get into a dangerous collision situation?*

*What if a line snaps? It'll be at least 30 seconds before I am on deck and in that time somebody could get badly injured.*

*What if somebody isn't clipped on up there? One lurch and they could get thrown overboard.*

*What if the sails aren't in proper trim? We aren't going as fast as we could be.*

At the most basic level, I knew I just didn't trust the crew yet. I didn't trust them to not make mistakes, to keep a good lookout and trim the sails correctly. They had been through the Clipper training programme and had been taught about all those things, but I wasn't willing to let them have responsibility for the boat just yet.

*Will they be ready by the time we reach the formidable Southern Ocean?*

*Will I trust them enough to drive the boat down those mountainous waves while I sleep soundly in my bunk?*

*Will they keep racing hard when I go to bed, or will they take it easy and stop trimming the sails?*

And most important of all…

*Could they get the boat to a safe port if I got knocked unconscious or killed?*

These were things I needed to think more about when I wasn't so tired.

We performed consistently in all of the training races and while we never came first, we were always in the top three. I was very pleased with our progress and we earned an early reputation of being a solid crew who sailed hard.

After the third of our four weeks, I sent this message in an email to the whole crew:

> Hi Team SPIRIT,
>
> I thought it was about time I sent out an email update on how things are going. I would like to start sending these more frequently, so everybody feels more involved.
>
> Firstly, the team spirit and attitude on board has been amazing. On each of our three courses thus far, I have been hugely impressed with the hard-working, focused, competitive and fun racing ethos that has emerged each time.
>
> Little things stand out in my mind. For example:
>
> People getting out of bed during their off-watch to help pack a spinnaker.

People moving bunks so others can manually pump the bilges beneath it.

Mother watch turning out improvised baked treats for the crew up on deck in the cold.

…and a hundred others.

It's little things like this that make the difference over the course of a long ocean race. One recurring theme has emerged on these last three races – **Persistence**.

No matter what the race or the weather throws at us, we fight on, improvise, make use of everything we can and never give up. In many races we have done, we have been in a very poor position early in the race, but as the hours and watches go by, we climb our way up the table and, so far, have always finished on the podium. Not because we are better sailors or our boat is faster, just because we don't give up and we keep our focus.

I noticed a pattern emerging during these practice races. During the first 12 hours, all of the boats would be racing hard and there was very little between us, speed-wise. The opportunities for overtaking were limited as all the crews were super-motivated, pushing as hard as possible.

After 12 hours, the fleet began to disperse. The skippers would be playing out their various race strategies and the boats went from being a few hundred feet from each other to being specks on the horizon, if even visible at all. Gains and losses were harder to measure with the naked eye and the motivation that came from having that competition so close started to wane. The only indication we had of our position in the fleet came every six hours in the form of our email scheds. Finding motivation during that time was definitely harder and it became clear that some crews stayed focused and others lost it and slowed down.

It was during this middle period of the race that we always seemed to creep from whatever position we were in to being near the front of the pack. We didn't speed up or do anything differently, we just didn't slow down. We kept our motivation going, even though the competition was not within eyesight. We kept reminding ourselves that they were still there, just over the horizon and pushing as hard as they could, and we had to do the same.

The final 12 hours of the race were like the first 12. The boats were converging again on the finish line. In the final push for the line all the boats were racing their hardest once more. By that time, though, the gaps between them were usually big enough that the finishing order was set. It became clear to us that the crews who stayed motivated and showed persistence for that middle section of the race, when the fleet was spread out, were consistently the ones who finished in the top half of the fleet.

There is a saying: *You don't win a race, you lose a race.* All you have to do to win is keep racing as hard as possible, don't make mistakes and stay motivated. If you can do that, the competition will eliminate themselves through their own mistakes or problems. This mentality became a key part of our racing philosophy.

This was all well and good on a four-day training race around the Channel, but would any of us skippers be able to keep our crew motivated for a whole *month* of ocean racing, out of sight of our competitors for weeks at a time? That was the real question.

I had seen all of my crew perform during those practice races and now had the tough decision of selecting two 'watch leaders'. The job of the watch leader is to be responsible for what is happening on deck when I'm not up there. They would supervise the helmsman and make sure they were steering the correct compass course and make sure the sails were being trimmed regularly. They would keep me informed of any changes to the conditions. Most importantly, they would wake me up if I was sleeping and something was amiss. It was a massive responsibility. On most sailing boats, the skipper has another professional sailor called a 'first mate' to fill this role. I was going to have to ask two of my amateur crew to step up into the role, knowing that the extra responsibility on their own shoulders might take some of the enjoyment from their own experience. Luckily, I had a handful of crew who wanted the job and were very capable.

Sticking true to my 80 per cent people skills, 20 per cent sailing skills breakdown, I selected two guys who I thought would do a good job. They were responsible, trustworthy and both could manage the expectations of the crew on their watch. Most importantly, though, I trusted them to come and wake me up if anything wasn't right.

I pictured that the three of us would make up a 'management team' and we could discuss issues and bounce ideas off each other, so I needed two people who would complement my strengths and make up for my weaknesses. A leader doesn't need to be well rounded, but a leadership team does. I needed two people who could get things done, work independently, and make the crew who were doing the work feel valued.

In the end, I chose two excellent watch leaders, who are the first of the characters you will meet from my crew.

Mike Hanssen was a 36-year-old construction manager from Perth, Australia. He had his own business doing the fit-outs of new apartments in high-rise buildings. He had done very well for himself and was now ready to take a break from work for ten months and have an adventure. He was brutally honest with people and from his own business life had a very results-driven attitude. He had great leadership qualities and less confident crew members would go to him and ask questions if they were unsure. He was also very competitive and his goals mirrored my own. He had done a lot of small boat racing in Perth, but had never crossed an ocean before. It became clear to me early on that Mike had a great eye for detail and this was something I didn't have. He saw problems emerging from quarters that I missed, because I was keeping a broader focus on the crew. He took steps himself to sort them out. Mike was a supportive leader and would take time to give instructions to people, explaining why and making them feel responsible for the outcomes.

Mike gladly accepted when I offered him the position of watch leader and his efforts were instrumental in our overall victory.

Steve Davis was a 52-year-old radiologist, also from Perth. He was the managing director of a private radiology practice. He was at home in the surgery, offering diagnoses and comfort to patients in his quiet but assured voice. Steve was a great people-person and was very hard not to like. He, too, had a high-performance approach and his goal was for us to win the race. Steve's style of leadership was 'executing'. He would give clear instructions before any manoeuvre and confirm, then reconfirm, that everyone understood their role. Some of the crew found the talking tiresome, but it meant mistakes were minimised and people were clear on their jobs.

Steve was also very good at offering me advice. He had been in positions of leadership and knew many of the pitfalls. He would often quietly offer me advice on how to tackle a crew issue or make certain people feel more included. It was always done in private and in a positive, constructive way. I was very grateful to have Steve as a sounding board. He was only doing the first three legs of the race, so I would need to think long and hard about who would replace him when he departed.

In a private briefing with these two guys, I told them what my expectations of them would be and what they should expect from me. I told them that sometimes they would have to order the crew on their watch to do things they didn't want to do. They would probably be criticised at various times for decisions they made. They may have to deal with some personal issues they would rather walk away from. They both accepted that these were just the realities of being a leader and I was confident that they would be loyal and trusted deputies. They both had my 100 per cent unwavering support, which gave them the confidence to be bold and decisive in their roles. But I had to warn them, too, that their place as watch leader was not set in stone and if they weren't doing a good enough job, then I would have to find somebody else.

Meanwhile, the sponsorship hunt for our boat had come to an end. I was taken out to lunch with the race director and informed that my boat was going to be named *Spirit of Australia*. An Australian sponsor had come on board and they decided on the name, partially based on the fact that we were already calling ourselves Team SPIRIT and also because 'Spirit of Australia' is the tagline for the iconic Australian airline QANTAS. I suspected our sponsor would be Australian (there were rumours going around) but to have it confirmed was brilliant. The fact that we could keep our Team SPIRIT brand alive was fortunate; all the crew had bought into it and were proudly telling people about it. As I walked back to the boat, I had a big grin as I imagined introducing myself to people – 'Hi, I'm Brendan, skipper of *Spirit of Australia*.' 'Welcome on board *Spirit of Australia*, I'm the skipper.'

The final sponsors were confirmed now and the boats all had names:

| Boat name | Skipper |
| --- | --- |
| *Edinburgh Inspiring Capital* | Matt Pike |
| *Jamaica Lightning Bolt* | Pete Stirling |
| *Uniquely Singapore* | Jim Dobie |
| *Cork* | Richie Fearon |
| *Team Finland* | Eero Lehtinen |
| *Qingdao* | Chris Stanmore-Major |
| *Cape Breton Island* | Jan Ridd |
| *Hull & Humber* | Piers Dudin |
| *Spirit of Australia* | Brendan Hall |
| *California* | Pete Rollason |

I put the word out to the team that we needed a mission statement, a short, snappy sentence that summed up the goals of our newly-named team. After a few days of discussion back and forward, one of my crew, Bob Bell, came up with this:

'Our goal is to sustain a campaign of continuous improvement. To do all we can to win the race and feel fulfilled.'

Bingo. That was perfect. The three key elements were continuous personal development, a clear articulation of our goal – winning – and acknowledging the importance of self-fulfilment and individual goals. It summed up our ethos perfectly and I immediately made a laminated copy of it in large bold lettering and stuck it to the wall of the communal saloon area on *Spirit of Australia*, where the crew would see it every day of the race.

I've always loved quotes and sayings, those small linguistic pearls of wisdom. I love reading about and trying to understand the wise and clever thoughts of great minds. I decided to select some of my favourite quotes that I thought reflected the three key elements in our mission statement and stick them up around the boat.

For the theme of continuous improvement, we began on the wall of the galley, with the saying of Solomon Ibn Gabirol, a Hebrew poet and philosopher:

> *'The first step in the acquisition of wisdom is silence, the second listening, the third memory, the fourth practice and the fifth teaching others.'*

On the theme of winning the race, the sayings all revolved around that one word I knew was going to make the biggest difference: Persistence.

Staying in the saloon, where the crew would spend much of their time eating meals and relaxing, the sayings on the walls left no doubt about our intention to never give up.

> *'Energy and persistence conquer all things.'*
> Benjamin Franklin

> *'Success is the sum of small efforts, repeated day in and day out.'*
> Robert Collier

> *'The rewards for those who persevere far outweigh the pain that must precede the victory.'*
> Ted W. Engstrom

For me, the most powerful of all, the words of US President Calvin Coolidge:

> *'Nothing in the world can take the place of Persistence.*
> *Talent will not; nothing is more common than unsuccessful men with talent.*
> *Genius will not; unrewarded genius is almost a proverb.*
> *Education will not; the world is full of educated derelicts.*
> *Persistence and determination alone are omnipotent.*
> *The slogan "Press On" has solved and always will solve the problems of the human race.'*

And finally, on the theme of personal fulfilment, I stuck up the quotes in the two heads (toilets), the only truly private places on board where one could contemplate.

> *'In learning to know other things, and other minds, we become more intimately acquainted with ourselves, and are to ourselves better worth knowing.'*
> Philip Gilbert Hamilton

> *'Exert your talents, and distinguish yourself, and don't think of retiring from the world, until the world will be sorry that you retire.'*
> Samuel Johnson

> *'The fact is, that to do anything in the world worth doing, we must not stand back shivering and thinking of the cold and danger, but jump in and scramble through as well as we can.'*
> Robert Cushing

Those sayings helped me, personally, get through some very hard times on the journey, particularly when the finish of a race seemed impossibly far away. The crew drew strength from them more and more as the race progressed and they saw the truth in them demonstrated. We relentlessly persisted through everything and it brought us victory.

## LEADERSHIP LESSONS

### Does it make the boat go faster?

This question was the filter through which I screened every new idea and it proved to be a very useful tool. It kept the crew focused on the overall objective, making the boat as fast and safe as possible. Weight was our critical factor – the less the boat weighed overall, the faster it would move – but there were other considerations and long-term implications. We could have saved even more weight by using lower-quality food or stopping the crew from bringing luxury items like books or music players on board, but the long-term detriment to crew morale would eventually slow down the boat. There was a balance to be struck and by asking the question every time we considered something, we found and kept that balance.

## What if?

In those early days of racing, when my trust in the crew hadn't fully developed, I found myself running through a lot of 'what if?' scenarios in my mind. In running through them, I was arming myself with the knowledge to deal with them. One question always led to others, for example:

'What happens if we had a man overboard?'

Leads to:

'Is the engine in neutral and ready to start?'

'Has it been checked since it was last used?'

'Who is wearing the climbing harness?' (They become the person lowered into the water to rescue the casualty.)

'How many extra crew from the off watch will I need on deck to perform the rescue?'

'Which is the nearest coastguard station and what VHF radio channel do they use?'

Systematically running through all these questions and answering each one to my satisfaction was the only way to be positively sure I was ready for every eventuality. A crew member's life could be on the line and if I wasn't fully prepared, a delay in rescuing them could be fatal. There was no room for error.

I couldn't plan for every possible eventuality, as you will read in further chapters, but I had a list of ten common disaster scenarios for which I had a fully formulated plan, based on my rhetorical 'what if?' questions. In having answers to those questions, I lowered my own anxiety about how I would deal with them if they arose, which in turn increased my confidence. As time progressed, I began using my 'what if?' questions on the crew, particularly the two watch leaders. I wanted them to be running through their own list of 'what if?' scenarios. I asked the same of our boat medic, to make sure they had a clear plan of action for the ten most common injuries they could imagine someone sustaining on board. They would need to be able to react and treat the casualty immediately, so forward planning was crucial.

In every walk of life, we ask ourselves 'what if?' questions, though they are usually generated by our short-term worries. What if the car doesn't start tomorrow morning? What if I don't get the job I'm applying for? What if I fail this exam?

For anybody, particularly if you're in a position of leadership, I would urge you to make the 'what if?' question a more important part of your internal monologue. Imagine the ten or twenty things that keep you up at night, make you worried or anxious. Pose yourself a simple, thoughtful 'what if?' question and keep generating more questions as you answer them, like I did with the man overboard. It won't stop the problems from happening, but it will help alleviate your worries about them and make you feel more prepared.

Worrying doesn't solve tomorrow's problems, it just takes away today's peace. Asking myself those 'what if?' questions made me confront my worries and feel more confident about dealing with them.

# 7

# RACING AT LAST

*Coming together is a beginning. Keeping together is progress. Working together is success*

*HENRY FORD*

The boat was ready. The food for one month at sea was packed into day bags and loaded. The crew were as ready as they could be. We had a short shake-down sail from Clipper HQ in Portsmouth harbour up to the city of Hull in north-east England for the official race start.

There was a big party for the boats leaving Portsmouth and hundreds of people lined the waterfront to watch the fleet leave. We motored out of the harbour in an arrowhead formation, with our stainless steel polished, battle flags flying, and sponsors' logos bright and shiny. The sails were white as snow and the scene looked exactly like that in Liverpool two years earlier, when I watched the fleet leave on the 07–08 race. Only now I was experiencing it from behind the wheel of one of these ten mighty racing yachts, with an inexperienced but loyal and hardworking crew.

The cheers of the crowd were loud and I spotted a few Australian flags being waved in among the sea of colour as we motored out the harbour. A flotilla of boats flocked around us, people shouting wishes of good luck. The send-off was very warm and heartfelt, but we were told it was nothing compared to the send-off we would receive in Hull at the official race start.

Once we had left the harbour and broke formation, I gave the order to hoist our headsails. It was a very straightforward manoeuvre, which the crew had done by themselves many times, so I went below to write an entry in the log book.

It was over before I had time to register it. I had only just turned my head to see what the noise was and now I was looking at the body of Barry, lying at the base of the companionway ladder with blood coming out of his head. I had just glimpsed the last moment of the 2-metre fall and seen him land on his head.

*Oh, shit. Spinal injury.*

I was sitting only a metre away and, after a second of disbelief, I jumped up and went to his aid, with the words 'cervical spine injury' ringing in my ears. We were less than 15 minutes from harbour and already had a potentially critical injury on board. Luckily, we had a qualified GP doctor on board, Felicity, who came immediately to Barry's aid as he came round to consciousness. Her initial diagnosis was not as severe as I was expecting. He had full consciousness and his spinal cord was undamaged. Felicity and a few helpers looked after Barry, while I got the boat turned around and we steamed back into Portsmouth harbour at full speed.

'How on earth did this happen?' I asked the crew on deck. They told me that Barry had been standing next to the open hatch pulling on the line for our running backstay (a line that helps support the mast). There was resistance in the line, so he gave it a good pull with all his body weight and the line slipped and he fell backwards, down the hatch.

We arrived at the marina, where an ambulance was waiting to take Barry to hospital. Though his shirt was covered in blood and looked a mess, he was able to walk off the boat himself with the help of the paramedics.

The crew were being quite positive about the whole thing – it was just an accident after all – but I knew that it would be a confidence killer if we didn't take the time to talk it through. I called a team meeting in the cockpit of the boat as soon as Barry had been taken away.

We discussed how the accident had happened and what we needed to do to stop it happening again. Everyone had a turn to provide input and, by the end, we decided as a group that to prevent any further injuries of this type, the companionway hatch would remain closed at all times, unless someone was going up or down. I knew this was the natural conclusion they would reach and I guided the discussion in that direction. I could have just said 'New rule – hatch stays closed from now on', but I knew that if I wanted them to *really* remember and ultimately self-police the rule, they would need to come up with it themselves.

A racing yacht is a workplace health and safety inspector's worst nightmare. The wet and slippery deck is festooned with trip hazards, deep hatches and lines under huge tension. We send crew up the mast wearing a helmet and a harness to inspect the rig without scaffolding or working permits. The sails are incredibly heavy and the crew have to lift and lug them around on slippery, uneven surfaces where proper bend-at-the-knees lifting is impossible. These are the things we all accept when we go racing. There are no warning signs, risk assessments or over-the-top procedures – just personal responsibility, common sense and practical safety equipment. It's a refreshing change from the overly litigious world ashore, where every day ambulance-chasing solicitors drive another nail into the coffin of personal responsibility. On the ocean, you really hold your own life in the palm of your hand and the lives of your fellow crew members too. It's an empowering feeling and it builds a self-belief and a trust in your team you rarely find ashore.

We got word later that afternoon that Barry was fine. It was a nasty cut on his head, but nothing more sinister. He was in good spirits on the phone and regretted that he wouldn't be able to join us on the sail up to Hull. He would see us in Qingdao, where he was joining us for the leg across the North Pacific to San Francisco. I gave him the nickname 'Head Banger' and promised I would bring a helmet for him to wear during the crossing.

The sail up to Hull was a testing one. The winds were blowing up to 50 knots and we were forced to sail with a minimal sail plan for the final part of the journey. We were sailing upwind, which meant the boat was heeled over at a 35-degree angle, making life on deck and below deck considerably harder. If you draw a 35-degree angle on paper it doesn't seem like much, but when your entire world is leaning over at 35 degrees it feels like much more. Add to that the fact that you are sailing into the waves, not with them, and the boat crashes and slams with each wave impact. As the boat takes off over the top of a wave and then all 32 tons slams down hard into the trough, the sound inside is truly gut-wrenching. As the boats are stripped out and largely empty, the sounds feel like a bass drum. It booms and reverberates and everything shakes and shudders. For some of the crew, this was their first taste of really heavy weather and the slamming sounds made some nervous about the strength of the boat in these conditions. It was hard sailing, but we got to Hull safely and without any more injuries.

In Hull the hurried preparations continued. The race fleet was the news of the city and there was a constant stream of people gathered around the walls of the marina, watching us diligently going about our jobs. The local TV and radio stations were buzzing with race fever and the vocal community support for the local boat *Hull & Humber* was fantastic to see.

The day before the race start, I booked a meeting room in a local office and brought my whole crew up there for our pre-race briefing. The first race was a short sprint to the city of La Rochelle in France, which would be a quick stopover before the long 5,000nm race to Rio de Janeiro, Brazil. In the briefing I stressed the importance of preserving our equipment. I told the crew that while I loved the fact they were brimming with energy and enthusiasm, they were still relatively inexperienced and we couldn't afford to break a spinnaker pole or tear a sail at this early stage. We had 35,000 miles of racetrack ahead of us and we had to stay focused on the bigger picture. I knew all the crews would be fired up and the skippers would be tempted to fly their sails above their maximum recommended wind speed on this short first race. It was good strategy for short-term speed, but the sail would quickly stretch and the shape would change, meaning it would be less efficient in the long term. I came up with the phrase 'Think long-term victory, not short-term glory' and told the crew to remind me of it if I looked tempted to push our sails above their limits.

I knew from my discussions with the past skippers that at least half the fleet would tear their spinnakers on the first leg, because of crew inexperience and flying the sails in more wind than they were designed for. There was a penalty system for breaking equipment or tearing sails. Any repair costing more than £500 would incur a one-point penalty, more than £1,000, two points, and so on. A destroyed spinnaker could cost up to four points to have replaced, which could easily be the difference between overall victory and coming second.

The scoring system on the race was simple. There were 14 races in total. On each race, the boat that came first got ten points, second got nine, third got eight and so on. We also had 'scoring gates' on the longer ocean legs. These gates were positioned about a third of the way into the race and were designed to reward the teams who pushed hard early on. They could be anything from 60 to 500 miles wide. The first boat to sail through the gate got three points, second got two and third got one. Any subsequent boats that went through the gate got nothing.

I didn't sleep a wink the night before the start, I just lay in my bunk and ran through the plan for the race over and over in my head. As dawn broke, my hands were shaking with nervous energy and anticipation.

It was an emotional morning, with the crew saying tearful goodbyes to family and friends. It was truly touching to see families embraced, children sobbing with sadness at the departure of a parent. Touching words of support, hugs, pats on the back and encouragement came to me from all directions and I smiled and thanked everyone, but my mind was somewhere else, turning over the latest weather information, the tidal stream data for the River Humber and how we would tackle the first night at sea. There was a race start ceremony held next to the marina and all the crews took turns in going up on stage with their boat's battle song blaring in front of a crowd of 10,000 cheering supporters. Once each team had had their moment in the spotlight, they walked down to their boats along a barricaded pathway, with friends, supporters and cheering locals lining the edge, smiling faces with arms outstretched.

As I walked down to *Spirit of Australia* with my crew, I saw a face in the crowd I recognised. It was a man named David Jack. I had met him two years ago during a sail-training course. David was a legger on the 07–08 Clipper race and was washed overboard in the fearsome Southern Ocean when he was pulled out of his lifejacket by the force of a large wave. His skipper, Hannah Jenner, and crew found and rescued him in nine minutes, in the middle of the night. He had taken off his boots and jacket to stay buoyant and was on the edge of hypothermia, only minutes from exhaustion and drowning. He had come as close to death as is possible and survived, thanks to his skipper and crewmates. I hadn't seen David since before the 07–08 race and seeing him now brought back the feeling of shock and relief I felt when I first heard the news of his incident. I broke ranks from the crew and walked over to him and shook his hand. He said a quick hello and wished us well, then said something I will never forget.

'Keep them safe, Brendan. *You keep them safe.*'

The tone of his voice and the deadly serious look in his eyes said it all and I found myself suddenly fighting back tears. Here was a man who understood the burden of responsibility I was shouldering and it brought my mind back to earth with a bang. He released my hand, wished me good luck, and I fell back in step with my happy, excited crew. They were unaware of the profound significance of the moment for me and I kept walking and waving to the crowd, not knowing that David's words would come back to me many times over the next ten months.

The final goodbyes were said and the crews climbed aboard their yachts and left the marina one by one, battle songs blaring from the loudspeakers. Our own battle song was 'Around the world' by Daft Punk, as voted by the crew.

We hoisted sails in the river, dialled up for the start and jostled for the best starting position with the other boats. The crowd cheered from the shore and, as the countdown reached zero, the deafening boom of the start cannon marked the beginning of our epic race around the world. The action was frantic. We manoeuvred the yacht well and as we left the mouth of the River Humber we were in a solid mid-fleet position. The race to La Rochelle was only 800nm and, with the predicted wind, it would be a fast, downwind sprint. Three days maximum.

This was the first real race and all the boats were pushing hard. Every boat length was hard fought and the fleet stayed relatively close together. As the wind came around behind us, the boats hoisted their spinnakers, the enormous, parachute-like sails that fly in front of the boat, pulling it along at high speed. Each of our spinnakers was the size of a tennis court and the power in them was formidable. The boat began to surf on the waves and we touched a top speed of 18 knots on a particularly long surf. The boat felt right, the sails were powered up, and we were racing hard with the other three leading boats.

The wind kept increasing and was approaching the maximum wind strength for our heavyweight spinnaker. The sail was new and I knew it could handle a little bit more than the recommended wind strength. None of the other boats were making any preparations to drop theirs. Who was going to fold first? The wind was now creeping above the maximum for the spinnaker. The process of dropping the sail and changing to our smaller, tougher Yankee headsail would cost us a lot of ground and we would be left behind.

Do I stick to my guns and my 'think long-term victory, not short-term glory' or stay with the pack, racing on the limit? The cautious skipper in me said one thing, the competitive skipper said another. It was the nautical equivalent to a game of chicken, seeing which skipper would hold their nerve the longest…

*No, no, no! This is stupid. This short race is not worth blowing a spinnaker for. Forget the other guys and remember what the past skippers said. Get that sail down quick.*

We were the first boat of the leading group to drop their spinnaker and slow down. I was expecting to see the others sail away from us, but obviously the other skippers were equally conflicted and they dropped their spinnakers shortly after. The racing remained close all the way down the length of the English Channel.

We encountered our first technical issue of the race as we were approaching the Atlantic. Up the front edge of our Yankee headsail there is a series of spring-loaded brass clips called hanks, spaced every metre, which connect the sail to the thick wire forestay. They are critical for the sail keeping its shape. As we accelerated and slowed with each passing wave, the sail flapped back and forward and three of the hanks became disconnected. They were 10 metres above the deck and in an area of the sail under heavy load. If we didn't reconnect them, then it would place extra load on the other hanks and one by one they would buckle and we could lose the sail. We had to act fast.

I had two options. One was to drop the sail, reconnect the hanks and then re-hoist the sail. This would cost us a lot of speed and distance on the others. The other option was to hoist a crew member up the forestay in a harness and have them reconnect the hanks in situ, which meant we wouldn't slow down, but if anything happened to the crew member we sent up there... my thoughts trailed off.

*You keep them safe, Brendan.* David's words from the previous day came back to me.

Sod it, I thought. This is a race and we're playing to win. It's not that dangerous and I knew at least five of the adrenalin junkies on the crew would volunteer to do it. We fetched the climbing harness and helmet and sent Tommy, our softly-spoken Irish legger, up to fix the hanks. He spent an exhausting 15 minutes swinging around, halfway up the rig, as the boat rocked and accelerated down the waves. He had real difficulty holding on to the wire forestay with one hand while trying to re-clip the hank with the other. By the time he came down, his forearms had seized up and his hands were shaking from the strain of holding on up there. His exact words, captured on video, were, 'That was the hardest thing I've done in my life and hopefully never again.'

We had a debrief on the exercise immediately and Tommy suggested using a shorter safety line, so the person up the rig can't swing around so much and can use both hands to fix the hanks. A positive discussion followed with others also suggesting ways of doing it better. Tommy was praised and publicly recognised for his efforts. Our procedures were already evolving and I was very happy that the crew were driving the process. I facilitated the debrief, but that was all. Our campaign of continuous improvement was coming along nicely.

We sailed hard for the rest of the race. *Team Finalnd* were hot favourites to win this early race, and they pulled out a comfortable lead and won the race easily. Their skipper, Eero, was the most experienced ocean racer of us all and it was certainly showing.

At the very end of the race, we found ourselves in a close race with *Hull & Humber* for third place. The wind was blowing around 20 knots. Staying true to our 'think long-term victory' strategy, we had one reef in our mainsail, reducing its size and power, but preserving its shape long term. *Hull & Humber* had their full mainsail up and were closing on us quickly. Their boat was overpowered, but they were keeping it under control and going fast. In the last half hour of the race, they overtook us and beat us over the line by 40 seconds.

It was a crushing disappointment. We had raced our hardest for three days and we knew we deserved a podium position. My decision to keep the reef in the mainsail had cost us a race place and I felt like I had let the crew down.

In La Rochelle, we had a big team debrief over some fresh croissants and coffee and one of the crew offered the advice that we should just forget about what happened and move on, to which another one replied that we *shouldn't* forget about it. We should make sure we all remember that feeling of bitter disappointment and let it motivate us to sail harder and faster, so we never have to feel that way again. Fighting talk – I liked it.

To our good fortune, we found out that *Cork* (second) and *Hull & Humber* (third) had both infringed a rule during the race and had very briefly sailed into an off-limits area designated for commercial shipping only. It didn't give them any significant advantage in the race, but rules are rules and the race rules are very clear on the penalties for such violations. They were both given time penalties, which bumped them down the rankings and us up into second place. We gladly accepted the red pennant at the prize-giving ceremony, but we knew in our hearts that we had been outsailed by those two teams on the water.

After a few days of doing light boat work and stocking up on fresh food, we were ready for the start of the next race. It was going to be around 30 days of racing to Rio and the marina was buzzing with anticipation. True to form, I didn't sleep the night before the start. In the morning, the two watches went for their individual breakfast briefings with the watch leaders Mike and Steve and came back to the boat looking energised and raring to go. We left the marina on the high tide and sailed out into the small bay outside La Rochelle.

The start of the race was not how you might imagine. There was zero wind and the boats just sat there, drifting on a flat calm sea. The crews were doing everything they could to coax some shape into the sails and get the boats moving. The energy required to get a 32-ton object moving through the water is significant and even getting the boat moving at 0.1 knots is an achievement. We crossed the start line barely moving, but we knew it wouldn't be long before the breeze kicked in.

A day later and we were tearing along downwind in the North Atlantic trade winds. The trade winds are very steady and predictable streams of air, which flow in a certain direction during the year. They were the basis for ship-based trade between continents. A ship's master knew that if he set his sails in Portugal and followed the wind, he would eventually end up in the Caribbean. The science of meteorology has advanced a long way since then and the patterns of the world's trade winds are well known and still used for anybody crossing oceans under sail.

For the 09–10 Clipper fleet, it meant very fast, exhilarating sailing along the coast of Portugal with the wind behind the boats, our enormous spinnakers flying proud and the waves pushing us along from behind as well. The crew were revelling in the conditions and we had a good turn of speed. Our game plan was to follow the trade winds to the Canary Islands, where our first big tactical decision would need to be made. That was many days in the future and I would worry about it when we were closer to the islands and had some more accurate weather information. For the moment, there was enough to occupy my mind with the crew.

I decided that, as early as I could, I would begin delegating responsibility to the crew. The conditions in the trade winds were stable and the crew's confidence was high, so I began to slowly take steps backwards, letting the crew fill the void. For example, when we performed one of our very common manoeuvres, like putting a reef in the mainsail, I would call for a briefing and ask the watch leader to talk through the manoeuvre. I asked them to delegate specific roles to the crew, making sure there was absolute clarity of communication. Once I was satisfied that there was a good plan and people were clear on their tasks, I would tell them that I would be down below at the navigation station and they could call me if they needed any help.

I sat at the navigation station, listening to the sounds on deck, the click-clicking of turning winches, the flap of the sail as it was depowered, and the grinding cracking sound of the reefing line as the crew winched it to maximum tension. Manoeuvre complete, I would pop my head up and check everything looked OK, then congratulate the crew on a job well done. The satisfaction of being left on their own to do an evolution was evident on their faces. We were only a few days into the race and they were taking responsibility for the safe and speedy handling of the sails.

As they performed manoeuvre after manoeuvre flawlessly, I began to step back further. When a reef needed to be put in, I would give it as a question to the watch on deck – 'You guys reckon it might be time for a reef now?' – and they would agree. I told them to have a good briefing about it beforehand and then execute when they were ready. The first time they put a reef in and I was lying in my bunk was a very satisfying feeling for me. I vowed to keep the process going, remembering the very sobering thought that the crew MUST be able to get the boat to a safe port without me, in case I was killed or incapacitated.

My ultimate goal was that by the end of the race, I would be acting as more of a consultant to the crew – they would be running the boat, deciding on the sail plan and executing the manoeuvres. That would free up my time for doing our tactical navigating and weather routing. These were the more 'cerebral' of my tasks and I knew that I would need to be well rested in order to do a thorough analysis of the weather and make good tactical decisions.

One of the past skippers I had spoken to said they felt the need to be personally involved in every manoeuvre and sail change, which greatly reduced their sleeping hours. They told me about how their lack of sleep made their thinking 'fuzzy' and they couldn't concentrate for long periods. On one race, their boat went the wrong side of a critical mark of the course because they weren't thinking straight, only realising hours later and having to backtrack and go around it correctly, costing them dearly. Their feeling of sole responsibility for the crew doing manoeuvres correctly drove them into the ground. Though their intention was good, their performance suffered greatly.

I also knew that I needed sleep to be a good leader. It's a fact of life that people get grumpy and short-tempered when tired. Not everybody, but I certainly do. I knew this from my list of things that would stop me being a race-winning skipper, so getting enough sleep was something I felt was important. Several of the past race skippers I had talked to had told me stories about how little sleep they had to cope with during parts of the race. They seemed proud of the fact that they battled on for so long without sleep and at the time I was duly impressed with their endurance. After speaking to some of their crew subsequently, they described the skipper as being an 'intolerant, grumpy bastard' during those same periods. I had to make sure I got enough sleep so as not to become an intolerant, grumpy bastard myself.

We were approaching the Canary Islands and it was time to make my decision on which route would be the best. The Canary Islands are towering volcanic islands 60nm off the Atlantic-facing coast of Morocco. The direct line from the start to the finish of the race, called the 'rhumb line', went through the middle of the island group. The three choices were to hug the African coastline, go between the islands, or go to the west, sailing further but staying in consistent wind. Each option had its pros and cons. To make the decision harder, Clipper had placed the first scoring gate off to the west, to entice boats to take the longer route. Going for the gate and the extra points could set a boat back a long way and sacrifice their chance of a top position in Rio.

Fortunately, the research we had done before the race swayed my mind. One of the crew had done a detailed piece of research on the islands and talked to weather experts about their effects. The towering islands play havoc with the prevailing winds and create large wind shadows on the leeward side of the islands. Boats have been known to stay becalmed for days in one of these wind shadows. The slogan 'west is best' is common in the sailing world when discussing how to go through the Canary Islands, so that was the decision I took. West, further out into the Atlantic and towards the scoring gate. Three boats went west with us, four went between the islands and two hugged the African coastline, and the tension went up a notch.

Through our tenacity and the crew's persistent hard work, we outmanoeuvred the three other westerly boats, *California*, *Hull & Humber* and *Qingdao*, and went through the scoring gate in first place, bagging a bonus three points. When we rejoined the trade winds south of the islands we had moved up from fourth to third, with *Team Finland* and *Cork* still leading the charge. We were elated with the result and our confidence climbed higher.

We continued our charge south, towards the equator and the doldrums. The trade winds were strong and the sailing was perfect – hot, sunny weather, clear skies and cloudless nights. The wind was still behind us, so the boat's motion was steady and our speed was fast. Champagne sailing, they call it. We regularly saw enormous pods of dolphins. They would swim over to the boat and swim around the bow in the waves we were creating, darting back and forward, jumping and playing. It was a familiar sight for me, having done many ocean crossings, but the crew were mesmerised and the boat camera quickly filled up with blurry photos of leaping dolphins.

I love being at sea and I love the perspective it brings. When I look at the horizon of water all around, I really *know* I'm looking at the curvature of the earth falling away from me. It gives a real feeling of crossing the surface of a spherical planet, a green and blue jewel rotating through space. During the day, our sun, the ultimate source of all earth's energy, beats down, dominating the sky with its billion-year-old brilliance. The clear nights give a spectacular view of the stars without the light pollution of a suburban setting. The Milky Way galaxy is clearly visible – a fuzzy, velvet band running across the sky. It's an aesthetically beautiful vista, but I also find it a confronting sight, forcing me to accept the immensity of the ocean, our planet and outer space. In philosophical moods, I have looked out at the universe and reflected on the corresponding minuteness of my own physical existence on earth and the inconsequential length of time my lifespan represents. At first I found it a dark and depressing thought, but after years of gazing upwards on many ocean crossings, I have decided that I should, instead, be grateful.

I, Brendan Hall, a tiny mote of consciousness, against unfathomable odds, have simply had the opportunity to enjoy a brief lucidity of life before returning forever to the endless naught from whence I came. I accept my own mortality with open arms, knowing that my life's brevity is what gives it intensity and richness.

What do I want my life to mean? Who do I want to spend it with? What are the important things in it and what aren't?

I find questions like this come more naturally at sea, away from the trappings of life ashore and surrounded by vast spaces. I firmly believe an ocean crossing is a journey everybody should undertake at some point in their life to experience this perspective.

Back in the race, the tension was beginning to show among certain members of my crew. We were now about two weeks from the start and the little niggles began to creep in. Tiny things, like somebody spending too long in the toilet or somebody taking more than their fair share of treats from the snack box. Things that no mature person would make a big deal about ashore, but out at sea these things begin to get on people's nerves. Ironically, in the very comfortable, stable conditions we were having, the crew seemed to get on each other's nerves more. I could see the beginnings of several mini falling-outs between certain individuals. The easy, fast sailing meant that up on deck there were only jobs for fewer of the crew, which were shared around on a rotation, but it also left room for boredom to creep in and boredom gives people time to dwell on tiny issues. The devil makes work for idle hands, as the saying goes. While I had to keep my finger on the pulse of the crew, I wasn't prepared to get involved in the small issues and mediate trivial disputes.

Instead, I brought the issues up in a general way at our daily meetings, explaining to the crew that it's natural to feel more edgy after a few weeks at sea when fatigue creeps in. Family, friends, comfort and privacy seem a long way away out here and it all contributes to people making a bigger deal out of something than it's really worth. On a sterner note, I warned them that the strongest teams can rot from the inside out very quickly if they let squabbling and minor issues distract them from their objective.

Everyone, including myself, had good days and bad days. The world doesn't stop when you're at sea and people were getting news from home and it affected their moods. The crew were great at supporting each other through the bad days. We had some very maternal ladies on board, who were good at offering comfort, advice and support to anyone who was feeling down. Support was one of our core values and we were sticking to it. A quiet word, a warm smile, or a gentle touch on the arm could be enough to bring somebody's mood back up if they were missing home. Support comes in many forms and doesn't always necessarily mean trying to talk and empathise.

There was an incident around this point of the leg where one of my core crew became very quiet and distracted. When he was not actively doing a job on deck, he would sit on the edge of the deck, looking out to sea rather than joining in the conversation and banter. Some of the others on his watch felt he was just being grumpy and not being a team player. They brought the issue to me and said I should try to talk him out of it. When talking to him, I discovered that he was mourning the death of one of his family members, who had died exactly one year previously. He didn't feel like sharing his loss with the others and was happy to just be by himself for a few days to contemplate. I urged to others on his watch to offer support by giving him space for a few days. They didn't know what the issue was, but they agreed and after a few days he was fine again.

The next big tactical decision was where to cross the doldrums. You probably know the word doldrums from the saying 'in the doldrums', meaning 'in low spirits'. It was originally a nautical phrase. The doldrums are a horizontal band of weather just north of the equator, where there is very little wind. Old sailing ships could be becalmed and stuck here for days or even weeks, hence the phrase.

The idea is to get across the doldrums as quickly and directly as you can to minimise your time in the windless area, even if it takes you off the rhumb line to your destination. Modern meteorological synoptic charts show the shape and size of the doldrums and it changes daily, pushed north and south by the seasons and the high-pressure systems in the North and South Atlantic.

The doldrums represented a big element of chance. The boats at the back of the fleet were hoping that the lead boats would 'park up' (racing lingo for being becalmed and stopping) and give them an opportunity to catch up. The lead boats were hoping they would find the fastest route through the light patch while everyone else got caught out. It was a great leveller, though to see weeks of hard work blown in a day because we sailed into a wind hole would feel grossly unfair. Like the Canary Islands, the fleet diverged, each skipper playing out their tactical decision on where to cross the doldrums. Once each boat got into the doldrums, they were committed to sailing south as quickly as possible and getting back into the strong wind to the south. We were in third place going into the doldrums and we could be anywhere from first to seventh when we came out the other side.

I briefed the crew on the experience of crossing the doldrums. It was important to set an expectation and give people time to prepare mentally for the change in conditions. Sadly, our days of champagne sailing were coming to an end.

Once we reached the doldrums, the days would be scorching hot and still. On deck, the temperature would be in the mid-30s. Below deck would be hotter. The concentration needed to get the boat moving would be great. Sleep would be difficult in the heat and sunburn and dehydration were big dangers. It would be a test of our mental resilience to cope with the uncomfortable conditions and stay working in the same high-performance way we had been up to that point. There is an old sailors' saying that any fool can make a yacht go fast in lots of wind, it's only the skilled sailor that can make one go fast in little wind. The difference would come down to persistence. I knew how frustrating and boring it could be to be stuck in the doldrums and I knew other crew would lose focus and stop pushing hard. This was going to be a big challenge, but it was also our opportunity to gain places through our dogged persistence, which I knew was our single strongest quality as a team.

We would also need to be ever vigilant for squalls, which were common in this area.

A squall is a very powerful localised wind, generated by a single cloud or bank of clouds. They are most common in the tropics, as they are generated by the energy of evaporating water. As far as a sailor is concerned, squalls equal danger. They hit very quickly, bringing winds of up to 45 knots, and usually last from a few minutes to half an hour. They usually also bring lashing rain and visibility goes down to zero. Our challenge would be dropping our large, light wind sails before the squall hit and tore them to pieces. Once the squall had passed, we would be left with zero wind again and we would need to re-hoist our lightweight sails. The boat and crew would quickly dry off and we'd be back to moving at a snail's pace under the scorching sun – until the next one.

The first squall we hit followed this exact pattern, but my decision to drop the sail came too late. The crew struggled to pull down the uncontrollably flogging Yankee. The mast was shaking violently and I thought we were going to break something. It was exhilarating and dangerous, as the crew struggled against the enormous sail. After that first incident, I knew I would need to decide sooner to give the crew more time to get the sail down. I called a debrief, apologised for my delay, and asked what we could do better next time. The result of the discussion was that if we saw a squall approaching, the crew would all get exactly into their positions for dropping the sail and wait there, greatly reducing the time it took to execute the manoeuvre. This strategy worked well for us and all our subsequent squalls were handled safely and quickly. With every sched, we saw our position creep forward. Our persistence in the light winds and our effective squall management paid off and we exited the doldrums in second place.

Crossing the equator holds a special significance for all sailors. It's only recently, with the advent of satellite navigation, that we can pinpoint the exact second when we swap hemispheres. Our equator crossing happened in the middle of the night, with the crew gathered around the GPS display, waiting for the moment when the little N (north) became a little S (south).

The next day we had our proper celebration during our lunchtime meeting. The tradition is that you have to give an offering to Neptune (Roman god of the sea) for you to be allowed safe passage across the equator. I dutifully tipped a generous dram of our 'celebrating whisky' over the side and threw in some ginger-nut biscuits for good measure. Other members of the crew had offerings of their own, which they sent into Neptune's watery domain. We had a funny ceremony, with core crew member Bob Bell dressed up as Neptune, complete with white beard made out of spare rope. As is tradition, he accused each member of the crew of the crimes they had committed in his domain and handed out silly punishments. Steve had spilled a mug of hot chocolate all over the deck a few nights previously, so his punishment was to make the rest of his night watch hot chocolate from now on. Josie, who was very softly-spoken, was ordered to give us three of her loudest screams, and so on. It was a great hour of entertainment and a welcome distraction from the pressure of racing. It was an important milestone on our journey and I knew that the time spent celebrating it would be a great morale booster after the doldrums. I firmly believe in setting and celebrating milestones on any sailing passage. Focusing on how far you have left to go is necessary, but it's equally important to look behind and enjoy how far you have come. We had natural milestones on the race, like the equator crossing or the International Date Line crossing, but we made some ourselves, just to help break the passage up into smaller, less intimidating chunks, and we had a mini celebration for each one.

We were now in the southern hemisphere trade winds and heading for the coast of Brazil. *Team Finland* had pulled out an impressive lead of more than 100nm. Eero had drawn on his many previous equator crossings and positioned his boat perfectly, slightly to the east of us. Now they were charging for the finish and we were chasing hard, with *Cork, Jamaica* and *Cape Breton Island* hot on our heels.

It was at this point of the race when we had our first major team decision to make. As I had previously noticed, the skill of the person helming the boat had a dramatic effect on our speed. We had six crew whom I considered highly skilled helms, eight average helms, and four quite poor helms. On each watch, the helming was being shared equally on a rotation, with everybody getting 45 minutes. The difference in speed and accuracy of course when a good helm handed over to a bad one or vice versa was obvious and I remember sitting at the navigation station when a poor helm was steering, grinding my teeth as I watched our course deviate and speed drop.

This was my big dilemma and I knew we would have to address it at some point on the race. Every crew member was paying an equal amount for their berth and each had an equal right to get experience doing every job on board. If a crew member who was a terrible helmsman wanted a go, then it was unfair of me to tell them they couldn't. Restricting the helming to only the best people would have big ramifications for crew morale, but I knew that if we were going to have any chance of catching *Team Finland* and outrunning the other two, then we would need to make a change.

It wasn't easy, but I called a crew meeting and laid the issue on the table. Some of the more competitive crew were in favour of limiting the helming to the best people. Others were opposed to it, saying they had an equal right to maximise their own experience. Others didn't believe me that it was making a big difference to our speed and yet others were happy just to go with the flow and would accept the decision the group came to. The helming issue was the key to higher performance, but if it would divide the crew and sink our good morale then it would not be a wise decision.

After giving the matter a lot of thought, I decided that we would conduct an experiment over the next 24 hours. For the first 12, we would carry on as we were, rotating through the helms equally. The following 12, we would go with our six best helms only. Using our navigation software, I could analyse the difference in speed and accuracy of steering between the two. I explained this to the crew and they agreed to try it. After 24 hours, the results were clear. Taking into account the wind strength and angle, we were on average 0.4 knots faster with the best helms only.

An average of 0.4 nautical miles per hour. That's 9.6nm every day. Over the course of a 30-day race, that's 288nm and that's a very significant difference. I explained this to the crew the following day and gauged the reactions. Everyone was now convinced of the difference it made. The numbers spoke for themselves, but opinions remained unchanged. Our unifying team mission statement of '…to do all we can to win the race and feel fulfilled' now seemed ironically divisive. There were those who wanted 'to do all we can to win the race' and others who wanted to 'feel fulfilled'. No matter which option I went for, one of the two groups was going to be disappointed. The arguments were already starting to have a detrimental effect on the crew morale.

*Can I find a balance here? Am I just being a win-at-all-costs jerk?*

I consulted with my two watch leaders, Mike and Steve, as well as some of the other core crew, and with their input we came up with a system we felt would strike a balance. The six 'primary' helms would do 75 per cent of the helming and the others would do the remaining 25 per cent, but during that time the focus would be on training and coaching them to improve. This was accepted by crew and that was how we proceeded for the rest of the round the world race. The model evolved as we got further into the race and the less experienced helms got more time when the conditions were steady and the helming was straightforward, to build their confidence. Conversely, there were times in the roughest weather, or when the racing was very close, when I only trusted the primary helms to steer.

Striking that balance between high performance and giving the crew a chance to experience everything was a sticking point for many teams on the race and they all tackled it in their own way. In the latter stages of the race, the crew who knew their helming was poor voluntarily opted out of helming, because they didn't want their poor performance to slow us down. They wanted what was best for the team and focused their energy on becoming an expert in another of the many roles on deck.

This focused and specialised approach worked its way into our general sailing ethos. While everybody still rotated through the jobs, everyone also had to become a specialist at something. Some people became specialist bowmen, others became specialist halyard handlers and yet others became specialist sail trimmers. The crew were free to choose their area of specialisation and a balance worked itself out naturally, with every role always filled. The crew could change to a different specialisation if they wanted to, but only once they had mastered one already.

This long-term approach to up-skilling the crew had some key benefits. It meant that when the pressure was on or the weather was rough, people would go into their specialist roles and would perform safely and confidently, without needing to be briefed. The crew enjoyed seeing the increased speed when performing manoeuvres, changing sails and reefing that this approach led to. Crew members took real ownership of their area of specialisation and insisted on high standards from others. They felt personally responsible for the job they were given and how it would contribute to our overall success.

The culture of knowledge sharing was beginning to emerge. During our daily meetings, the crew would share suggestions on how to speed up or improve communication during a particular manoeuvre. One of our bowmen, Kelvin, took it upon himself to write a comprehensive guide to being a bowman, which he expected people to read if they wanted to become a bowman themselves. It was great to see and the crew were doing this without my input. There were a few key players who were more vocal than others, but the rest were quickly swept along in the enthusiasm. Nobody wanted to let the team down and that's the way it stayed for the next ten months.

We were gaining on *Team Finland*. Their lead was down from more than 100nm to 60nm. When the six-hourly scheds came in, it was a very nervous time for all of us. The crew would gather around the navigation station as the email slowly downloaded and then, with crossed fingers, I would open the text file and see if we had gained miles or lost miles on the fleet. If we had gained, the mood of the crew was lifted. Fists were pumped in the air and there were pats on the back all round. If we had lost miles, the mood was sombre.

This was where I made my first big people-management mistake of the race. I let my own mood become too affected by the sched results. If we'd had a good one, I would come on deck cheery and happy, tell the crew they were doing a great job and to keep it up. I enjoyed seeing people getting recognition for the hard work they had put in and I was generous with my praise. If we'd had a bad sched, I would come on deck and immediately check the trim of the sails. I was short with some crew members who asked me how we did on the sched. I would tell the crew we all needed to lift our game and try harder and we needed to make the next sched a good one. I was despondent, unhappy and fearful that our position in the race was going to be lost. Every six hours the crew on deck would sit there wondering if the skipper who came up out the hatch would be a happy one or a stroppy one. The crew were genuinely trying their hardest – they worked hard for each other and to prove to me they could do it. The lost miles on the sched were in most cases down to the wind strength. The fleet was spread out and all the boats were likely experiencing different wind strengths based on localised weather effects. At the time, I was convinced that our gains and losses were the result of how well we were sailing, and so my mood went up and down with the sched results.

As a skipper, your mood counts for at *least* 50 per cent of the mood of your crew. Under the pressure of racing, I had become too results-focused and had lost my sense of self-awareness. I found out later that the crew called it 'sched whiplash', the emotional jolting from having a leader swinging from being happy to annoyed on a six-hourly cycle. I was becoming too emotionally attached to the performance of the boat and dragging the crew with me through the highs and lows of the day. People do this all the time. Fail an exam, screw up a job interview or lose a contract – it is natural for these things to disappoint us and affect our mood, but if you are a leader it's part of your responsibility to minimise the impact of your mood on those working for you. The shadow you cast is great and you need to be self-aware of your moods and how they affect others.

The crew talked about this issue among themselves and one of the core crew, Kirsty, brought it up with me. It was hard to hear, but what she said was absolutely true. What I was doing was unacceptable and it was becoming detrimental to the morale of the whole boat.

*No! I'm doing what needs to be done! If you guys can't handle a little criticism then you need to toughen the hell up!*

This was my initial knee-jerk response to the criticism. Luckily, I bit my tongue and let the moment of anger pass. I needed to think more about this before speaking to the crew. I said thanks to Kirsty for bringing it to my attention and let her get back on deck. I needed some time alone to think, so I briefed the watch leader and went to my bunk.

The feeling of disappointment hit me like a cannonball. I was disappointed in myself and how I had failed to keep my emotions in check. I felt the crew would have lost respect for me and would be writing home to their families and friends describing how their skipper was some immature, manic-depressive 28-year-old. I was supposed to be the rock at the centre of the team. I was the one with the responsibility and the crew needed to have absolute trust in my abilities and judgement. I had to provide stability and be under control at all times. I lay there and beat myself up about it for a while longer and then, with a deep sigh, I let it go. What was done was done and I had to think of a way to turn things around, *fast*.

Firstly, I reached into my locker, pulled out a biro and on the bottom of the bunk above mine, I wrote myself a note – YOUR MOOD BECOMES THEIR MOOD – so I would be reminded every time I lay down.

The solution was simple – I just had to keep my emotions under better control. If we had a good sched, be cool about it. Give the crew the news and give them a big well done. If the sched was bad, be calm and philosophical about it. Don't sweat it if we get a bad one. Let the crew know the sched wasn't great, but they were doing well and we just had to make sure we were doing the best we possibly could. We were only three weeks into a ten-month race, so I had to keep my mind on the bigger picture. A happy, stable crew needed a happy, stable skipper.

I didn't formally acknowledge or apologise to the crew for the 'sched whiplash', but they quickly saw that I had taken on board their criticism and things were now different. I just had to make sure I kept my emotions in check and it didn't come back. I had moments of sched whiplash over the course of the rest of the race, but they were very occasional and I was quick to remind myself of this valuable lesson I learned early on.

We were getting close to Rio now. *Team Finland* were still 60nm ahead of us and in the distance we had left it was unlikely that we would catch them. *Cork*, *Cape Breton Island* and *Jamaica* were chasing us hard and were less than 20nm away. If I didn't make the right tactical calls on our final approach to the line, we could be fifth as easily as second. The coastline of Brazil is very congested, with oil rigs, supply ships, off-limits military areas, fishing vessels and normal commercial shipping traffic. The crew had to be hawk-eyed at night to make sure we stayed clear of all these dangers. The weather added another tactical element. The winds inshore were lighter than the winds further off the coast, but the shortest route to the finish was inshore. We opted for the inshore route and, with our skill at sailing fast in light winds, we stayed ahead of the chasing pack. We limped over the finish line off Cape Frio in the middle of the night, doing less than 1 knot as the wind finally died off. I watched the navigation computer screen as our boat icon crept over the line. The feeling of excitement was electric. All the crew were awake and ready to celebrate. As the icon finally crossed the line and our GPS confirmed we had finished, the cheer that rang out from the crew gathered around me was deafening. A wave of relief washed over me, and my body relaxed the muscles that had been gradually tensing over the last few days. The moment passed and was swept away in the celebration.

We had done it, second place after 5,000 miles! We cheered and hugged each other, congratulating warmly with a mixture of joy, relief and triumph. Our persistence had paid off. We had come through the fast racing in the trade winds, the dash for the scoring gate, the frustration and heat of the doldrums, the frantic upwind sprint south of the equator and, finally, the tactical chess game of the Brazilian coast. We could have lost it at any of those points, but we didn't. We persevered and kept pushing hard and the reward was ours. *Team Finland* had sailed a great race, leading from the start, but we had chased hard and kept them honest to the end. We deserved this second place and knew we had outsailed the eight boats behind us fair and square.

We dropped sails, kicked the engine into life and set off at full speed towards Rio. The crew of *Team Finland* were waiting on the dock to welcome us in, along with our friends, family and supporters. We made the boat secure to the dock and after some photos were taken, it was time to spray some champagne! A crate of beer quickly found its way onto the boat and it didn't take long to be demolished by a very thirsty crew, who quickly went off in search of more. The celebrations carried on all morning.

## LEADERSHIP LESSONS

### Delegate

I began delegating responsibility to the crew very early on in the race and, looking back, that decision was one of the largest factors in our overall success. I didn't make a song and dance about it or give a speech telling them that I felt they were ready for it now. I just slowly took those backward steps and reduced my presence on deck. I wanted them to feel that sailing the boat without me supervising was the normal state of affairs, rather than that they were being given some special privilege of responsibility.

I wasn't sure if they would be ready to take the responsibility, but my doubts were alleviated after a few days, when every manoeuvre on deck was being performed quickly and safely and the boat was sailing at close to its maximum speed all the time. The crew were lifting their game, collectively, to the challenge of performing without supervision. I wasn't there to spot mistakes before they happened, so each crew member made sure they were absolutely clear on their role during a manoeuvre before it began, forcing them to learn faster and take *complete* responsibility for their assigned role.

It also engendered a trust between the crew and myself. The crew felt that I trusted them and had confidence in them. They didn't want to lose that trust and confidence, so they went to great pains to minimise the potential for mistakes or problems that would require me to come up on deck to solve. Although I was always available if anything went wrong or if they needed advice, they liked being an empowered crew and took pride in their self-sufficiency. It was this attitude that would allow them to grow as a team and exceed every expectation of them in life-threatening conditions, as you will read in a later chapter.

This allowed me to focus more of my time on the tactics and weather routing, the area where I could add the most value to our race performance. I could keep a broad focus and work uninterrupted on the complex calculations needed to give us the fastest route through the wind patterns ahead of us.

A leader needs to understand that in order for a team to grow and perform, they need to delegate and empower the team. Start the process slowly, taking those small steps backward and encouraging the team to take the responsibility left to them. It can be a difficult process, particularly for a leader who is passionate and likes to stay in control, but the control strings have to be loosened for the team to reach its potential.

An overbearing, micro-managing leader will never get the same results from their team as a leader who is prepared to delegate effectively and share responsibility, partly because their team won't feel trusted and will be less likely to use their own initiative and partly because a disproportionate amount of their energy is spent managing small details, rather than focusing on the big picture.

## Look after yourself

I knew that for me to be making the best decisions and concentrate on the weather routing, I would need to be well rested. I didn't have set sleeping hours, like the crew did, I just had to fit sleep in when it was possible. When the sailing was easy and straightforward, I would 'stock up' on sleep, knowing I might not get another chance later on. I was always conscious of the fact that I needed to 'keep my tank half full' to deal with an emergency if it happened. If we had a disaster situation, I might not be able to get any sleep for two days or more, so I needed to keep a reserve of energy in case that happened. If I worked myself to exhaustion and *then* a disaster situation occurred, I might not have the mental acuity to make the best decisions and keep my crew safe.

I also needed to make sure I was rested in order to be a good leader and manage my crew well. I knew that I got cranky when tired and had a tendency to snap at people or make negative remarks, so keeping myself well rested was in the best interests of everyone. None of the crew were going to applaud my endurance if I forced myself to stay awake and in control all hours of the day, but they certainly would criticise me if I became that 'grumpy, intolerant bastard' that some previous skippers had become.

To be the best leader I could be, I needed to look after myself.

## Squalls

I think the squall at sea is a great analogy for short-term difficulties in life. We knew that we would experience squalls in the doldrums, so they weren't entirely unexpected, but each individual squall was an intense and short-lived problem, with the potential for inflicting long-term damage to our sails. Avoiding damage from the fierce gusts of wind in the squall relied upon extremely fast and coordinated action by the crew. We had a plan to take down our large headsails and executed it as each squall approached us. There was no time for briefing or delay; the crew had to react instantly.

What are the squalls in your life?

Are you in an area where squalls are likely?

Do you have a plan to deal with them?

## Performance focus *v.* personal fulfilment

Finding the balance between having a performance focus and making sure each individual got exactly what they wanted out of the experience was one of my biggest challenges of the race.

It came to a head with the helming issue, a topic that threatened to divide the crew and kill our team morale. The race was an unusual situation, as the crew were all paying for the experience and had a right to provide input on the way we ran the boat. There was nothing stopping me using my authority to order the change in helm rotation, which would have probably worked in the short term but done more damage in the long term. If I wanted to increase performance and sustain it, then a balance would need to be found and accepted collectively.

A good leader acknowledges the need for the individuals in

their team to feel fulfilled and makes an effort to find a balance between receiving their high performance and giving them that fulfilment.

## Be self-aware

Self-awareness is an absolutely critical thing that every leader needs. Your mood and attitude becomes the mood and attitude of your team. The shadow you cast as a leader is bigger than you might imagine. Your words and actions become magnified because of your position.

During my moments of sched whiplash, I was letting my emotions overcome my need to be a role model for the crew. I had been warned about this before the race, it was something some past race skippers also did and regretted. Yet I found myself repeating their mistakes and letting my passion for high performance get the better of me. It was a lesson I needed to learn for myself and I am thankful that my crew challenged me on it so quickly. If they had been a weaker team, they might have kept quiet and allowed it to continue until it became a critical problem.

I think every leader needs a reminder somewhere in their life of that clear statement, 'Your mood becomes their mood.' As a leader, whether it's at sea or ashore, you are still an ordinary, fallible human being. You will have bad days and good days, so small fluctuations in behaviour are only natural. On a larger scale, it's part of the responsibility to control your moods and keep a positive attitude, for the benefit of your team, not just yourself.

## The Tuckman model of team development

The Forming – Storming – Norming – Performing model of group development was first proposed by Bruce Tuckman in 1965. He maintained that these four phases are necessary and inevitable in order for a team to grow, to face up to challenges, to tackle problems, to find solutions, to plan work, and to deliver results.

I asked one of my crew to do some research on the Tuckman model and create something we could put up on the wall of the boat to remind us of the stages we would go through. She wrote an excellent description, which we stuck on the wall of the toilet, where it would be impossible to not read. It was such an important reminder, and so well written, I feel it warrants reproduction here.

Any group of people who spend time together will cycle through essentially four stages. By understanding how these phases work, we can realise that we are on-track to becoming a team that produces the desired outcomes! We have the added challenge of having our group constantly changing and therefore, with each change of crew, the group will begin at the first phase again. The progression through these stages is important as it ensures that the team becomes fully cohesive and functional as a unit. We therefore need to be patient at the beginning of each leg and work through the phases again. Since there are quite a number of 'core crew', the process may become streamlined; however, it is important to allow the group the time to work through each of the phases and not try to skip to the last phase, as important learning will be lost.

So what are the phases?

*Forming (Like the birth phase of life)*

In the beginning phases, the group members are usually polite and superficial with their interactions. Members seek out people that are similar to them and share common needs. There may be confusion, anxiety and ambiguity as people compare reasons for being there. They are determining what price they are willing to pay to be part of the group and whether they will be accepted.

Communication patterns and relationship styles emerge and usually reflect what people feel as 'safe' (what has worked for them in the past). Individuals will be looking for leadership to guide them and give them direction. This stage can be quite enjoyable and exciting as the members are all exploring, as long as they tolerate the ambiguity.

The key here is to be aware that frustration levels will be high at times and to respect that. Establishing a leader or leadership group will assist to move the group forward. Naturally, we will have a watch leader to run the boat in terms of sailing; however, other leaders may well emerge outside the parameters of the watches as the group gravitates to a particular style or person.

### Storming (Youth)

Criteria for membership are established and people know why they joined the group, why they chose to 'play the game'. This stage is similar to youth power playing and storming to establish power. In this phase, individuals challenge each other for power or influence in the form of direct confrontation, covert actions or non-support of established leaders. This may be directed towards the watch leader or other leaders that have emerged. This can be a difficult stage and there will often be attempts by the group to move away from this phase; however, unless skills required are gained in this phase, the group will have to revisit this stage until these skills are gained.

In our situation, one of the most important things to establish or learn is how we will make decisions as a group. If this is not achieved, there will be discontent whenever a decision needs to be made and individuals are unhappy with the way it is dealt with. There is a need to establish the 'ground rules' for this team and how it will work in terms of relating to others and task allocation. As this develops and leadership qualities emerge, the group can move on.

*Norming (Mature phase)*

This phase sees the group starting to function well. The frustration and confusion of the previous level diminishes as individuals know what to expect from each other, trust develops and tasks are accomplished by working together. Group members can share ideas about how their goals are being realised and a sense of achievement develops. There is a common goal and movement towards it as a team with a unified identity. The foundations are built as the group is able to work together to strengthen bonds and improve skills ready for the final phase.

*Performing*

A group at this level develops trust, which in turn generates fulfilment leading to increased commitment to the team and often more energy. The group is able to stand united and powerfully together against challenges and by overcoming these obstacles, they learn and grow. Relationships within groups in the performing group are well established and few leadership issues exist. A group in this phase produces results and is able to self-manage without too much effort.

While this is a very basic outline of the stages of groups, it highlights what we will be going through on each leg of the race.

For those doing the full circumnavigation, it will be interesting for you to observe the changeover of crew and how the dynamics change. Be prepared for that; no group will function the same even if only one member is added or removed.

Those joining along the way will need to be aware that there was a previous group that had certain ways of doing things and appreciate that it will be a struggle for those remaining from the 'old' team to readjust.

Through all of this, remember that the process is totally natural and will be happening on every boat. The more we embrace it and work together to keep moving forwards through the phases, the quicker we will be in the performing phase and therefore creating the results we want!

Having this text displayed in a prominent place made people understand the importance of the stages we were going through. In retrospect, I think its biggest benefit was explaining that conflict is a natural and necessary part of the storming phase and isn't something to be shied away from. By making the crew aware of the stages we were going through, it made the transition from one to the next faster with each subsequent leg of the race.

# 8

# JUDGEMENT

*A man should learn to sail in all winds*
*ITALIAN PROVERB*

Rio was the changeover between legs one and two and there was a lot of work to be done before we set off again. We lost three leggers and gained three new ones. I wanted us to do an activity as a team before setting off again, so on a hot and sunny day we all took a cable car to the top of Sugarloaf Mountain, an impressive rocky pinnacle overlooking Guanabara Bay and the city of Rio de Janeiro. It wasn't much of a focused team-building exercise, but it was an excellent chance for the new leggers to socialise with the rest of the crew, away from the boat. Their anxiety at joining a high-performance crew was noticeable – they didn't want to let the side down. It was great to see them coming on board with this attitude, it meant they would be motivated to learn quickly and take on the high-performance habits we had developed on leg one.

The prize-giving ceremony was excellent and we proudly accepted our red second-place pennant from the Commodore of the yacht club. *Team Finland* skipper Eero was invited to make a short speech after his team were presented with their yellow first-place pennant. He graciously gave recognition to all ten competing crews, but gave a special mention to *Spirit of Australia* for pushing them so hard, right to the finish.

I had one-to-one debriefs with each of the crew during the stopover and while the overall mood was good, there were a few personal problems beginning to creep in. Certain individuals didn't get along and there was friction between one watch leader and another core crew member. I took this information and made some changes to the watches, moving people from one to the other to accommodate their requests. It wasn't always possible – each watch needed to retain a specialist for every role and have enough physically strong crew to perform any sail change on its own. I also had to find places for the new leggers to slot into and assign them mentors for the first few days at sea.

Apart from the socialising and fun, there was a lot of work to be done. It was 18 days of racing to Cape Town and, with 18 crew, there was a huge amount of food to be bought, sorted, divided into day bags and stowed on board. As well as this, I insisted that in every stopover port we did a thorough check of every single one of our sails, repairing any small nicks or holes that might have been overlooked at sea. As the past skippers had predicted, several of the boats had torn their spinnakers by pushing them too hard. *Cork* had utterly destroyed their medium-weight spinnaker and were going to incur a harsh points penalty for getting a replacement. I was very happy that all of our sails were in excellent condition. We were conservative with them and looked after them meticulously. We would need them to be in good shape for the race to Cape Town, particularly our three downwind spinnakers.

The race to Cape Town was going to be a downwind drag race through the South Atlantic. From Rio, we would head almost directly south for a few days before turning east and heading for the African continent. The reason for this indirect route is the St Helena high-pressure system, which sits in the middle of the South Atlantic Ocean. If we took the direct route from Rio to Cape Town, we would sail into this high-pressure system, where there is virtually no wind. It would be like the doldrums all over again. The route I had planned took us south of the swirling high-pressure zone, using the wind around the bottom as a slingshot to push us towards Cape Town. The wind would be behind us most of the way and the South Atlantic has a fearsome reputation for the conditions being far heavier than predicted, so a conservative approach to choosing our sails would be needed.

In my crew briefing, we discussed the expected conditions and gave a special briefing to the watch leaders about making the decision to reduce our sail plan sooner rather than later. We all agreed that we needed to treat this leg as a warm-up for the next leg from Cape Town to Australia, when we would be sailing through the Southern Ocean and the weather conditions would be even heavier.

On the day of the race start, all ten crews assembled at the yacht club marina. One by one, they were introduced to the modest crowd of supporters and given the instruction to 'man your boat' by the race director.

Once we had slipped from the marina, it was time to get ready for the starting sequence. Each boat selected the sails it would be starting with and did a few practice runs at the starting line. Even after only ten days of not sailing, it was clear the crew had become a bit rusty and the practice was much needed before we hit the line at full speed. The new crew were working well and even if things were taking a little longer than before, they were all sailing safely. Accidents on the start line are a common thing in yacht racing, when the adrenalin is at maximum and the crew become totally focused on their job and not completely aware of everything else going on around them. If one of them were to be hit with a flogging sail control line, it could mean a broken arm. Years ago I had seen somebody get hit in the face with a flogging line and have six teeth knocked out instantly. I had to keep an eagle eye on all the crew and make sure they weren't moving into an unsafe position.

In addition to this, I had to manoeuvre the boat into the best position for the start. The stress levels were at a maximum for all the skippers, with ten 32-ton yachts all charging for a short starting line and no fast way of slowing down. Start-line collisions between boats are also a common thing in competitive yacht racing, so I had to be careful not to get into a collision situation. If I messed up and crashed into another boat, then our race would be over before it had begun. I decided I would play it cautiously and hang back while some of the other skippers pushed aggressively for the best position on the line. With the huge number of tactical decisions to come over the next 18 days, being ten seconds late over the line was not going to make any difference at all.

*Think long-term victory, not short-term glory.*

The countdown reached zero and the starting gun boomed. We were racing again and the feeling was electric. The boats charged at one another, one ducking around behind another at the last second. The shouts of the skippers and crews could be heard above the sound of the waves crashing against the rocks. We jockeyed and pushed our way into a solid position and by nightfall the fleet was quite spread out. Some skippers' tactics were to head directly south and others headed east first. Our racetrack was 3,000 miles long by 2,000 miles wide and we could move within it any way we wanted. It was clear that each skipper had a very different strategic plan and, once they had committed to it, changing was difficult.

That first night out of Rio, most of the crew were seasick. The conditions became rougher and rougher as the night went on and, one by one, the crew that were prone to seasickness retreated to their bunks to rest. When somebody is violently seasick, the only thing you can do with them is get them to lie down and make sure they keep drinking plenty of fluids. Seasickness can quickly lead to dehydration. On past Clipper races, badly seasick crew have needed intravenous drips inserted to keep them hydrated.

Seasickness left the burden of labour on progressively fewer shoulders, but nobody complained. A badly seasick crew member is a liability on deck. Seasickness saps physical strength and mental acuity, so a seasick crew member is far more likely to get injured. The best thing for them and for everyone else is to get them rested and keep them hydrated until it passes, generally after 48 hours.

If my crew thought they were suffering, the crew of *Jamaica Lightning*

*Bolt* were worse. They had forgotten to use the water sterilisation pills supplied in Rio and their tanks were full of contaminated local water. Almost everyone on board contracted giardia and the two boat toilets were in use non-stop for days. They quickly fell off the pace.

We were in the group of boats that dived south early on. The weather quickly cooled and before long the conditions were starting to live up to our expectations. The waves were building in size and we shot down each one with a surf. The seasick crew began to emerge from their bunks, ravenously hungry and ready to get stuck in. We were racing hard and changing sails around once per watch. The racing was close and *Cork, Hull & Humber* and *Uniquely Singapore* were leading the charge.

The waves continued to build the further south we went and we began to see albatross, the masters of this desolate seascape. I had never seen one in the flesh before and they are truly amazing creatures. They are enormous birds with a wingspan of 3 metres (10ft) and they live for up to 70 years. They were curious about us and there was barely a day in the South Atlantic when we didn't have an albatross or two for company. They would fly behind the boat, just gliding on their enormous wings, never flapping them. The crew would watch intently as they'd dive and catch a fish and quickly ascend again. They never became distracting and their presence was always welcome.

In my email inbox the following day was a message from the race organisers that sent a chill down my spine. *Hull & Humber* had a man overboard. The crew member, Arthur Bowers, had been safely picked up by skipper Piers Dudin and the crew in 17 minutes and was uninjured.

A man overboard is a skipper's worst nightmare. In water that cold, hypothermia is a big danger and the dangers associated with rescuing the casualty are significant. Firstly, you have to manoeuvre the boat sideways under engine next to the casualty in the water, lower another crew member down in a harness and get them clipped together, and then winch the two of them back onto the deck. It's a fairly straightforward procedure on a calm day in the English Channel, but in a big South Atlantic swell the danger of rescue is actually crushing them with the boat as you manoeuvre close to them. If they get sucked under the hull, they could get dragged into the propeller, which would slice them to ribbons. Nightmare.

The main thing was that Arthur was alive and well. The message said that he was on deck and was in the process of unclipping his safety tether to go down the companionway into the boat when it was struck by a big wave and lurched sideways. Arthur lost his balance, fell down the deck and was washed overboard, underneath the protective guard wires.

A lump caught in my throat. I knew this news was going to scare the crew. We had a few crew members who were already very anxious about the conditions ahead. One of them even asked that they be excluded from going on deck at night, because they were so scared. The news of an MOB on another boat was going to terrify them.

I broke the news to the crew at our daily lunchtime meeting. As soon as I'd started telling them, I could hear the gasps and muttered curses. I glanced at one crew member who I knew would be more scared by the news – his eyes were like dinner plates and his hands were shaking. All the crew were relieved that Arthur was safe and sound. After going around the circle and asking everybody to describe how the news made them feel, we spent an hour running over and over our man overboard recovery drill. We also made some new rules about when we clip on our safety tethers. We would not unclip ourselves from the boat until we were safely down inside the hatchway.

I sent Piers an email that afternoon, telling him how good it was that he got Arthur safely back so quickly and without further injury to crew. I knew it would be affecting him badly and he had my sympathies. He was a good guy and great competitor and I didn't want to see him lose confidence or start second-guessing himself because of it.

We were 12 days into the race and I was working hard on our weather tactics, assisted by three analytically-minded crew members, whom I referred to as my three wise men. The weather files were being emailed to the boat every second day and we would pore over them for hours and make a decision on the course we would take. One of them was always in favour of taking the most direct route possible, the second was more of a risk taker, and the third insisted on a mathematical approach of examining every possible option. Each of them made valid points and the interplay between their opposing analyses helped me decide on the plan. Having that shared responsibility took a huge weight off my mind and they provided a check so I couldn't make a poor tactical decision because I was tired and not thinking straight.

The wind was forecast to increase over the next two days. There was a large depression to the south of us in the Southern Ocean and as it passed underneath us the wind would build to a predicted 40 knots, which was a lot, but nothing we hadn't seen before. We were in sixth place and I was desperate to get us climbing back up the table into the top three. It was this combination of competitive desperation and building wind that led to our first disaster on the race. I had no idea at the time as I sat there at the navigation station, but the next 96 hours were going to be some of the toughest of the entire race.

I've always believed in trusting my gut instinct, particularly when it comes to sailing. There have been times when I know something just isn't right. I can't exactly put my finger on it or articulate it into words, but something inside of me knows danger is approaching. Maybe it's a subtle change in the air pressure, an increase in moisture on the wind or a change in shade of the clouds but, whatever the reason, I know we need to reduce sail, *now*. It doesn't happen often, but I know it when it comes. As darkness fell on that night in the South Atlantic my senses were tingling. I knew we would get hit with some big wind overnight and it should build gradually, giving us ample warning to take sails down and prepare. As predicted, the wind was beginning to build and the barometer was dropping steadily. According to every instrument on board, all appeared normal, but *something* didn't feel right and I just couldn't shake that uneasy gut feeling that we should start reducing sail now.

*Sod it, Brendan, you're jumping at shadows. Reduce sails now and you'll just give away more miles to the leaders. There will be plenty of time later, and we're racing after all. Trust your instruments and the ability of the crew.*

In the end, I let my subconscious gut feeling be overwhelmed by my rational conscious mind. Maybe I was jumping at shadows after all? Was it just nervousness about the safety of the new leggers in their first big blow? Was I just losing my nerve in the face of a bit of heavy weather? These were questions that flashed into my mind.

As predicted, the wind and seas built. We were *absolutely bombing* along, surfing down a long swell at up to 25 knots. I was excited about the next sched, seeing how much we had gained on the race leaders. We had a lot of sail up – a single reef in the mainsail and the number two Yankee up front. It was too much, but the boat seemed under control and the helmsmen weren't struggling. By now, we were running with only our four best helms; they were the only ones good enough to keep us on course with this much power in the rig. It was a knife-edge balance – if we could keep this speed up, then we would be back up with the leading group in the next 12 hours, but if we lost control and wiped out, then we would damage the boat for sure. I sat in the navigation station, lit by the soft glow of the computer screen, gritted my teeth, and watched the instruments.

Outside, the night was absolutely pitch black. There was no moon and the sky was clouded over; the darkness had a thick quality that seemed to devour the light of our head torches. The roar and crash of the waves behind us was extremely unsettling. We couldn't see their size, and in the darkness our minds probably exaggerated their height. A wave would pick us up from astern and the whole boat would tip forward and get steeper and steeper, like a rollercoaster on the precipice of a terrifying drop. Then gravity would kick in and, with a jolt, the boat would begin surfing, 32 tons surging forward into pitch darkness. The powerful feeling of momentum was heightened by our blindness to the seascape; all we could see was the white, frothing water cascading down the deck. If somebody wasn't holding on, then the force of the water was enough to sweep their legs out from under them and wash them down the deck. Everyone was gripping on tight and the white-knuckle ride went on, watch after watch.

I knew we had too much sail up. The wind was now increasing past the 40 knots predicted and I could feel the helmsman having to pull harder on the wheel to make the boat respond. Watch leader Mike was on the helm and he was one of our very best. He had an instinctive feel for the motion of the boat and, with a lack of any visual reference, was keeping us on course using only the magnetic steering compass. He was doing a great job and our speed was phenomenal. The midnight sched came through and we had made a lot of ground on the leading group. Brilliant! A few more like this and we'll be…

'*Fuck! The compass light! The light's gone! Get a torch on this thing!*'

Mike was screaming from behind the wheel. The 5p LED light bulb that illuminates the compass had blown. Without the compass, he would be sailing blind. He was a great helm, but without a compass even he would struggle. The backup helmsman was fumbling with his head torch, trying to get light onto the compass. We were still howling along, on the edge of control. I was in overdrive and was scrambling up the companionway steps, looking towards Mike on the helm. I saw him correct the course as we came down a massive wave, but he was turning the wheel the wrong way.

I didn't even have time to scream for the crew to hit the deck.

The boat lurched away from the wind and swung into a violent crash-gybe. Our overpowered 250kg mainsail backed. The double-preventer lines, with a combined breaking strain of 16 tons, snapped like parcel string under the load. The 400kg alloy boom swung across the deck at head height, like a woodsman's axe swinging at a tree, and slammed with sledgehammer force into the rigging on the opposite side. It was over in a second.

If anybody had been hit by that boom, it would have been fatal. The crew were all safe, but they were deer in the headlights and had no idea what to do. There was panicked shouting coming from down below. Mike was swearing and the boat was lying over in the water, with the mainsail now on the wrong side.

I clipped my safety line on and shot up on deck to take control. I was told later by my crew that my first words were, 'Everyone calm the fuck down!'

I did the world's fastest headcount and then bellowed down the hatch for all hands to get on deck, *now*! I looked up at the mainsail and saw that it was torn, ripped somehow during the crash-gybe. We needed to get it down, *fast*. The sail was flogging and the vertical hole was getting bigger by the minute. The well-drilled and practised crew leapt into action and were in the process of reefing down the flogging mainsail when…

Bang!

As soon as I heard the sound, I knew what it was. It was one of the brass hanks on the front edge of the Yankee headsail snapping. I looked up and saw it was the one at the very top.

Bang! Bang! The next two down snapped off. Bang, bang! Two more.

Before we had time to blink, every one of the 20 brass hanks on the front edge of the sail had snapped off, like an unzipping jumper, and suddenly we had two sails flogging out of control. The mainsail was still flogging violently and the Yankee was slamming backwards and forwards with a deep, resonating WHUMP! that shook my bones. The flogging sails were pulling the mast in opposite directions and the whole boat was violently shaking. There were more crew emerging from the hatchway onto a deck where carnage was now king.

*What to do?*

The hole in the mainsail was getting bigger, but if we didn't get that Yankee down, we may well snap the mast.

With a gut-wrenching tear, the bottom of the Yankee tore off. It wasn't surprising; the forces acting upon the canvas were more than it was ever designed to handle.

*Quick!*

I sent everybody up onto the foredeck, where they struggled and heaved and fought with the sail, trying to get it down. The power in that piece of heavy canvas was ferocious and it was hitting them with the power to break fingers and noses. The hanks along the front edge of the sail now had sharp edges from where they had snapped and were tearing up the crew's Gore-tex oilskins. The crew would all grab the sail together, trying desperately to get their body weight on top of it to weigh it down, but the wind would catch the sail again and flick them off like ants. It was a battle against an indifferent and impossibly powerful force. And we were losing.

Eventually, we half dumped the sail overboard and the crew wrestled for a further five minutes, dragging it out of the water and back onto the deck. Half of them stayed up there and lashed the sail down, like imprisoning a dangerous criminal, while the rest came back and brought the mainsail down to its smallest setting and made it secure. One of them vomited from physical exhaustion and the others were collapsed on deck, gasping in huge breaths of air. With our mainsail now reefed all the way down, the boat was slower, but far more controllable. We secured the boom so it couldn't swing back again and regrouped.

The adrenalin was starting to wear off and I knew at least a few of the more scared crew would soon be in shock. I made sure everything was safe on deck, and then ordered the off-watch back to bed. After they were safely down below, I got the on-deck watch to clear up and hoist our small staysail to give us some more stability. The crew were still on a survivors' high, just happy to be safe and sound. They thanked me for handling the crisis situation so well and getting them through. I knew in my heart that, while I kept them safe, the whole situation was my fault.

*Idiot! You stupid bastard! All your talk of preserving the sails and thinking about long-term victory and then you charge off like a reckless fanatic, ignoring your own rules. We had been overpowered for hours and you did nothing! Damn you!*

It was my fault. Yes, the compass light failure was unexpected, but if we hadn't been so overpowered then we wouldn't be looking at two badly ripped sails. I felt incredibly guilty for the situation. I ignored my gut feeling in my desire to see us have a great sched and now we were in deep trouble. With a damaged mainsail, we couldn't sail at optimum speed and we were sure to have a bad result on this leg, but the point penalty we would incur for the repair of those two sails could undo all our hard work from the last race to Rio.

My feeling of guilt made me feel personally obliged to fix the situation.

I had made the mistake and I felt I needed to atone for it. It felt like a virtuous attitude to have, the brave skipper working non-stop to fix the situation and get his boat back in the race. In retrospect, it was a selfish motivation: I needed to soothe my guilty conscience and I became fixated on repairing the damage I had caused. I lost sight of the bigger picture, our high performance and my greater responsibilities as a leader.

The mainsail repair was something I could easily have delegated – we had some very clever people on board and I knew they could have engineered a solution to close the hole in the mainsail and strap it up until we reached Cape Town, but my pride and my guilty conscience wouldn't let me.

Big mistake.

By first light, I had made a plan. I would get into the climbing harness, ascend the mast and inspect the hole. Bob and I had come up with a solution of drilling holes through the sail and bolting a piece of solid plastic batten next to the vertical hole and then using thin cord to pull it closed. It sounded good and would be an easy job on a stable workbench, but suspended 12 metres above the deck of a rocking boat that was still moving quite fast was a different story.

With Bob's help, I spent the best part of ten hours up the mast that day and by dinnertime that night the hole was closed and the repair looked solid. It wasn't difficult work, once we knew how we were going to tackle the problem, and it could have easily been done by somebody else, but I stayed up there, gripping the mast so tightly my legs went numb. When I came down I was shivering and dehydrated, but my guilty conscience was assuaged.

During that day, we had no daily meeting at lunchtime. The flow of information stopped. I was the only person who had the password to get the sched emails, so the crew had no idea how we were doing in the race. Anxiety. They weren't able to download the weather files either, so they had no idea if this bad weather was going to continue or abate. Uncertainty. To suddenly rob a high-performance team of critical information is going to make them anxious and uncertain and is the surest way to watch morale drop.

With my attention distracted by the repair, I lost my team focus, too. I should have spent time that day making sure the more affected crew were coping. A big wipeout incident like that one can be a real confidence killer and I needed to be providing support to the crew, especially Mike. If I felt guilty, I can't imagine how he felt. He was on the wheel at the time of the gybe and although his error was the result of equipment failure, he would be feeling personally responsible – that's the kind of person he is.

During that day, the wind had shifted south, allowing us to sail a more direct route towards Cape Town, but as I was up the mast and not looking at the navigation instruments, I didn't notice and we denied ourselves the advantage of the wind shift. The rest of the fleet reacted to the shift immediately and we lost many miles to all of them. The latest sched was a shocker and we were back to seventh place, but the wind had eased and we had the correct sails up, so we were still in with a chance of a top five position.

Just like the previous night, this one felt dark and ominous. For the night-time hours, I restricted the helming to our six primary helms. None of the others complained – nobody wanted to be on the wheel if we were in another dangerous situation like that. I was exhausted from my time up the mast and just wanted to sleep. We were on course, the boat wasn't overpowered and the helms seemed to be coping with the conditions well, so I briefed the crew and went to bed. I was unconscious in moments.

It was about two hours later when it happened. All I remember was feeling the boat tip over suddenly and immediately I knew what was coming. Crash-gybe number two. Time slowed down as I lay there, pinned against the wall of my bunk, hoping the new preventer lines would hold the strain.

*Crack!*

The new preventer lines snapped.

Just like the night before, the mainsail and metal boom swung across the deck with terrifying power and slammed into the rigging on the opposite side with a sound like a thunderclap. The boat shuddered under the impact. Shouting from on deck and more shouting below. In a second I had extricated myself from my sleeping bag and was pulling my lifejacket over my shoulders. My mind was racing.

*How in the hell did this happen?*

*Is anybody hurt?*

*Do we have a man overboard?*

And finally…

*Are we going to lose the mast this time?*

Up on deck, it was a familiar sight. The boat was leaning the opposite way to how it should, with the mainsail now on the wrong side. I did a headcount – all present and uninjured. I started breathing again.

I looked up, expecting to see the repair on the mainsail torn to shreds, but it held. Impressive.

The tired and exhausted crew were firing on all cylinders again with the new surge of adrenalin. Thankfully, the damage was minimal and we spent two hours securing the boom with two new preventer lines, which we were positive wouldn't break. They were the strongest, most high-tech ropes we had on the boat, so it was the best we could do in any case.

Bob was on the helm when it had happened. He was the best and most experienced helm we had on board. It was almost unthinkable that he could crash-gybe the boat because of an honest error. He was too good for that and he hadn't made a mistake like this before.

Once the situation on deck was sorted out and we were back on our proper course, I went down below to check on Bob. He was so upset he was in tears. He was an experienced sailor and knew that while we got away with minimal damage and no injuries, it could have been deadly if somebody had been standing in the wrong place when it happened. A strike on the head from a swinging boom with that much energy behind it would have been instantly fatal.

Bob couldn't even really explain what had happened. He made no excuses and never tried to put the blame onto anybody else. He knew he was at fault and he accepted it. He felt responsible, guilty, and I could almost see his confidence draining away with the colour in his face. I knew exactly how that felt and my own painful feeling of guilt returned.

His helming error was probably a result of not sleeping much over the last 24 hours, a knock-on from my own mistake, which caused the accident the night before. I put my arm around Bob and sat there with him for a few minutes as tears streamed down his face.

I offered support. I told him that there are two types of helmsmen in the sailing world: those who have crash-gybed a boat and those who lie about it. I told him that he was our best helm and my biggest concern was that he would lose belief in himself. He was going to have to get back on the horse as soon as possible and get his confidence back. I didn't need to say much, but the support meant a lot to Bob at the time. In my own mind, it helped me overcome my own sense of guilt and, in a way, I forgave myself too.

The crew were great with Bob, very encouraging and supportive. The 'no-blame' culture we had on board really showed itself in these times of crisis. We weren't trying to pretend that it had never happened or not worry about it. There was a lot we could learn from the experience and in the next day's daily meeting we came up with a new, safer way of attaching a preventer line in case another one broke.

Two nights, two crash-gybes. What are the chances?

The wind had decreased further, so we dropped our small Yankee and hoisted the spinnaker to keep our speed up. While the crew were a bit disheartened by our run of bad luck, there was still a fighting spirit and we would push hard to claw back as much as we could, even if we couldn't gain an extra place. We wanted to make the boat in sixth place nervous, if nothing else. The scheds were a depressing sight – our main rivals, *Team Finland*, were sailing fast and were lying in second place behind *Cork*. Realistically, a podium position was out of the question for us by this stage and that had an effect on the motivation of the crew. They seemed less interested in the scheds when they came in and didn't ask questions about the next likely sail change.

My own motivation was being tested by the two setbacks. Neither of them was disastrous by any means, but they were brick walls and it takes energy to climb over them and keep running 24 hours a day, seven days a week, while trying to motivate 18 others to do the same. A nice relaxing weekend at home would have sorted me out and given me time to take stock and come back with renewed vigour, but sadly this wasn't an option.

As the sun set over the South Atlantic waves that evening, I could feel the tension on the boat, the feeling of anticipation mixed with dread. The sky was overcast and there was still no moon, so the oppressive, inky darkness was going to be upon us again within the hour.

What disaster is going to befall us tonight? I'm sure the crew were thinking that very thought. I certainly was, half seriously, half cynically. Another crash-gybe, perhaps? How about a halyard failure? Maybe we'll have a collision with a whale; it's the right season for them. Let's spin *Spirit of Australia*'s wheel of disaster and stay tuned. This thought brought a chuckle, my first in a few days.

I obviously didn't knock on wood after thinking that thought, because a few hours later I was up on deck and we were preparing to drop the spinnaker as the wind was building again when one of the heavy-duty, stainless-steel shackles that attach the spinnaker to the control line exploded.

The sail, now free from the massive tension keeping it in shape, began violently flapping out beside the boat. Another of the control lines was still attached to the rogue sail and was thrashing backwards and forwards, like a bullwhip. We had experienced a similar shackle blow-out on leg one in calmer conditions, so we knew what to do. The 35-metre long spinnaker control line whipping across the deck meant nobody was safe. We could see the enormous white sail flogging, but we couldn't see the control line, connected to its corner. We could hear it slicing through the air as it screamed towards the boat, the whip crack as it hit something and then flew back out into the darkness. Every ten seconds. The power in that thrashing line could break an arm and knock teeth out. Keeping low, the crew dashed into position for an emergency sail drop. I was just about to give the command to drop when the line whipped across the deck, lashed me right across the middle of my back and threw me to the deck. Even through my Gore-tex oilskins and thermal layers, it was excruciating. I howled with pain and bellowed at the crew to get the sail down, now!

I could still move my fingers and toes, so I knew my spine was undamaged. The crew were frantically heaving down the spinnaker and stuffing it down the hatch in big armfuls. Once it was contained inside the boat, I instructed the crew to get the number three Yankee (smallest of the three) up and flying, before gingerly making my way below and collapsing in the navigation station. I reached up underneath my clothing and when I drew my hand out, there was no blood. Lucky escape. If this had happened on a hot leg and I was just wearing a T-shirt, I'm sure it would have been far worse.

Our on-board medic was watch leader Steve. He had a look and while there was a nasty welt, which would later become a big bruise, there didn't appear to be any more serious damage. He gave me some painkillers and said I needed some more sleep. I eased my way into my bunk, rolled onto my side and lay there. The adrenalin was still in my system, so I couldn't sleep just yet, and my thoughts turned over in a downward spiral.

*Let's just get there. If we can get to Cape Town without trashing the boat any further or hurting anybody else, then I'm happy.*

Hitting a brick wall every night for three nights in a row had drained my energy and this last one, which had left me personally injured, was the final straw. For all my talk and rhetoric about persistence and energy and victory, I knew I had lost my motivation. I was cold, tired, exhausted and in pain. Just getting there became the objective. The race win – the single goal I had been pushing towards for the past two years – seemed unimportant at that moment.

It pains my ego to write it, but I had given up.

I slept for nearly 36 hours. My body and mind needed the rest, but all that time I was in my bunk, I was not being a leader. After three big setbacks in a row was when the crew needed me the most. As I was the only person with the email password, when I was asleep the crew couldn't access the scheds or the weather information being sent to us. The flow of information stopped once more and, in my absence, the crew became despondent themselves. We sailed slowly onwards toward Cape Town.

When I awoke, I felt 100 per cent better. My back wasn't so sore and I felt refreshed. I quickly gauged the mood of the crew and it wasn't good. I checked the latest sched and it showed us still in seventh place and not far behind *Qingdao* in sixth. They must have been having their own problems. The weather between us and the finish looked stable and the sailing would be quite easy in comparison to the last three nights.

We needed to have a good meeting and debrief on the last few days. At that lunchtime meeting, we all talked about the run of bad luck we'd had. Some of the crew were disappointed that we had lost positions in the race. Others were just glad to be safe. Some wanted to get back to hardcore racing as soon as possible and others wanted to take the slow and steady approach. There was a lot of stress on board, caused by the incidents themselves, the anxiety of having a skipper who wasn't being a good leader, and the uncertainty of not having any information on the weather or our position in the race. The stress was evident in their body language, their facial expressions and the tone of voice they used.

I read an article in a science magazine years ago explaining how stress manifests itself physically. Heart attacks and strokes at the extreme end of the spectrum, but day-to-day stress can lead to tensed muscles, joint problems and high blood pressure. The article said that shouting and screaming can help to purge stress physically out of your body. The exertion of projecting your voice and the primal outlet of pent-up frustration can be beneficial.

I can't explain why, but my memory of this article came back to me as we were having the debrief and I could sense the stress of the crew. And so without further ado, I asked everybody to gather around the stern of the boat, facing outwards away from everybody else. We were going to have a 30-second shout and scream at the South Atlantic Ocean. We could shout anything we wanted – abuse, swearing, condemnation or just a good old shout of nothing at all. I made it clear that we weren't shouting at each other or the boat.

What followed was an 18-person tirade of words and phrases not fit for printing. At full volume, on a sailing yacht in the middle of the ocean. It was a truly surreal moment. Some crew had to cover their ears from the volume of it all, but they kept shouting. For my own part, I shouted at the ocean, calling it a bastard and telling it to stop making life hard for us. Just give us a bloody break and let us get to Cape Town. My language was possibly more colourful than that, but you get the picture. It was clear from what I was hearing that many of the crew shared my exact sentiments.

By the end, we were all laughing. It's a very rare thing to be able to do and even be encouraged to let out stress and frustration in this way. Shouting in general life is frowned upon and a leader who shouts at his team needs more practice at being a leader, but in a carefully controlled environment, I think it can be beneficial. While it didn't take away any of our root causes of stress, the very act of letting it all out made people more relaxed. I also saw it as a way of closing the book on the events of the last few days and consigning them to the past. That was then and this is now, sort of thing. We had three days of racing left and we could still catch *Qingdao* and get sixth place. That was our new goal. Forget about the front-runners. Barring a catastrophe, they were out of our reach now.

I opened the floor to the crew and the comments made were generally positive. The crew hadn't given up and I wasn't going to let them down. I had given up temporarily, a lapse in motivation, but after a long sleep and giving the South Atlantic a good bollocking, I was ready to go again.

The sail into Cape Town was an amazing one. The sun was setting, the glorious vista of Table Mountain and Table Bay beneath it. A pod of 50 porpoises came and swam with us for an hour, jumping and playing in our bow wake. An hour or so later, *Qingdao* appeared on the horizon, abreast of us. We were an equal distance from the finish line and both pushing hard. They had a little more wind but we had a better angle. We converged and raced neck and neck for three hours, as the sun set behind us, bathing Table Mountain in a soft, amber light.

We were in overdrive. It didn't matter that we were fighting for sixth position. It was a race between two boats and two crews and no quarter was given. As we came under the wind shadow of Table Mountain, the wind quickly dropped away. The race was now to see which crew could hoist their spinnaker quicker to keep the boat moving in the light wind. The *Spirit of Australia* crew leapt to the task, working quickly and efficiently in the darkness. There was excellent communication as the procedure for hoisting the tennis-court-sized sail was played out. Our spinnaker was up and flying well before *Qingdao*, and we left them in our wake and crossed the finish line to claim sixth place.

From the cheer that went up, you could have mistaken us for the boat that came first. We had made it. Our final race with *Qingdao* proved to us that we were a great team and we were still fiercely competitive even after all the brick walls we had hit on the way there. It was a minor victory, but a significant one to all of us.

Looking back now, that finish into Cape Town was the most satisfying of any race finish. We had been through a lot over the last 18 days and the relief of arriving safely with all of my crew uninjured and in remarkably good spirits felt like a real achievement. We had a custom on *Spirit of Australia*, before the start and after the finish of each race, where we would have a team huddle on the foredeck of the boat. We'd stand in a circle, arms around each other's shoulders, and I would make a short speech. After that race I made a speech in our team huddle, telling the crew how well we had done to get through all those setbacks and remain in such good spirits. I told them that brick walls are good – they remind us how much we want something. And we do still want to win this race. I had played with fire, had my fingers burnt on this leg, and I wasn't going to let it happen again. We had all learned lessons that we needed to reflect on, talk about and take forward with us into the fearsome Southern Ocean on the next race from Cape Town to Australia.

I told the crew they were the best crew a skipper could want and, asked with a nod in his direction, our most fair-dinkum, true-blue Aussie, Ian King, gave us an *Aussie! Aussie! Aussie!* To which we all chorused back *OI! OI! OI!*

We were welcomed to the Royal Cape Yacht Club by the other crews who had arrived earlier that day and the beer flowed all night long. Their stories were similar to our own; every boat had a taste of

**Above** The 10 Race Skippers. (L to R) Pete Stirling (*Jamaica Lightning Bolt*), Jim Dobie (*Uniquely Singapore*), Chris Stanmore-Major (*Qingdao*), Pete Rollason (*California*), Eero Leitinen (*Team Finland*), Richie Fearon (*Cork*), Me (*Spirit of Australia*), Matt Pike (*Edinburgh*), Jan Ridd (*Cape Breton Island*), Piers Dudin (*Hull & Humber*).

**Below** The highs of being a skipper. Elation in the navigation station as we cross the scoring gate off the Canary Islands.

**Opposite top** The Clipper Fleet at rest in La Rochelle. The crews were frantically preparing for their first ocean crossing to Rio de Janeiro, one month away.

**Opposite bottom** Pushing hard.

**Left** Sunset at sea is a great time for reflection.

**Below** A close pass with *Cork* at the Rio start line.

**Opposite** Bob and me repairing our badly damaged mainsail. The repair took 11 hours.

**Above** The Clipper Fleet blasting out of Cape Town, heading into the dangerous Southern Ocean.

**Below** Approaching the finish line in Geraldton, Western Australia. Great teamwork and a great result.

**Above** Punishing conditions on the way up to Qingdao. The foredeck crew struggle valiantly against icy waves as they perform another headsail change. The volume of water was so great, their lifejackets kept automatically inflating.

**Below** As well as the punishing conditions, I had to navigate us safely through one of the most congested shipping areas in Asia. Each of those green triangles is a tanker ship, moving at twice our speed. *Spirit of Australia* is the black one in the middle.

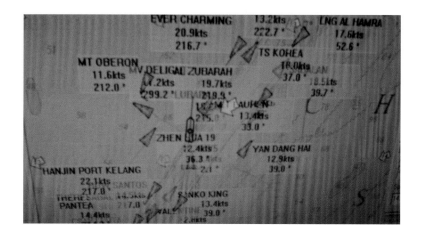

The reward for our relentless effort. The reception at the dockside in Qingdao was phenomenal.

**Above** The waves at the start of the storm in which Piers would break his leg. Me at the helm, looking serious.

**Below** Me in my dry suit, preparing to transfer onto *Hull & Humber*. Bob (at the helm) would become acting skipper of *Spirit of Australia* and Gareth and Mike, the two watch leaders, would be responsible for getting our boat and crew safely through the dangerous North Pacific Ocean. If anybody could do it, they could.

**Above** Saying an emotional goodbye to my crew before departing. Getting off *Spirit of Australia* was the hardest thing I have ever had to do.

**Below** Transfer successful. Me being winched up onto the deck of *Hull & Humber*.

**Opposite top** Bob and the *Spirit of Australia* crew hold their first daily meeting without me.

**Opposite middle** Dismasted *California* speeding down the face of an enormous North Pacific wave, as seen from *Hull & Humber*. These waves were the biggest I have seen.

**Opposite bottom** The waves begin to build in the North Pacific.

**Above** After a much-needed break in San Francisco, the fleet heads out under the Golden Gate Bridge and into the Pacific Ocean once more. Next stop, Panama.

**Opposite** Stuck in a wind hole, with our lightweight spinnaker hanging limply.

**Above** The fleet leaving Cape Breton Island, Canada under spinnaker.

**Below** The *Spirit of Australia* crew and me in Cork, Ireland after our final ocean crossing.

**Above** On the dockside in Ijmuiden, Netherlands, having just won the overall Race!

**Left** *Spirit of Australia* charging towards the finish line in Hull under our largest spinnaker.

**Opposite** In time-honoured tradition, lighting the red flare to signify our victory.

Holding the trophy: the achievement of a lifetime.

accidents and breakages on this trip. We were not the only boat to need sail repairs.

Luckily, the cost of labour in South Africa is quite low, so we got away with the repair on the mainsail and the number two Yankee for £485 in total. Another £15 and it would have cost us a penalty point. Lucky break.

During the stopover in Cape Town, I booked a meeting room in the Yacht Club and organised a full debrief with the whole crew, including the new leggers who would be joining us for leg three. I thought long and hard about what to say in the meeting and decided that the theme should be 'Improvement'. The agenda had three items on it:

- How to improve the way we do things?
- How to improve the way everyone gets along?
- How can I improve as your skipper?

I didn't want my presence to be a censoring factor for the last question, so I told the crew that I would leave the meeting for that part. They needed to elect somebody to summarise the discussion and come to me with the points. It wasn't an easy thing to ask for personal feedback and I had to mentally prepare myself for the comments they made. Criticism, even constructive criticism, is never pleasant to hear, but it's essential to improvement. There were no politics in play, as might be the case in an office environment, where honest 180-degree feedback might negatively affect a worker's chance of promotion. If people wanted their comments brought to me anonymously, then that was fine.

The first two items on the agenda brought a raft of ideas, from the knots we use to tie our lines onto the sails to the methods for pumping the bilge and tweaks we could make to the mother watch rotation to make it easier. Somebody said we didn't play enough music on board and we should have more music down below deck. There were concerns that there wasn't enough fun stuff to keep the mood light when we were racing. There was honest communication and positive conflict over issues that people felt were important. No idea was shot down or ridiculed and everyone valued the input of the others. Nobody sat back in silence, every person at the table was engaged and wanted to have input into improving things.

When we reached the final point on the agenda, I excused myself and waited downstairs in the yacht club bar while the meeting carried on for what seemed like a very long time. Was that a good thing or a bad thing? Eventually, watch leader Steve and Gareth Rees, another core crew member, came and sat with me and gave me the points that had been raised.

The consensus was that I was not giving enough training to the crew and they wanted me to spend more time on deck teaching them things.

The other key point was that they wanted me to give them more responsibility. Up until that point, the crew came to me and suggested that we changed sails and I would say yes or no. From now on, they wanted to make those decisions themselves as a collective. I could overrule them if I felt the decision was incorrect, but I felt they were experienced enough now to start making these decisions.

There was one final point, which wasn't raised at the meeting but by a crew member who came and spoke to me privately later that day. He cautioned that I should never go up the mast again, or put myself in a position where I was in danger. His argument was that inside my head was all the navigation knowledge – knowledge of the safety routines, knowledge of the boat systems, my sailing knowledge from years of training and experience and the skills to lead the crew in a crisis situation. He made the point quite eloquently when he said, 'If we had a man overboard, I'd want you coming back for me, not us coming back for you.'

It was a point I hadn't really considered up until then, but he was absolutely right. I needed to keep myself safe to keep the crew safe. This runs contrary to the mentality that, as a leader, you cannot ask one of your crew to do something you're not prepared to do yourself, but when you have 18 lives depending on you, the risk is just too great. I thanked him for his insight and assured him that I would keep my boots firmly on deck from now on.

Besides these points, the crew were generally happy with the way I did things. We knew our performance on this leg was just a 'blip', a blemish on an otherwise very strong track record. On the next leg, armed with everything we had learned, we were going to be back up the front of the fleet where we deserved to be. The next leg was a race into our home port, the town of Geraldton on the Western Australian coast, 400km north of Perth. The Clipper race is fabled for the 'home port curse', meaning no boat ever wins the race into its home port. In all seven Clipper races, the curse had only been broken twice, by *Victoria* in the 05–06 race and *New York* in the 07–08 race. I felt this was a good omen, as *Victoria* and *New York* were the two previous names of our boat, *Spirit of Australia*. She wanted to win this leg as much as we did and make it three from three.

## LEADERSHIP LESSONS

### Trust your gut feeling

The phenomenon we know commonly as our 'gut feeling' or 'intuition' is known in the world of psychology as *thin slicing*. It describes an innate ability in humans to subconsciously find patterns and make very fast decisions based on small amounts, or 'thin slices', of information. Our ability to *thin slice* is an evolved survival mechanism. If one of our ancestors in prehistoric Africa was confronted with a hungry lion, he would need to make a snap decision on what to do to escape. In the blink of an eye, his subconscious mind would assess the danger, based on his knowledge of lions and any past experiences with them, and his gut feeling would be to run away. If he waited, carefully weighing up his options and thoughtfully deciding on a plan of action, he would be killed.

Our gut feeling is a hard thing to explain rationally. We usually hear it referred to when people say things like 'Something just didn't *feel* right,' or 'Looking at it, I could just tell something was wrong,' If you ask them to explain or clarify exactly what they mean, they usually can't put their finger on an exact reason. Somehow, they just *know* it.

That, very simply, is *thin slicing*.

I made the big mistake of not listening to my gut feeling on that night in the South Atlantic. My gut feeling was definitely telling me to reduce our sail area, but I ignored it. If somebody had asked me why I felt this way, I couldn't have articulated it in a meaningful way, I just *knew* we should.

The trouble is that the conscious, logical, explanation-seeking part of our mind has trouble making sense of thin-sliced gut feelings and often overrides or dismisses them.

In my case, my conscious, analytical mind subverted my gut feeling, rationalising it as a momentary hit of paranoia. After all, the boat's instruments were telling me that the wind was within acceptable limits and so I made the decision to keep our sail plan as it was.

If I had listened to my gut feeling and reduced our sail area, we would have avoided the awful sequence of events over the following three nights. Since that night, I have never ignored my gut feeling again and it has always been proved right.

As a skipper, you need to be aware of your gut feelings. Listen to them and don't dismiss them as I did. If you just *know* something, without being able to explain it, take the time to explore that line of thought and see where it leads. That feeling is there for a *reason* and in my experience, it's usually correct.

### Stay focused on the big picture

In the aftermath of the crash-gybe that ripped our mainsail, I lost my focus on the big picture. I became fixated with making the repair myself, and my guilt was a powerful motivator. For those hours I was up the mast, I was totally neglecting my greater responsibilities as a leader.

What I *should* have done was delegate the laborious, time-consuming work of the repair to others. It wasn't a specialist repair that needed my expert attention, but I felt it would be unfair to put somebody else up the mast to get swung around and beaten up to fix *my* mistake.

I let my emotions get in the way of making a good decision and the consequences cost us a lot. As the team's leader, I needed to keep my boots on the deck, making sure the boat was being sailed safely and quickly and the crew felt supported after the accident. Their confidence was severely knocked and this was the hour where they needed my support the most. Unfortunately, this only became clear with the benefit of hindsight.

As a leader, you need to remember your responsibilities: the well-being and performance of your team.

If you de-prioritise these responsibilities in the face of an unexpected setback or problem, then the detriment of lost leadership will far exceed the detriment of the problem itself. If you are personally involved, try to assess the situation dispassionately, delegate accordingly and make sure you keep your eyes firmly on the big picture.

## Create a no-blame culture

A no-blame culture was something that quickly became one of our core team values. Given that this was a race for amateur sailors, it was to be expected that mistakes would be more frequent than with a seasoned and experienced crew of professionals. As a team, being able to openly discuss and collectively learn from an individual's mistake and then letting it go would be critical to our long-term team development. From the earliest stages of training, I made sure it was ingrained in the whole team that mistakes were inevitable. Everyone would make them, including myself, and it was *how* we dealt with them that was important. They could either be a positive learning experience, or a negative, blaming, confidence-sapping experience. The fact that mistakes weren't stigmatised made people comfortable with admitting to them and taking responsibility for them. There was no need to cast the blame elsewhere, to make excuses or run away.

From a morale perspective, this was a great strength. Every crew member made their mistakes, some bigger than others, but nobody was ever humiliated, blamed or snubbed as a result. I can recall touching scenes of crew members comforting somebody who had made a big mistake and felt they should be rightly criticised and blamed. The support for them was always unreserved and sincere and it bred a feeling of team solidarity that became stronger as the race went on.

After the fact, our priority was rebuilding their lost confidence and making sure we all learned from it. After we had discussed the mistake and all learned from it, we would 'leave it on the last wave' and put it behind us.

As a leader, creating and sustaining a no-blame culture is a challenge. It doesn't mean accepting repeated mistakes or blithely shrugging off poor performance. The members of your team are accountable for their actions, but they *will* make mistakes. Nobody is infallible. If you have created a culture where mistakes can be accepted, not stigmatised, learned from and then left behind, it will avoid a lot of the negative politics that can become rife in a competitive team environment. How a team deals with its individual members' mistakes can be its greatest strength, or its greatest weakness.

### Draw a line

Say what you will about our act of collectively shouting

profanities at the South Atlantic Ocean, but it *worked*. The act of shouting seemed to take the edge off the stress people were feeling and acknowledged our collective frustration. More importantly, it mentally drew a line in our minds between the past and the present. The last three days were in the past and we couldn't change what had happened.

I wanted to use this as a fresh start and a chance to 'reset' all our high-performance team behaviours. We were going to finish our race in the same manner as we started. I fully intended to revisit those three nights of disasters in a thorough debrief once we reached port. For the time being, we needed to focus, without distraction, on racing as hard as possible to the finish line.

A good leader recognises when a fresh start is needed, particularly after a bad setback. Do something novel to signify the occasion. It doesn't have to be anything big or extravagant, just something symbolic that your team can participate in and will remember. Getting over setbacks can be a drawn-out process and performance always suffers in the meantime. A leader who can quickly draw that line and turn their team's focus from the past to the future will see the recovery process dramatically shortened.

## Get feedback

There is no such thing as a perfect leader. Every leader has room to improve, no matter how long they've been doing it. Only an egotist would argue otherwise.

I knew from the outset that getting feedback from my crew was going to be a factor in me improving as a leader. After all, I was 'practising' my skills on them every day, so they were ideally placed to tell me what I needed to hear. Of course, what I *needed* to hear wasn't necessarily what I *wanted* to hear. Even well-intended, constructive criticism is never a pleasant thing to listen to, but is absolutely essential for development as a leader. I thought I was doing a pretty good job, but there were certainly things I could do better.

By inviting the feedback, with the stated goal of improvement, it gave the crew a chance to air their criticisms of my leadership in an open forum, which I felt was far preferable to them complaining to each other behind my back on night watch. I was going to be criticised in any case – at least this way I could address their criticisms and learn from the experience.

In the feedback I was eventually given by the nominated messenger, it was clear that our boat ethos of having a no-blame culture extended to me as well. They accepted me as a fallible human being and a young leader, who was doing his best and wanted to improve, which they respected. The constructive criticisms they gave me were honest and I took them in good spirit. Our team goal was to 'sustain a campaign of continuous improvement' and this was an opportunity for me to do exactly that.

I believe that any leader who wants to improve needs to seek feedback, knowing it's not always going to be positive. Your team are the best ones to provide that feedback and they will provide it to each other, whether you are listening or not. A good skipper should give them the opportunity to provide it in a controlled, constructive forum and see it not as a threat, but as an opportunity to grow.

# 9

# ATTITUDE

*Attitude is a little thing that makes a big difference*
*WINSTON CHURCHILL*

The Southern Ocean has the reputation of destroying boats.

The region of the notorious Cape Horn, at the bottom tip of South America, is the most treacherous of all, but in general it is a place to be feared and respected. It's the only unbroken ocean in the world, going all the way around the globe and meeting itself again. With no continents to get in the way, the waves and the ferocious winds circle the Southern Ocean indefinitely, building in size and power, seeking any seagoing vessel on which to vent their terrible energy.

The area of sea we would be sailing through would be between latitude 40 and 50 degrees south. It goes by the moniker of 'the Roaring Forties', from the size of the sea and ferocity of the wind. Below latitude 50 degrees south, it becomes the 'Furious Fifties' and then into the 'Shrieking Sixties', at which point you get to the continent of Antarctica. Basically, the further south you go, the worse it gets.

I had never sailed the Southern Ocean before this race. It's rare for sailing yachts to go down there without a good reason. Most ocean crossings can be done further north at the right time of year, with far easier conditions. The Southern Ocean is the final frontier for an ocean sailor and there is a lot of kudos attached to having sailed a yacht between continents through that dangerous place.

With the danger comes the excitement, though. Those enormous waves and roaring winds can propel a well-sailed yacht at huge speeds, surfing down the faces of the long grey waves. If any crew wanted an adrenalin-fuelled, downwind ride, this was the race they were going to get it. I was looking forward to it – with trepidation, of course, knowing that I was about to lead my crew into an environment where very few sailors ever go.

I had done my homework and spent hours every day in Cape Town analysing the latest Southern Ocean weather patterns as they developed. The low-pressure systems were following their regular patterns and we would be in for a rough ride, right from the outset.

On the day before we left Cape Town, I gave the crew a full briefing, trying my best to strike a balance of setting realistic expectations while not scaring them unduly. These were going to be the hardest weather conditions we had experienced thus far. We were going to see more wind and bigger waves than we did in the South Atlantic and would have to endure it for 25 long days. The pressure was on us to win this race; I had already done some telephone interviews with the Australian sporting press. They were following us intently and expecting a win. There was also a scoring gate in this race, positioned about 1500nm along the course. It was a chance to pick up some more points to make up for our poor result coming into Cape Town.

In traditional fashion, I didn't sleep a wink the night before the race start. The core crew were ready and the new leggers were keen as mustard. Most of them had chosen to sign up for this leg because they wanted to experience the harsh conditions of the Southern Ocean and, on the whole, they seemed to be a fairly hardy bunch.

With an amazing fanfare, the fleet slipped line from the Victoria and Alfred waterfront marina in Cape Town and motored out into Table Bay. We all hoisted sails and began preparing for the start sequence. As with Rio, I told the crew that we were going to play it safe on the start line and keep clear of the other boats. Aggressive pre-start tactics were being used by some of the skippers, forcing competitors to tack out of the way or change course and go behind them. The wind was blowing a stiff 25 knots and most of the boats were overpowered, but we had learned our lesson and were keeping our sail plan conservative until we had a little more sea room to play with.

One minute to the start cannon and all boats were on their final approach to the line, powered up and thundering along, all pushing to get their nose over the line first. I looked over my left shoulder and saw *Cork* powering directly towards *Hull & Humber*, who were perpendicular to them on the other tack. It was going to be a close pass.

*Are they? …oh my g..*

SMASH!

The sound rang out across Table Bay like a cannon shot and lingered in the air. *Cork* had T-boned *Hull & Humber*, slamming into them at full pace, 2 metres from the stern. The boats came apart and quickly started taking sails down and assessing damage. I knew instantly that neither of these two boats would be taking part in the race. The damage was too extensive and would take weeks to repair.

*Unbelievable. How the hell had that happened?*

It really brought the 'think long-term victory, not short-term glory' mentality home for all of us. *Cork* had pushed too hard and paid the price, just like we did with our sails on the previous leg. I felt sorry for the two crews, not being able to race with us on this leg, but there was nothing any of us could do about it. We had our own race to worry about.

We left Cape Town in our wake, as the sun set and bathed the beautiful Table Mountain in soft light. My strategy was to dive south as quickly as possible and get away from the continental shelf. The shelf to the south of Cape Agulhas is renowned for treacherous sailing conditions and many wrecked ships. When the depth of the ocean changes from 4,000 metres deep and almost instantly shelves to 200 metres deep, the waves increase in size massively. On the nautical chart I was examining, there were stark warnings written all over the area, warning of unexpected, heavy, breaking swell. An area best avoided if at all possible.

So, head south into the Southern Ocean, hang a left when the time is right, then hold on until we reach Australia. Simple.

Things were going smoothly. As with leaving Rio, we had our 48 hours of seasick crew, but we had systems in place to make sure we could still sail at full speed with fewer people on deck. We pushed south, following a hard-charging *Team Finland*. The sailing was hard, we had the wind on the bow, so the boat was heeled over at a 35-degree angle and bouncing and bashing through the waves. It didn't take long for conditions to become very cold – the wind was blowing straight off Antarctica and had a fresh, icy feel to it.

The Southern Ocean was everything we expected – the enormous, slate-grey waves with foaming crests, called 'greybeards', marched east with power and purpose. A wave would come from behind us, lifting the stern of the boat, higher and higher, then surging us forward with a roar from behind. We surfed and surfed, the momentum of the wave was overpowering and irresistible. After 20 seconds, it would loosen its grip and then roll underneath us.

Day and night, we surged along through the enormous grey valleys between the crests. The seascape was desolate, inhospitable and monochrome. The sky was mostly overcast and a sunny day just meant a slightly lighter shade of grey light. The size and power of the waves made the hairs on the back of my neck stand up and we all had that feeling of awe known only to sailors who visit this place.

My focus was on making sure we were placing the boat in the right position to take advantage of the next weather system. The weather systems were coming up from behind us, heading east, but moving at around four times our speed, so they would eventually catch and overtake us. If we were too far south, we would get caught too close to the centre of the system, where the wind was too strong. If we were too far north, we wouldn't get enough wind and we would lose speed. There was a band of wind that gave us optimum speed and it was my job, with the assistance of my three wise men, to make sure we stayed in it.

There was a frantic race to the scoring gate, which I am proud to say we won, adding an extra three points to our tally. *Team Finland* crossed just an hour behind us, picking up two points. *These guys never bloody let up.*

The following weeks we sailed hard, jostling for the race lead with *Team Finland*. The team were working well and were relishing the tough conditions. In the heavy weather, the energy used to do a big job like a headsail change is much greater. It involves getting six to eight people to lug a 70kg sail up a hatch onto the foredeck, where they get soaked to the bone by the waves coming over the bow. They take it out of its bag and attach the hanks to the wire forestay. They then have to wrestle down the working sail and un-hank it, then finally hoist the new one. It doesn't stop there – the old sail, wet and heavy, needs to be brought off the foredeck, folded neatly into its bag and then put away down below. In total, this is a good 40 minutes of hard, wet, exhausting work for everyone. In the middle of the night, with freezing cold water cascading over the bow, there was a strong temptation to not bother with the sail change. The crew on deck were shivering, tired and just wanted the watch to finish so they could get back into the warmth of their sleeping bags. They never faltered though. As the wind dropped, no matter what hour of the day or the conditions, they would change sails. Even if one hour later they had to change it back, they would do it. There was no question of being too tired or exhausted, there was work to be done and they would do whatever it took to keep *Spirit of Australia* going at full speed.

There were many moments on this race when my judgement was tested. The wind would build rapidly as the Southern Ocean weather systems caught up with us. The lessons of leg two were fresh in my mind and we played on the side of caution, reducing sail early and keeping the boat under better control. Our speed might have been slightly less, but we were far less likely to have a scary wipeout situation that might knock us out of the race. It was a trade-off I now gladly made. As the old saying goes – to finish first, first you have to finish.

The weather and racing weren't the only things occupying my

mind. During this race, I had a problem with a certain crew member. It was a lesson for me in managing a very strong and difficult personality and also the effect a personality like that has on a team. The male crew member was a supremely gifted individual, he was technically excellent in his role and he showed amazing persistence. He was definitely one of the hardest-working people on the boat, but he lacked self-awareness and people skills. He would criticise other crew members harshly and directly if they took longer to get something done. Some leggers struggled at times with tying the knots in our sail control lines. He would get frustrated watching them and eventually grab the rope out of their hands and tie the knot himself, then walk off, muttering under his breath. He left some female crew in tears with his attitude and sharp tongue, all the while completely unaware of his effect on others. Over time, his behaviour became a very negative influence on the team. The inexperienced crew became afraid of making a mistake in front of him, tying a knot incorrectly or not coiling a line in the way he liked it done. As a result, they shied away from doing tasks they weren't 100 per cent sure of, for fear of being criticised. He was task-focused to the extreme, but this came at the expense of his ability to sense his influence on others.

I had spoken to him at length about his attitude and lack of self-awareness on the first two legs and after each talk he made an improvement for a few days, but then slipped back into his old ways. I was in the difficult position of needing him for his skill and ability, but not actually wanting him on board, because of his attitude and his effect on the team.

Which is worth more? Technical skills or people skills? I remembered back to what Duggie had told me before the race. He said he would rather have a clueless amateur crew member who was a good team player and had a willingness to learn over a technically great sailor who had a bad attitude and couldn't get along with others. This crew member was a case-in-point for me and changed my opinion on the value of both. While I found him difficult to deal with, I couldn't blame him for the way he was. Each of us is a product of our life experiences and the core character traits we learn during our childhood and teenage years remain largely unchanged throughout adulthood. In the end, I realised that no matter how much I tried to make him see how his attitude and behaviour were detrimental, I wasn't going to be able to undo 30+ years of programming. He was who he was. We had to accept him for his strong points and grit our teeth and live with his negative points. Thousands of miles from land, there really weren't any other options.

He was only doing the first three legs and so would be leaving the boat in Australia. In a way, I felt bad that he would probably leave the race with a negative opinion of the whole experience. Could a better skipper have come up with a way of making him change or work better with others?

I had tried empathetic understanding – trying to figure out why he got so frustrated with people over small issues. I asked probing questions about his life and work up until now, but he didn't want to talk about it.

I tried negotiation, appealing to his sense of fairness and 'do unto others'. 'How would you like being cursed at and having things snatched away from you?' I asked on many occasions.

When these methods failed to improve matters, I even tried flexing my skipper's authority and flat-out ordering him to improve his attitude. This didn't work either; I couldn't punish him or stop him from coming on deck. He was a paying customer and the fact was that we needed him on deck because he was so skilled and capable, *and he knew it.*

*Attitude over aptitude.*

My other concern on this leg was replacing watch leader Steve Davis. He, too, was leaving the boat in Australia and selecting a replacement would be difficult. I intended to select a core crew member who would remain as watch leader for the rest of the round the world race. There were several very good candidates, some of which had expressed interest in taking on the role.

The person I chose to become the new watch leader was Gareth Rees, a 33-year-old corporate treasurer. He had not expected to be asked to replace Steve as watch leader and he thought long and hard about it before finally accepting. He had never sailed before signing up for Clipper, but he had learned quickly and was becoming a skilled sailor. I chose Gareth on the strength of his leadership and people skills. I trusted him and felt he would work well with me. He would be an effective conduit of information between his watch and me. He felt he lacked technical experience, but I told him that I could train and help him with that. It was his personal characteristics – a great attitude and ability to communicate well with the rest of the crew – that made him the obvious choice in my mind. There were far more experienced sailors I could have chosen, making my life as skipper easier in the short term, but my gut feeling was that Gareth would be the best choice for the duration of our campaign.

*Attitude over aptitude.*

I teamed him up with Steve for this leg, acting as assistant watch leader, watching and learning all he could. This handover process was very valuable as it gave the watch time to acclimatise to working with Gareth as their watch leader and let him develop confidence in his own abilities to lead and manage them. When we left Australia on the next leg, heading north towards Singapore, I needed him to be 100 per cent ready and on the ball and the Southern Ocean was a thoroughly testing apprenticeship.

Meanwhile, with no apparent reason, *Team Finland* began to storm away from us. We were pushing as hard as we dared, but sched by sched they were building a lead ahead of us. This was *our homecoming race*! We had worked so hard and deserved to win it, for our own sake and also for the people of Australia, who were so vocal in their support for us and were willing us home in first place. The weight of expectation on my shoulders was heavy and I needed to vent my frustration to a sympathetic, confidential listener.

From: Brendan Hall Spirit of Australia Ops
Sent: 08 December 2009 16:57

To: Zoe Williamson

Heya Zoe,

How's it going?

Things here are ok. We seem to be in a bit of a slump at the moment, losing ground on every sched and not really being able to explain why.

We are sailing as well as we can, but we just seem to be off the pace at the moment. It's really hard to have to give the crew the sched news, after they've worked their arses off for the last 4 hours, hopeful that their extra effort will bring the reward, only to have another loss to *Finland* on the sched.

It's hard not to become despondent. I really try to keep a strong, positive face to the crew, but I think they see past it sometimes when I am worn out and then the general mood on board goes down (and the boat speed with it). I'm sure the same thing happens to a greater or lesser degree on all the boats and maybe we are just at that time in the race where energy is dropping and we lose our focus a bit.

Anyway, I gave a nice little pick-us-up speech at our midday meeting, where I tore up all our previous scheds and said we are starting a new sheet as of right now and not to think of ourselves as past race leaders now slipping behind, but as Finnish reindeer hunters, now closing in for the kill. We'll see how things pan out over the final week of this tough race. Can't wait to get in.

Brendan

The pick-us-up speech worked and a few days later we had closed the gap on our Finnish rivals. I felt better for getting my frustrations off my chest and threw myself into the racing with renewed energy.

The miles quickly ticked down. We were in a two-boat drag race to the finish line with *Team Finland* just 5 miles ahead of us, their sail clearly visible on the horizon ahead. We both had our afterburners on and were storming towards Australia. We desperately wanted the home port victory and they were intent on denying us.

The first thing I remember about reaching Australia was the smell. We could smell the land before we could see it on the horizon. It's a smell I remember well from my childhood growing up in Brisbane, the smoky smell of a bushfire. It's amazing how sensitised your nose becomes to new smells after weeks at sea. The only smells on the boat were mouldy dampness, diesel, anti-bacterial spray, body odour and sea salt. Don't get me wrong, the smell of the sea is something I love, but after weeks it becomes the norm and the smell of the land has a welcoming 'earthy' scent that is always pleasant. It was particularly pleasant in our case, because it signified we were nearly at the end of this race. We did everything we could and were making small gains on our Finnish rivals, but in the end they were too fast and beat us over the line by 33 minutes.

As we approached the finish, a small flotilla of powerboats and jet skis came out to meet us. We were the home boat and the community of Geraldton was going to put on a show for us. The marina breakwater wall was lined with hundreds of people, cheering, shouting and holding signs. We sailed directly at the breakwater wall, going as close as we safely could before throwing in a slick tack.

Call it showboating, but hey, we *were* the home boat and we were going to give the crowd a great show. We were paying in advance for the great Australian hospitality we were about to receive.

The crowd's cheering doubled in volume as we sailed over the coordinates of the line and finished the race.

It was an amazing moment – 4,900nm of heavy, Southern Ocean conditions and we had come through with flying colours and got our third podium position of the race. We cheered and hugged each other as it dawned on us that the race was over. Very few sailing yachts venture into the Southern Ocean and even fewer go down there to race. To have raced through that treacherous body of water and come through safely was a great achievement, but to have come an incredibly close second in a fiercely contested yacht race was epic. We were disappointed to be coming second to *Team Finland* for a third time, but we'd beaten them to the scoring gate, so we equalled their 12 points for this race. The last 25 days had been every bit as testing as we expected. We had endured, persisted and kept each other safe in a wild and powerful wilderness, and now it was time to celebrate.

*Team Finland* were waiting to greet us as we crossed the line and they were gracious in their applause, though it was ruined when some of the crew turned their backs on us, pointing over their shoulders to the bold 'They'll never catch us' slogan on the back of their team shirts.

*Yeah yeah. We'll get you next time…*

*…Bastards.*

The reception we received as we entered the marina was amazing. Hundreds of supporters, spectators, friends and family cheering us home as I parked our sturdy boat in its berth. The national anthem of Australia, *Advance Australia Fair*, was blaring from the speakers and the crowd was singing along and waving flags. I was home at last.

The bottle of champagne was handed to me and I popped it, spraying the ecstatic crew while the sound of clicking camera shutters and the cheering crowd rang in our ears. On the pontoon were my parents, both in tears. I had not seen them in nearly two years and as soon as the photographers had finished getting their champagne shots, I leapt off the back of the boat and into their warm embrace. Standing there on the pontoon, in the loving arms of the two people who brought me into the world 28 years ago, my rufty-tufty skipper's persona crumbled under a wave of emotions.

I felt comforting relief that the race was over and we were all safe. I felt an intense pride in the crew, who had pushed themselves harder than ever before and achieved something great. I felt a powerful nostalgia at being home again in the country where I grew up after my long absence, and I felt euphoric at having achieved one of my life's goals – sailing through the Southern Ocean. It was a moment that will stay with me for ever.

This stopover in Geraldton was going to be the longest of the whole race, three weeks long over Christmas. A long stopover was needed after the two hard races we had just completed. All ten boats were going to be hauled out of the water with a crane and put up on blocks in a boatyard for a few days, during which time we would have to repaint the bottom of them with protective anti-foul paint.

The theme of the stopover for me was family. It was Christmas, normally a time when families come together, and many crew flew from Australia back to the UK to spend Christmas with their loved ones. Spending precious time with family was the happy place that got many of our crew through some very tough times in the Southern Ocean. When the rain was pelting down, the howling southerly wind blowing off Antarctica was chilling the crew on deck to the bone and their bodies wanted nothing more than warmth and rest, they needed that happy place in their minds that they could retreat to and enjoy until the watch was over. I needed it, too – the stress of constant worry and concern about the crew and the conditions made it hard for me to relax. The mental film reel of having a long break over Christmas in Australia with my parents and girlfriend, Lois, was the comforting thought that soothed my mind and also fired my determination to finish the race as quickly as possible.

The crew had become family over the last four months. The core crew especially, who had lived together almost non-stop. Most of them knew each other better than some of their closest friends off the boat. On those long night watches, some people shared things with the other crew they hadn't shared with anyone else – secret dreams, hopes, concerns about their family and more. An ocean racing yacht is, in my mind, the best place in the world to form lifelong friendships and bonds. The crew see each other at their very best and at their very worst. Everyone realises that they are not the well-rounded people they might believe they are ashore. But being well-rounded isn't necessarily a virtue to be striven for.

Take a cylindrical container and fill it with round objects and they will only occupy 70 per cent of the total volume and only touch each other lightly. Take that same container and fill it with oddly-shaped, asymmetric objects of different sizes, give it a good shake, and you will see that they come together, interlocking, tessellating and filling gaps in each other's shapes. They are pressed together and more closely connected to each other. The same was true of us. Our personalities were the oddly-shaped objects and the race had certainly given us a good shaking. Our physical proximity to each other and the trials we had endured together forged us into a great team and a close family. Everyone had their strengths, weaknesses, fears, hopes, motivations and irritations. Seeing these things in each other made us see them in ourselves and a meaningful mutual acceptance grew.

This theme of family was highlighted to me when one of our core crew members, Dawn, decided to leave the race to be with her fiancé. She had loved the race and it had been an emotional journey for her, but she missed him and the thought of spending another six months apart was too much for her. The terms of her contract with the race organisers meant that she would not be refunded the money for the rest of her journey, but this didn't change her mind. The race had done its work – given her the perspective she needed and made her realise what the most important thing in her life was. It was sad to see her leave, but it was the right decision for her life.

Eero Lehtinen, *Team Finland*'s iconic skipper, also decided to leave the race in Australia for family reasons. It pained him greatly to walk away from his star performing crew, but his responsibilities as a father of three children came first, as they must do. I was sad to see him leave, even though his team were our biggest rivals and I had cursed his name a hundred times when scheds showed *Team Finland* pulling further ahead of us. Beating Eero had become my personal mission. Just once would do, and having his respect as a racing equal would be worth more than any podium pennant. I told him this before he departed Geraldton and, with a gracious smile, he told me I was exactly that – a racing equal and he respected me greatly. It was a touching compliment from somebody I admired and it spurred me on further to make sure *Spirit of Australia* took control of the leader board on the next leg up to Qingdao, China.

Eero was being replaced by Rob McInally, a highly respected and experienced ocean racing skipper. Rob had completed the whole of the 07–08 Clipper race as skipper of *Nova Scotia*. He knew the boats inside out and knew exactly how to handle the responsibilities of being the skipper of an amateur crew. I knew Rob was a hardcore racer and *Team Finland* weren't going to slow down one bit under their new leader.

## LEADERSHIP LESSONS

### Short-term glory *v.* long-term victory

The start-line collision of *Cork* and *Hull & Humber*, on top of our own disasters on the previous race to Cape Town, really brought the lesson on long-term victory into sharp focus. This race was a ten-month endurance event and overall victory would only come by playing the 'long game'. Taking risky decisions and pushing too hard for a short-term gain wouldn't suffice.

I had made this mistake in the South Atlantic, and in the end it cost us far more than it was worth. The most powerful example of this mentality would be the short-sighted greed of Wall Street bankers and financiers, chasing big bonuses at the expense of long-term sustainability. It was their desire for short-term glory that precipitated the global economic meltdown. I'm sure you can think of examples from your life about people who have had this attitude.

I believe that, as humans, our brains are wired to be motivated by short-term rewards. They are close, tangible, and achievable.

*We can have them now.* We live in a microwave society, where instant gratification is aspired to and we seem to want everything faster than before. Our society is a product, not a cause, of this hard-wired way of thinking.

Long-term goals are further away, abstract, hypothetical, fuzzy. We can't visualise them easily and they don't provide that same visceral motivating force. To stick with the Wall Street analogy, the idea of corporate sustainability and stable growth over the next ten years cannot compete on the scale of human motivation with the idea of a fat, six-figure bonus at the end of the year.

Because of this, I think there will always be a natural tendency to push harder for short-term gains, and as a leader this can have disastrous results for your team. A leader needs to recognise this tendency in their thinking and guard against it if they aspire to long-term success.

### Attitude over aptitude

I could write a separate book on this topic alone, such an important one is it to any leader.

I was told before the race that my job as a skipper would be about 20 per cent sailing skills, 80 per cent people skills. It was especially important for me to realise this as a leader, given my position of authority, but the same ratio held true for the crew. As the race progressed, my conception on the relative value of these skills changed in favour of people skills over technical skills. Of course, my hypothetical 'ideal' crew member would have both, but if I had to choose one over the other, it would definitely be in favour of people skills. For the team to work well, there had to be chemistry and a momentum that came from a positive collective attitude. It astounded me how much a single person with an intolerant attitude can bring down the energy and cohesiveness of the team, even if they are technically adept. If I had several characters like this on the boat at any given time, then there would have been no chance of us achieving the same level of slick teamwork and cohesion as we had prior to them joining.

The skills to race a large yacht could be learned in a relatively short space of time compared with the time needed to adjust one's attitude, if indeed one wanted to adjust it at all.

My collective experiences on the race led me to the conclusion that if somebody is to be a part of a high-performing team, then the leader in charge needs to make sure their people skills and attitude are up to the task. Their technical skills need to be present, but without the people skills to work well in a team, they won't perform at their best and can often stop others from doing so as well.

*Attitude over aptitude.*

*Always.*

# 10

# PERSISTENCE

*No great achievement is possible without persistent work*
BERTRAND RUSSELL

The hospitality of the town of Geraldton was amazing. They held a street parade that we all took part in, all ten crews marching down the high street in our team uniforms, with hundreds of cheering supporters waving flags. It wasn't as rigorously organised or choreographed as some of the ceremonies in other stopover ports, but it came from the heart of a small country town and we all appreciated the supportive spirit of the people. Christmas and New Year were typical Aussie affairs – barbecues, seafood and cold beers by the swimming pool.

Every day I was logging in to the Australian Bureau of Meteorology website and checking the latest weather. There was a tropical revolving storm, the first stage of a developing cyclone, forming out in the Indian Ocean. It would be getting close to the north-west Australian coast by the date we were due to be leaving. The race office was also monitoring the situation. If it developed into a cyclone and was going to be anywhere near the path of the fleet, then the start would be delayed until it had passed. It would throw a spanner in the works, from an organisational point of view, but I didn't hear any complaints from the crew about spending more time relaxing in the sunshine. Luckily, it moved past the expected track of the fleet and fizzled out once it hit the continent.

The leg four route was divided into two separate races. The route would take us from Geraldton north to Indonesia, where we would pass through the Sunda Strait, the narrow passage between the large Indonesian islands of Java and Sumatra. Once through the straits, we would be in the Java Sea, renowned for its dangerous reefs, high volume of commercial shipping, unpredictable fishing vessels, vicious squalls and, most worryingly, piracy. The race finish was in the Singapore straits, near some of the busiest shipping lanes in the world. We would have a stopover in Singapore and then continue.

The second race was the one I was dreading. The race from Singapore to Qingdao (pronounced ching-dow) would see us facing some of the harshest upwind sailing anywhere in the world. We would head north from Singapore, past the islands of the Philippines and then into the Luzon Strait. The Luzon Strait has a reputation for destroying boats. Like the Agulhas bank at the tip of Africa, the sea floor rises sharply and the waves coming in from the vast Pacific Ocean suddenly increase in size and power. In the last Volvo Ocean Race, three boats had suffered major damage near the Luzon Strait and had to turn back for shelter behind the land mass of the Philippines. Once we were through the Luzon Strait, we would sail around the outside of Taiwan and into the East China Sea and Yellow Sea. At that time of year, there would be violent 50+ knot winds blowing down from the north and we would have to sail against them all the way to our finish in Qingdao in northern China. The temperature was expected to be below zero and we weren't heartened by the fact that the city of Qingdao was experiencing a record snowfall while we were sipping beers under the scorching Australian sunshine.

The day of the race start came and, as usual, I'd not slept a wink. The crew were all back from a much-needed break over Christmas and were raring to go. We had a new group of leggers and their fresh energy and enthusiasm was great to see. There was a great fanfare and the town of

Geraldton once again showed us its warmth and support by turning out en masse to see the fleet off. I had said a tearful goodbye to my parents and Lois earlier in the day and I knew there was still a big part of me that didn't want to leave, but the sea was calling and I had a race to win. I had a good feeling about this one. We had done a lot of pre-race research on this tricky area and I felt confident it would pay off once we got into the Java Sea.

In our pre-race team huddle, I stressed our need to have a conservative start to the race – everyone was going to be a bit rusty after the long break and we couldn't afford to make a silly mistake that could end in a breakage or injury. These carefully chosen words went straight out the window as we crossed the start line. We were sailing as hard as we could right from the outset. That was the only way we knew how. There were no mistakes, no breakages, and we rounded the first mark of the course, just off the beach, in first place. The crowd went wild and sent us off with a massive cheer. The flotilla of supporters' powerboats that escorted us into Geraldton followed us out to sea, and one by one they peeled off as we surged away from land, heading north-west towards Indonesia.

On the way up to the Sunda Strait, we had the privilege of sailing over the spot where an Australian warship, HMAS *Sydney (II)*, had been sunk by a disguised German warship, the *Kormoran*, in the Second World War. The 645 crew on board were killed as the ship quickly flooded and sank.

Each Clipper yacht was given a wreath to drop in the ocean as we passed over the site of the wreck. As we approached the point, my imagination began to turn over. What would it have been like, being on board the ship as it sank, the water level rising and rising and knowing there was no escape? Thinking of the terror, panic and dread those 645 sailors must have felt in their last moments alive sent a chill up my spine. As we passed over the wreckage, kilometres below us in pitch darkness, I laid the wreath upon the waves and said a small thank you to those brave men who died to keep Australia free. It was a small gesture, but a meaningful one to all of us.

The race for the scoring gate was on, though it wasn't the high-speed affair we were used to. An area of high pressure had developed over the fleet and we were becalmed once more. We were closest to the scoring gate and knew that anybody coming up behind us would park up as soon as they got close. The sun beat down heavily. The crew on deck were sitting in a row under the narrow shadow of the boom, moving with it as it crept over the deck. We had our largest and lightest spinnaker flying and sometimes we would get a zephyr and begin to move, but it would quickly pass and we would go back to drifting.

The high-pressure system crept over us and slowly the wind returned. We were in pole position to get to the scoring gate and only a mistake on our part would see us lose it. We had seen that saying 'you don't win a race, you lose a race' proven correct over the last four months. We had cost ourselves the race in the South Atlantic through our own mistakes and my poor judgement. We had seen ourselves get a podium finish in Australia by having a very trouble-free Southern Ocean leg where we made virtually no mistakes, sailed conservatively and had no breakages.

Now we were in the leading position, knowing that even a small mistake would cost us the scoring gate. The crew sailed perfectly and my weather routing plan was spot on. We crossed the scoring gate to clinch another three points, which we were all ecstatic about.

From the gate, we sailed further north and into the Sunda Strait. We had been warned of pirates in this area and were vigilantly looking out for them. Piracy here isn't the organised and militarised type you read about in Somalia. It's more a crime of opportunity by some poor fishermen who would just try and rob all the valuables off the boat. They might have a basic, home-made gun or a machete, but nothing heavier. We had been briefed on the dangers of piracy back in Geraldton and were told that if we saw a suspicious vessel coming towards us, we should get all 18 crew on deck and standing together in a line as a show of force. We were told that if everybody is wearing the same shirt, this further adds to the impression of solidarity. Hopefully that sight would deter the would-be pirates from trying to rob us.

That was all we had – besides the knives in the galley and the winch handles on deck, we had no weapons to defend ourselves. I had briefed the crew and told them to have their *Spirit of Australia* crew T-shirts handy by their bunks. If I called down that pirates were coming, then they had to whip their T-shirt on and get on deck right away. The problem was that as we sailed up through the strait we drew a lot of attention. We had our spinnaker up and were moving quite quickly. To the local fishermen in their rickety wooden boats we must have looked a genuinely curious sight and some of them came closer to check us out. Naturally, I was pretty paranoid, so every time one of them approached I would call for all hands on deck and the off-watch came charging up with their crew shirts on and formed a line on the side deck of the boat. The fishermen must have thought we were putting on a show for them. After a while they got bored of us and went away and everybody relaxed. Better safe than sorry, I would tell the sleepy off-watch as they went back to bed.

We were now sailing up through Indonesia and it was the middle of the night. There were ships everywhere, most of them heading from Singapore down to Australia or Jakarta. We were still in the lead by the skin of our teeth, with *Jamaica Lightning Bolt* and *Cape Breton Island* charging up behind us. I was in the navigation station when the satellite phone rang. A lump formed in my throat – when you get an unexpected call on the satellite phone, it is never good news.

I answered the phone and it was James Allen, the Clipper training director, on the other end. He told me that *Cork* had just struck a reef. She was hard aground and the crew were attempting to abandon ship in their liferafts. He told us to turn around and go back and help them in any way we could. He gave me their location – the boat was stuck upon a small atoll called Gosong Mampango. We had passed it about two hours ago. I told James I would get sails down and motor back as quickly as possible.

I shouted for everyone to get out of their bunks and for all spare deck crew to get below. I briefed them on the situation and told them to get ready for some long days ahead. There was no hesitation, no complaint.

The race was now irrelevant – all that mattered was helping our friends on *Cork*.

*Hell's teeth. They're abandoning ship into liferafts; she must be breaking up on the reef. People get killed in these sorts of accidents*, I thought to myself as I did a quick check of the engine before starting it. The crew on deck had begun to take sails down and their minds were completely focused on getting back to *Cork* and rescuing their crew as quickly as possible.

Ten minutes later the satellite phone rang again and James told me to cancel the order to turn back. There were other boats closer to the reef that could assist sooner. We were ordered to turn back around and continue racing to Singapore. With a deep sigh I put the phone down, threw out a few choice swear words, called all crew to the cockpit and gave them their second briefing for the night. We quickly turned the boat around, put sails back up and, with grave concern for our friends in our hearts, began racing again.

We were relieved to hear the following day that all of the *Cork* crew were rescued safely and were now on board *Team Finland* and *California*, and the fleet was moving onwards towards Singapore. *Cork* was lost, too badly damaged to be salvaged. Gosong Mampango would be its resting place. Why the accident happened was not yet apparent, but the main thing was that all the crew were safe. The boat and its contents could be replaced, its crew could not.

It took us a few days to put the *Cork* incident behind us and focus entirely on the racing again. As we headed further north, beating our way up the Java Sea, we began to enter squall territory again. I hated squalls and the state of constant anxiety they put me in. Sometimes they would pass overhead and the wind would increase only a little, other times the wind strength would double or even triple in seconds – a sure recipe for torn sails and injured crew. At night-time there was no way of knowing and so we always assumed the worst.

We had one squall that caught us out completely. It was at night and we didn't get sails down in time. The squall hit us with rain so hard it stung the skin and the wind shot up from 18 to 45 knots. The boat slew violently towards the wind and tipped over on its side. The horizontal deck was now nearly vertical and people were clinging to winches and lifelines, their legs flailing in the air. The rudder and the keel of the boat were out of the water, so there was nothing we could do to change course or control ourselves. We just had to hang on, literally, until it passed and the wind eased off. The sails were flogging violently and I was sure one of them was going to rip, but they survived the punishment. The squall passed a minute later and the wind eased back off. The rain suddenly stopped and we were back to sailing along in 18 knots with the sails perfectly trimmed, like it never happened. The crew and I looked at each other with disbelief for a moment, then shrugged our wet shoulders and carried on racing.

We had a very close race with *Cape Breton Island*, who made a bold tactical decision that paid off and put them less than 2 miles in front of us. We did everything we could, but we just couldn't catch them before the finish. We crossed the finish line 10 minutes behind them. We were bitterly disappointed about coming second, again, but the nine points for second place plus the three scoring gate points meant we overtook *Team Finland* on the overall points table.

*Spirit of Australia, Number One!*

The stopover in Singapore was a great time to rest and gather our strength for the next leg up to Qingdao. With the loss of *Cork*, the decision was made that the crew would be divided evenly among the remaining nine boats. *Spirit of Australia* gained some great crew members as a result of *Cork*'s loss, so while we were upset that a very competitive boat was now gone, we were happy to take on the *Cork* crew and make them feel welcome.

In our pre-race team briefing, I explained how testing the conditions were going to be. I spoke at length about the monsoonal weather systems that were going to affect us, the average wind speeds and the swell height. There was a lot of data we had researched and I enjoyed sharing it with the crew, though I could see some of their eyes glaze over.

I printed out some race journals from the Volvo Ocean Race, where those hardened professional sailors described the violent conditions that wrought havoc upon their lightweight carbon fibre boats.

I also read some race journals from the 07–08 Clipper race. The crew member writing the journal described the soaking wet, freezing, uncomfortable conditions in great detail, but it was the following quote that made me pause:

> Things between the crew got fractious, and of course when the new watch is late taking over at 3am and it's really, really cold, tensions rise – at one point even to the extent of a couple of punches being thrown between disagreeing crewmates. Not a huge deal – though if it happens again the culprits will be thrown off – but definitely a sign we'd reached breaking point.

That's the part that worried me the most. *Throwing punches.* We had never even been close to a situation becoming physically violent on *Spirit of Australia*. There had been a few terse words used and some minor falling-outs, but nothing like that. This leg was going to be the ultimate test of team solidarity. The conditions in the East China Sea would push each crew member beyond their perceived limits of endurance, both mental and physical. The challenge for me as skipper was going to be managing them when they were in such a state and preventing small issues from escalating into problems they were prepared to fight about.

We spoke about this fact openly during the briefing and talked about what we would do if tensions were rising too high. We talked about the effect a lack of sleep and proper rest can have on our mental state. We talked about how we were going to look after each other and not let the conditions grind us down. We were discussing practical solutions to a very practical problem – what happens to a team of people in extreme conditions.

Remember, these guys weren't specially selected to do the race. They weren't army commandos, trained to be part of an elite team in extreme conditions. They were amateur volunteers of all ages and from all walks of life. Sandra the accountant, Rob the teacher, Pen the journalist and John the wine merchant, to name a few. Together, they were a strong crew with great mental fortitude, but we had not faced conditions like the ones we were about to go into.

How would they cope, individually and as a unit?

I read the rest of the journal to the crew. The vivid picture it painted had the crew enthralled and it set a visual expectation, one they could imagine and picture themselves in. The weather data was abstract and hard to put into context, but the anecdotal description was far more valuable. The crew could relate to it and their expectations became more realistic. Far from being scared, most of the crew looked forward to the rough stuff. This is what they had paid for – to experience something extreme, something that makes their adrenalin surge and reminds them they're alive. This was going to be something to tell the grandkids about.

On top of the challenges of keeping the team safe and cohesive in extreme conditions, the pressure of the race would be ever present. I had to be careful that my own tiredness and worry didn't manifest itself as 'sched whiplash' again and that I remained the steady, unfaltering rock at the centre of the team. My own people skills, mental resilience and emotional intelligence were going to be tested on this leg and I was going to have to lift my game to meet the conditions ahead.

The race began a few miles off the coast of Singapore in very light wind under the blisteringly hot sun. The deck was too hot to walk on in bare feet and if the crew wanted to sit down, they had to pour water on the deck first to cool it off. The choice phrase for describing the boat was 'disgusting sweatbox'.

The fleet quickly spread out with seven boats heading east right away, while *Team Finland* and ourselves stayed further west. After a few days it became clear that the easterly route was the better one and, for the first time in the race, *Team Finland* and *Spirit of Australia* were in eighth and ninth place. It was intense match racing, though, with no other boats around to distract us. The two heavy hitters of the fleet slugging it out in a private race and both crews had their pride on the line.

The crew did everything they possibly could. The sails were perfectly trimmed, the balance of the helm was excellent, and the crew were sitting on the upwind side of the boat, where their body weight was most beneficial. Despite all of this, three days into our private duel *Team Finland* just picked up speed and sailed past us and by nightfall they were over the horizon. It was incredibly frustrating, particularly as we couldn't think of a single thing we could be doing better. We looked under the boat to check we didn't have anything caught around the keel or rudder that might create drag. No such luck. We were dead last and with no explanation for why.

This was not where we were used to being. We should be up the front of the fleet with the others, racing hard for the scoring gate. The wind was very steady and the opportunities to pass the yachts ahead would be minimal, until we got into the rough weather north of Taiwan. The effect on morale was noticeable – we were prepared to be fighting hard against the elements and in a way I had assumed we would be up the front of the fleet, racing hard for the top spot, not lagging behind in last place, struggling to regain miles on the usual backmarkers. Had I become overconfident, making assumptions like that?

The bulk of the fleet were jostling for position around 80nm ahead of us and were approaching the straits of Luzon.

The weather patterns looked favourable in the short term. We should be able to cross the treacherous 200nm strait in steady wind. The seas would be lumpy, but nothing too bad. The longer-term synoptic situation looked worse. There was an enormous low-pressure system developing over Mongolia and by the time we were up past Taiwan it would be right above it, bringing the huge winds and big seas we were expecting.

We wouldn't make the scoring gate, I knew that for certain. We would need to take a risk if we were going to get back in touch with the fleet – simply following the pack wouldn't make the miles up quickly enough.

In the ocean racing world, breaking from the fleet in a risky tactical decision is referred to as 'going on a flyer'. It's the classic big risk, big reward strategy. I had seen other boats take flyers on previous legs, sailing 50 or even 100 miles away from the rest of the fleet in an effort to pick up stronger winds they hope will catapult them into the lead.

Sometimes it works and the pack gets a new leader, but usually it causes a boat to go from a respectable mid-fleet position to dead last. Boom or bust.

Up until this point, I hadn't taken us on a single flyer. Every race, we stayed as close as possible to the rhumb line and tried always to sail the shortest distance to the finish. It doesn't always work, but it's statistically proven that the boat that sails the fewest miles *generally* wins, so it's a good starting point. I had made a rule that if we were in the top six on any given race, we wouldn't take a flyer – our persistence and ability to grind our way through any conditions counted for a lot and even from sixth place we could fight back to a top-half result or even a podium position if we were lucky.

From ninth position, a flyer looked like a pretty good idea. We had nothing to lose and everything to gain. Thankfully, the opportunity for a flyer was about to be present. Running up the eastern coast of the Philippines is a warm water current called the Kuroshio Current. It flows north past the eastern sides of Taiwan and Japan. It's one of the fastest-flowing oceanic currents in the world, reaching speeds of 3 to 4 knots, and is known more colloquially by the name 'the black tide'. The fleet would be sailing to the west of the current and wouldn't get any boost from it. My flyer strategy was to break dramatically from the rhumb line, sail out into the current and then turn north again, where the extra speed and slightly better wind angle we got from the current should put us back up with the leaders.

I briefed the crew and asked for their input on the strategy. Some were enthused by the idea of trying something different, while others cautioned that it might put us even further behind and completely out of touch. I ran the numbers through the computer and spent hours analysing the current flow diagrams, weather patterns, and the speed data of the boat. Numbers began swimming in front of my eyes. I could spend days analysing the data in front of me, but I had to make a decision now. Play it safe or roll the dice?

*Sod it! Let's go for it.*

With all my fingers and toes crossed, I called for the helm to tack the boat over and set a course due east. The finish line was north. The crew knew what that meant. We would need to sail east for about 11 hours before turning our sights north again. The tactic would mean that, on the scheds, it would appear as though we were falling further and further behind. We were mentally prepared for this and decided that we wouldn't look at the next sched, lest it discourage us from our strategy.

We made great speed and reached the fastest-flowing part of the current in around ten hours. As we entered the current the sea started to build up. The wind was blowing in the opposite direction to the current and this heaps the waves up and makes their faces steeper. The heavy upwind slamming had begun and wasn't going to let up for another seven days.

I called for the helm to tack the boat back north again and watched the computer screen anxiously to see how much extra speed we would get from the current. Our speed shot up from 7 knots to 11 immediately, but the ride was brutal. The boat surged forward into the faces of short, steep-sided waves, ploughing through them more than riding up over them. We were heeled over at a 35-degree angle again and with every wave we hit, a wall of solid green water crashed over the bow. One cubic metre of water weighs one metric ton and I estimated we were getting two or three tons of water coming over the bow with the bigger waves. The force of that much water would wash somebody clean off their feet, sweep them down the deck into something hard, or worse – over the side. The foredeck was off-limits to everyone without my permission.

The flyer was working. Our average speed was well above the rest of the fleet and after ten hours of making no gains on them, we were now catching up at a rapid rate. We just had to hold on and not break anything or injure anybody up on deck. Memories of the South Atlantic flashed back into my mind, visions of our boat hugely overpowered and careering down waves on the edge of control. I knew what we were doing here was risky, but it didn't feel dangerous in the same way. We were expecting to get a battering and that's exactly what we got.

With Lady Luck on our side, we climbed back up the fleet sched after sched. The flyer had paid off massively. We had sailed around the outside of three boats and were lying in sixth place. I received emails from home and from other boats with a mixture of surprise and congratulations on our sudden charge up the leader board. While the rest of the fleet were concentrating on the dash to the scoring gate, we had charged up the outside of the course and back into a solid position. We were ecstatic and the feeling of being back in the fight spurred the crew on to race harder.

As we got north of Taiwan, the temperature dropped sharply, like somebody had flicked a switch. From the uncomfortable stinking sweatbox conditions of a week ago, we could now see our breath inside our three-layered sleeping bags. On deck, the temperature was below zero, counting the wind chill. We were wearing every layer we owned, but it still made no difference. After one 30-minute stint on the helm, one of our core crew members, Bluey, came down below literally in tears from the excruciating pain his hands were in. Even inside thick, supposedly waterproof mittens, his hands had become wet and numb and his knuckle joints had locked up. As his hands began to thaw, the pins and needles sensation had him gritting his teeth in agony. It was the coldest most of the crew had been in their lives. The other problem was the dampness. It wasn't a dry cold, like we might get on the ski slopes, but a damp cold that got under our skin and chilled us to the bone.

The conditions down below were no better. Everything was wet and cold. There was no ventilation, so people's breath was condensing on the fibreglass roof and dripping back down. The water poured down the small leaks under our deck fittings and into the bilge, which needed pumping every half an hour. The soaking wet sails lay on the floor of the accommodation area and damp socks, beanies and thermal underwear festooned the crew bunks. The crew's Gore-tex oilskins were permanently soaking wet and when they weren't being worn they hung in the boat's wet locker, getting colder and colder. The only place on board that was dry was the inside of our sleeping bags and even there it took nearly an hour for the warmth to work its way back into our extremities.

The wind continued building as the low-pressure system intensified

– 25 knots quickly became 35 and within another 12 hours it was up to 50. The sea was large and the waves were quickly becoming higher. The bow of the boat would hit them almost head-on, spearing through the top of the wave and sending a wall of water cascading back down the deck. At the same time, the crest of the wave would pass and we would then slam down into the trough behind the wave. The crew on deck would frequently be tossed in the air as the boat bucked and slammed through the waves. It was the skill of the helmsman to quickly steer away from the axis of the wave to avoid the worst of the slamming. The noise down below was gut-wrenching. Every blow made us cringe and the reverberation of the impact rattled through every part of the hull. Some of the bigger impacts were enough to shake up the electrical circuits in the navigation station and set off our boat alarms; shrieking, high-pitched sirens that cut the air and gave a general sense of panic. We had six more days of this before the finish.

While these conditions were dangerous, there was also opportunity here. The wind speed was beginning to fluctuate between 35 and 45 knots. At 35 knots we needed our small, tough, number three Yankee and at 45 knots we would need our storm jib, a tiny headsail made from the thickest, toughest sailcloth, designed to withstand any conditions. We could see three other yachts as they bounced and bashed their way north, though we couldn't make out their names. They all kept ploughing on with their storm jibs, even when the wind dropped to 35 knots and they were underpowered. It was late afternoon and the sun was beginning to set; I figured that they would probably stay with their storm jibs all night.

*If we keep changing between our number three Yankee and our storm jib as the wind fluctuates, we could make some serious miles on these guys.*

I briefed the crew and told them the plan. Despite being exhausted already, they were up for it. The next three days were going to be some of the hardest, meanest sailing they had ever done, but their determination, skill and relentless persistence would see us on the podium. With encouragement, fighting talk and slaps on the back, we promised that we would grind our way to the head of the fleet before reaching Qingdao, whatever it took. The conditions were enough to make most sailors batten down the hatches and run for shelter, but not us. We were here to race, not just to survive. This was where we would plant our flag in the ground and prove to the rest of the fleet that we were the hardest, toughest racing crew of the lot.

The headsail changes were brutal. The cold water crashed over the deck and the wind whipped the sail out of the crew's numb hands as they tried to gather it in. The hanks had become jammed with encrusted salt and our bowman, Andy, was using pliers to open them. The bow of the boat rocketed off the tops of the waves, leaving the crew airborne for a moment before slamming down and jolting them back to the deck. The torrents of freezing salt water flooding down the deck knocked the crew off their feet and flooded down inside their oilskin jackets. But they would get up and carry on with the job. It was a struggle manhandling a wet 60kg sail, tying it up, refolding it and reattaching it in preparation for the next sail change. The teamwork in those conditions was as professional as you would find on any all-pro racing boat. The crew bellowed clear instructions to each other over the howling wind and set about every sail change with a safe and well-practised approach. Everyone had their position and knew exactly what they had to do. There was no room for errors, hesitation or confusion and the sail changes were surprisingly slick, taking the conditions into account.

At the end of the headsail change, the crew would come back to the cockpit of the boat, bruised and battered, aching fingers, but surprisingly, with beaming smiles. The achievement of collectively changing that sail, struggling as a team against the power of the elements and winning, was significant. Each sail change was a small victory, a lesson in the power of persistence and great teamwork. Then the adrenalin would wear off and the crew would slowly go back down below, waiting in the saloon for their turn on deck, falling asleep from exhaustion anywhere they could. One or two hours later, the headsail would need changing again and, without any complaint, they would get back up on deck and repeat the gruelling task with the same grim determination.

And it worked. In nine hours, we shot from sixth to second place. I was expecting us to overtake the others slowly over the next two days, so to see the results of our efforts paying off so soon was amazing. The boost in morale was huge and the news gave the crew a surge of fresh energy. We couldn't let up now; we were on the home straight with only 600nm to the finish. With a final overnight push, we charged past *Jamaica Lightning Bolt* and into the lead.

As I downloaded the next sched email, I received a shocking message from the race office informing us that *Team Finland* had been dismasted. The circumstances were unknown at the time, but all crew were safe and well. The mast had snapped about 5 metres above the deck and toppled sideways into the water next to the boat. It was still connected to the hull by a myriad of wires and ropes, which were all cut in sequence and the mast fell away from the boat and sank. *Team Finland* was motoring back towards the port of Hualien in Taiwan to refuel and assess the damage. Speaking after the race to their skipper, Rob, he just remembers the boat climbing a particularly steep wave then slamming down hard. With a loud bang the mast buckled and collapsed, ending their race to Qingdao instantly.

Dismasting is not an uncommon thing in ocean yacht racing, particularly at the highest levels, where the carbon fibre masts are designed to be as light as possible. Even though the Clipper race is an amateur event, the boats are not immune from gear failure and metal fatigue. On the 07–08 Clipper race, two boats were dismasted in the North Pacific. We were glad *Team Finland*'s crew were all safe and we felt sorry for them being unable to race for the rest of this leg. We wanted nothing more than to beat them fair and square, but now this would have to wait until later. The race organisers were scrambling resources from all over the world to have a new mast flown to Qingdao to be fitted in time for the start of the next leg.

Back on board *Spirit of Australia*, the effort of the multiple heavy headsail changes was taking its toll on all of us. They were doing the hard work up on deck; I was doing the hard work on the weather routing and calculating our tacking angles. The team was working brilliantly. Rather than the extreme elements being a divisive influence that would make people less tolerant and cause friction, we found it to be a unifying force. The crew pulled together, worked harder, supported each other and communicated better than ever before. We were in this thing together, fighting against a common enemy. Having spoken back in Singapore about the necessity for us to stay cohesive during the rough weather was paying off now. Even though they wanted nothing more than to stay in the warmth of their sleeping bags, the off-watch dragged themselves up extra early to make sure they weren't late for watch changeover. The effort was appreciated by the on-watch, who did the same thing at the next changeover.

Now we were getting closer to mainland China, the wind, waves and race weren't the only things on my mind. The Chinese fishing fleets have to be seen to be believed – 200 fishing vessels with powerful spotlights on the stern, all trawling along in a grid formation. They stretched all the way along the horizon ahead of us. I could see them on the radar and hear the chatter in Mandarin between the boats. I tried making a call on the VHF radio, but received no reply – I doubted any of them spoke English. We sailed between two 'rows' of the fishing boat grid formation. The boats shone their powerful spotlights on us from all directions, robbing us of our night vision. My heart was in my throat the whole time – the rules of the sea state that a sailing boat has to give way to a fishing boat, so if the fishermen decided to tighten their formation, we could become trapped in among them with nowhere to go and probably get our keel caught on their trawling nets. Luckily, we came out the other side with no incident, only to see another fleet of 200 vessels on the horizon in the distance. The commercial shipping was also very heavy, with bulk containers, gas tankers and container ships powering along in every direction. Keeping clear of them demanded my constant attention and I got very little sleep.

The low-pressure weather system that had been pounding the fleet moved off to the east, and we finally got the respite we had been waiting for. The seas calmed down and the wind reduced to around 15 knots, which now seemed like no wind at all after the last few days of heavy, upwind slogging. We had done it! We were in first place with a 30nm lead over *Jamaica Lightning Bolt* in second. We just had to hang on for another 24 hours and victory would be ours.

The final hour of the race was emotional for all of us. Six hours before the finish, the clouds cleared to reveal a bright, but hazy sunshine. It was still cold, but the air was dry and fresh. The wind had come around behind us and we had our spinnaker up. We were so close we could taste it. It was Bob's birthday, so we had a little celebration and I told him we would all be honoured if he would helm us over the finish line. He had worked tirelessly on this leg and he was definitely our best heavy-weather helmsman, so it was a fitting present.

Our persistence had done it. Eight days previously, we were in last position and in my own mind the prospect of a podium finish, let alone an outright win, looked bleak. A lucky flyer and four days of persistent heavy work in punishing conditions had paid off; we had leapfrogged the whole fleet and beaten them to the finish. It was a powerful lesson to all of us on the value of persistence.

Being stuck in ninth place was a brick wall and a big obstacle to overcome. I had to remind myself of the lesson I learned in the South Atlantic: brick walls are good, they remind you how much you want something. We wanted to win, even though it didn't seem like a realistic prospect. In the end, it didn't matter; it was the winning attitude and frame of mind that made the difference.

'Persistence and energy conquer all things,' says our inspirational quote from Benjamin Franklin, stuck to the wall of the saloon. On this race, we had proved it absolutely correct.

As we approached the line, we were joined by a swarm of small RIBs loaded down with Chinese journalists, photographers and media presenters, cheering, shouting and trying to get us to look their way for a photograph. We had been so focused on the race that we hadn't given much thought to the media frenzy that would soon surround us. It was like nothing we had ever experienced.

We crossed the finish line minutes later and the cheer that rang out was electric. Our first win of the Clipper race! The shouting journalists and snapping cameras were momentarily forgotten. The public victory would come later – now it was time for us to celebrate our achievement, individually and as a team. The hugs and handshakes were longer than before, there was a depth of emotion that came from the hardship we had endured together, and there were more than a few misty eyes behind dark sunglasses, I can assure you.

As before, we dropped sails, kicked the engine to life and set off at full speed towards the enormous Olympic marina in Qingdao, with the press boats following us all the way in. Our entry into the marina was choreographed with fireworks exploding as we came into view of the crowd of 10,000 people who had come to see us in. The Clipper race strikes a deep resonance with the citizens of Qingdao. The fact that the people participating are ordinary people, not professional sailors, makes the race a greater challenge in their eyes. Their support was amazing and my eyes bulged as I looked up at the size of the crowd lining the dockside, waiting patiently in the freezing cold to catch a glimpse of the winning boat.

Once we moored up, we were quickly escorted up onto an elaborate stage where the mayor of the city bestowed gifts on us and presented me with a flowing, floor-length cape – the traditional gift given to a victorious general returning from battle. The flashes of the thousands of cameras reached a crescendo as I was handed a bottle of champagne and sprayed it all over the delighted crew. The rest of the ceremony is a blur in my mind. There were dancing dragons, entertainers, and an ensemble of 60 female drummers hammering out a powerful rhythm.

After a few hours, the fanfare died down. The photographers and journalists left with interviews to print in the next day's newspaper. I went back to the boat, signed the final entry in the log book and turned off all the lights. I was taken to a nearby hotel, which the city had kindly paid for me to stay in.

My body craved sleep, but my mind wouldn't stop turning over, despite the many flutes of celebratory champagne I had consumed that afternoon. I lay between the soft, warm sheets in the darkness and reflected on the race.

We had pushed hard, harder than ever before. While the rest of the fleet were snugged down with only their storm sails, we were furiously changing headsails every few hours. The crew on the foredeck could have been badly injured. The volume of water that was coming over the top of them could have washed them into something solid and broken a bone. They knew the risks and went up there anyway. Should I have stopped them? My responsibility was to keep them safe, but safety is a relative term in those kinds of conditions. Nothing is 'safe' by conventional standards. Injuries are a part of yacht racing and can happen at any time at all – just ask 'Head Banger' Barry, who fell down the hatch when the boat was barely moving. The crew were becoming better and more confident, they were willing to push themselves and the boat harder than at the start of the race. I would have to make sure they found their limits and kept them there – beyond that point was a world of torn sails and broken bones. This was something I was going to have to think more about before we set off across the North Pacific.

How did I do, as a skipper, on this leg? The result was great, but I was pleased with the way I had led the team. I had set realistic expectations at the beginning, using a descriptive journal. I had managed to keep my disappointment at our poor position in check. The tactical flyer had worked a treat, though there was a lot of luck involved too. The punishing conditions north of Taiwan had tested my nerve. I listened to my gut feeling and reduced sail as soon as I felt it was necessary. I had mentally prepared myself for every possible disaster scenario, from dismasting to having a man overboard, but thankfully I didn't need to draw on it. I had kept my amateur crew safe, stayed calm through the rough weather, and kept them going with support and encouragement.

*Well done, Brendan. One gold star for you.*

# LEADERSHIP LESSONS

## Give good briefings and set expectations

Briefings were a way of life for us on *Spirit of Australia*. We would have a long and detailed one before each race and then, every day on the race, part of our lunchtime meeting would be me giving a mini briefing on the weather conditions ahead. Before each manoeuvre, there would be a small briefing given by the watch leader, so there was no confusion in the allocation of roles.

The question 'What's going to happen next?' is the largest source of human anxiety in the world, whether somebody is contemplating their weekend, their career, the state of the world or even the question of life after death. It was certainly an anxiety for my crew, with a gruelling ocean race ahead of them. As a leader, it was important for me to remove this anxiety as far as possible and the best way to do that was to give thorough briefings and set very clear expectations.

In the briefing, I would lay a planning chart on the table and show the crew the route drawn on it. I would explain to them why I had chosen the route we would use. Many of them didn't understand the technicalities of my explanation, but it didn't matter – they were reassured that I had given the matter a lot of time and consideration. They had confidence and trust in me and their anxiety about the race ahead diminished.

More by accident than intention, I stumbled upon the most effective tool for briefing and setting expectations – the candid memoirs of others who had gone before us. The past crew diaries were something my crew could really understand and relate to. They put things into a personal context and painted a picture that included the emotional effects of such a big challenge. They also described the importance of teamwork and persistence and demonstrated how they worked through the challenges and overcame them. It set an expectation in a way that I wasn't able to and the five minutes I spent reading those diary extracts was some of the most valuable briefing time I had given to my crew thus far. It was a case of illustrating a point, rather than explaining it.

## Show persistence

The persistence shown by the crew of *Spirit of Australia* was the single thing, above all else, that gave us the overall victory in the round the world race. It was especially highlighted on this race up to Qingdao, where we went from a lowly ninth position into first, through sheer persistence and hard work. There were entire days when giving up would have been easy and very understandable, but we didn't even consider it an option. We persisted right to the bitter end and were justly rewarded.

I fundamentally believe that persistence is the single most important quality for any person to have and is the differentiator between a strong character and a weak one. There are minds far greater than my own who have articulated this idea and which have served as a source of inspiration for me over the years – some of them you have already read in past chapters.

Here are some more of my favourites:

*'Great works are performed not by strength, but by perseverance.'*
Samuel Johnson

*'A little more persistence, a little more effort, and what seemed hopeless failure may turn to glorious success.'*
Elbert Hubbard

*'When I meet successful people I ask 100 questions as to what they attribute their success to. It is usually the same: persistence, hard work and hiring good people.'*
Kiana Tom

'*Money grows on the tree of persistence.*'
Japanese proverb

'*My first six years in the business were hopeless. There are a lot of times when you sit and you say "Why am I doing this? I'll never make it. It's just not going to happen. I should go out and get a real job, and try to survive."*'
George Lucas (creator of *Star Wars* and the *Indiana Jones* movies)

# 11

# DANGER

*He that will not sail till all dangers are over must never put to sea*

*THOMAS FULLER*

The prize-giving in Qingdao was a gala spectacular and was beamed out across all of China. Famous Chinese performers were brought in to perform on stage, from a Mongolian rock band to Shaolin warrior monks. We were honoured to go on stage in a line and receive our first-place pennant from the mayor of the city. Naturally, the biggest celebration was reserved for the home boat, *Qingdao*, who had finished in third place – their first podium finish of the race. They were joined on stage by a troop of singers and dancers and they all performed the theme song from the Beijing Olympics, 'Forever Friends'. It was a grand spectacle and they received a standing ovation at the end from all present. If we weren't able to win the race into our home port of Geraldton, then this one was definitely the second best to win, we decided.

With the prize-giving ceremony behind us, my mind turned to the challenges of the next leg of the race, from Qingdao to San Francisco,

California. It was 6,200 nautical miles of racing, equalling around 35 days at sea. The longest we had been at sea up until that point was 30 days, on the race from La Rochelle to Rio – but that was nice, warm, trade-wind sailing, easy as pie compared to the North Pacific.

Ask somebody to visualise the Pacific Ocean and invariably they imagine the South Pacific islands or the Hawaiian islands – tropical islands and atolls nestled in perfect turquoise water. Warm breezes, sunshine and fruity cocktails. Mention to them that you are about to sail across the Pacific and they will generally think you're about to embark upon a relaxing and thoroughly enjoyable voyage.

This is not the case with the North Pacific in winter. The weather systems are extremely powerful and the seas become massive – bigger than the Southern Ocean. Oceanographic stations in Alaska record wave sets up to 27m (90ft) in height and terrifying rogue waves over 30m (100ft) high are often reported by ships crossing the North Pacific. The thought of a 68ft yacht being struck by a rogue wave that large didn't bear thinking about.

On the 07–08 Clipper race, two boats were dismasted here. One of them lost their mast after a devastating crash-gybe in nearly 60 knots of wind. Like the Southern Ocean, this is a place that commands fear and respect. Although the rest of the fleet would be relatively close if something happened to us, we would be weeks from land in any direction. If we had a medical emergency, our only option would be trying to evacuate the casualty onto a passing merchant ship that could get them to land sooner. Once we were 200nm from Japan, there would be no option of a helicopter rescue until we were 200nm from America.

This leg was going to test every crew member on every boat. The physical challenges would be huge. Every day would be a day of hard work, reefing and changing headsails. The cold wind, the icy sea spray and the dampness below deck would be with us for the entire journey. These were challenges we had seen before and overcome, but only for short periods. This leg was going to be a five-week-long endurance test of all the challenges and hardships we had experienced thus far. After our win into Qingdao, the crew were positive and confident. Our keyword of 'persistence' had delivered us thus far and it would get us safely to San Francisco.

In our pre-race team briefing, I told the crew very frankly that there was a chance that one boat in the fleet might have a big disaster on board. If it was going to happen anywhere on the race, it would probably happen here – it certainly did on the 07–08 race. We would do everything we could to make sure *Spirit of Australia* didn't have a disaster, but we had to be prepared for the worst and the eventuality that we might be called to go to the assistance of another boat in trouble.

The briefing went on a long time and, as with the briefing in Singapore, the more we talked about and addressed the dangers and challenges of this leg, the less fearful the crew became. I am an advocate of the maxim that knowledge dispels fear, so I wanted the briefing to be a chance to arm the crew, particularly the new leggers, with as much knowledge as possible about the race ahead. We talked through our 'what if' scenarios and made plans to deal with each one. There was a lot of trepidation and one of our core crew members was unsure if she could even do the leg. She was so frightened by the conditions ahead that she was contemplating flying from Qingdao to America and rejoining us there. With encouragement, we talked her into staying with us on the boat – we would look after her and make sure she came to no harm.

To lighten the mood, I presented 'Head Banger' Barry with a bicycle helmet I had kept aboard just for him to wear on this leg, and told him he had to wear it 24/7 until we reached San Francisco. It was a good laugh, but there was a serious subtext. The forces of nature we would likely encounter on this leg were greater than anything we had seen thus far and not taking the correct safety precautions could see somebody killed or badly hurt. We all shared the responsibility for ourselves and each other. We felt comforted by the fact that one of our leggers on this leg, Joan, was an accident and emergency consultant. If anything serious did happen, we had the most experienced medic in the fleet to look after us.

Until we left, I was engrossed in the world of meteorology. I studied the synoptic charts, meticulously tracking the movement of the low-pressure systems over the North Pacific. I estimated that on our 35-day crossing we would get hit by three or four of these systems, each one bringing between 40 and 70 knots of wind. 40 knots is scary, but manageable. 70 knots is terrifying.

The departure ceremony was another enormous Chinese festival. The dragons, drummers and performers were back, along with hundreds of press and photographers. It was the closest I have ever felt to being a celebrity. Each skipper was presented with a battle-flag on a 2.5m (8ft) long spear, a gift from the grateful people of Qingdao. The mayor made a speech, referring to the collective Clipper crews as 'brave warriors' setting out on a long and dangerous voyage. One by one, the crews were taken to their boats, their battle song played over the PA system, and they motored out of the marina to huge cheers from the thousands of supporters.

At the last minute, the crew member who was scared during the briefing decided she couldn't do the leg. She was paralysed with fear and was talking about leaving. We had two minutes before we had to leave the marina. I talked to her and tried again to convince her to stay aboard. She was pacing up and down the pontoon next to the boat in tears, torn between her fear of the leg to come and her dream of sailing around the world. In the end, I had to tell her that she had to make a decision *right now*, so we could give her bags and passport back. With more tears, she reluctantly agreed to do the leg and climbed back on board. I told her that by facing this leg and her fears head-on, she would overcome them – there was no other way.

I told her about my extreme fear of heights, which I overcame by forcing myself to climb to the top of sailing yacht masts. Years ago, my fear was so strong that my body would shake and teeth chatter as soon as I was more than a few metres off the deck. My body was willing, but my mind was filled with visions of me falling to my death. My muscles would freeze up and all I could think of doing was clinging on to the safety of the mast and shouting to be lowered back down. It took me a long time to face and overcome this, forcing myself to endure a few minutes of fear and discomfort and gradually going higher each time. For my crew member, the fear and discomfort wasn't a few minutes, but five long weeks at sea, with no option of turning back or escaping a storm heading for us. Once we were out there in the middle of the North Pacific Ocean, rescue of any kind was a long way away. We all knew this and accepted it, but for my scared crew member the fear was overwhelming. I was happy to have her back on board, but knew that her fear would be a big issue for her on this leg.

Fear is infectious and it only takes one person saying how much danger we are in and how they think we are going to die for some others to start believing it, too. I knew the strength of the crew and most of the other core crew would ignore her if she began talking like that, but I worried about the effect she would have on the less experienced leggers, many of whom were keeping their own fear under close guard. It also meant I would have to instruct her watch to keep her away from any critical job on deck if she was panicking. At the crucial moment, the safety of the boat could rely on her easing a line in a hurry or cutting a snagged line with her knife. If we couldn't depend on her to act decisively at those critical moments, then we couldn't let her take on that role to begin with. She would probably feel it was unfair of me to restrict her from doing certain things, but I wasn't willing to take the chance.

With an explosion of fireworks and a cheer from the massive crowd, our battle song, 'Around the world', began playing. We slipped our mooring lines and motored out of the marina – our final act as Qingdao celebrities.

The race began an hour later outside the harbour. The temperature was still freezing and the crew on deck were wrapped up under every stitch they owned. It was a clear and crisp day, though the city was soon made invisible by the heavy cloud of smog surrounding it. The fleet was compressed and the competition was close. The crew slipped back into their watch system and, before long, the first cups of tea and biscuits were coming up from the galley to keep the crew on deck hydrated and warm.

We were aiming for the southern tip of Japan, where we would take a left turn and head out into the expanse of the North Pacific bound for San Francisco, one month away.

The conditions were the same as when we came north to Qingdao – big seas, strong wind, huge fishing fleets and lots of shipping between Japan, Korea and China. The wind quickly built. That same wind we had been beating and slogging our way into on the way up here was now behind us, pushing the fleet south at great speed. Sailing downwind is far more comfortable than sailing upwind. Downwind, the boat sits flatter in the water, goes faster, and as we are moving in the same direction as the waves, we surf down their faces rather than crash into them. The downside is that the risks are greater sailing downwind. Enormous crash-gybe wipeout scenarios, like we experienced in the South Atlantic, are far more likely when sailing downwind.

From my pre-race weather analysis, I chose a more northerly route than the rest of the fleet and as such avoided the worst of a wind hole in the East China Sea, which slowed everybody else down. As we rounded the bottom of Japan, we were sailing hard. The core crew were driving the leggers hard, so they learned as much as they could before the conditions got worse. Things aboard the green and gold missile were going brilliantly. Morale was high, the high-performance teamwork was ever present and we were in first place. *Top job!*

The crew on deck were reaching the point where verbal communication became less important, particularly with the core crew, who had sailed over halfway round the world by this point. They communicated with meaningful eye contact, gestures and nods; each crew member knew their role so well it was like poetry in motion. Sometimes, my involvement was more of a hindrance than a help, the crew's routines were so slick. The team was maturing to the point where they didn't need me at all on deck unless there was a problem. It was a great testament to their skill and attitude, but on a personal level it made me worry that their independence would begin to undermine my authority and lead to a 'we don't need him any more' attitude further down the line.

I reflected on this point as I sat awake in the navigation station one night as we neared Japan. My goal was to build the team to the point where they could sail the boat to a safe port without my input, basically making me redundant. I saw this redundancy as the sign of a mature team and it meant I had reached my goal. From a personal point of view, the feeling of being redundant is not an affirming one. Back at the beginning of the race, I was the font of all knowledge, the directive leader shouting instructions to a willing crew. I was involved in everything and played a part in every decision. I was the rock at the centre of the team, I had 18 novices looking up to me for everything and I *felt* important. Now, this feeling of importance was fading as I gave the crew more responsibility and the space to grow. I came to realise that *feeling important* had been a big motivator for me in the early part of the race; it made me work harder and give more of myself. Now that feeling was fading, part of my motivation was fading with it. I knew I could try to make myself feel important again by flexing my authority, spending more time on deck actively taking charge of every manoeuvre. I could take responsibility for sail-plan decisions back from the crew and do it all myself. I would definitely feel important again and my ego would be bolstered, but it definitely wouldn't be best for the team. I had to accept that my role as skipper was changing as the race went on. To cling on to that feeling of importance from earlier would be to selfishly stifle the full potential of my crew. I had to find private satisfaction in the fact that my crew was a mature, high-performing team and even though I was less involved with the sail-plan decisions and manoeuvres on deck, it was my leadership that got them to that point.

We sped around the southern tip of Japan on a gloriously clear day. The Japanese coastline looked verdant. To the south of us were the off-lying islands of Takeshima, steep-sided spires of ebon rock towering out of the sea. We had our spinnaker up and the waves were pushing us along with small surfs. The warmth of the sun began to creep its way back into our bones and we sat on deck that day for our daily lunchtime meeting, soaking up the pleasant weather. My briefing on the weather for the next two days wasn't so nice. We would be hit by our first big storm of the Pacific crossing in around 48 hours. It was a big one. We wouldn't feel the full force of the storm, as it was a long way north of us, but we could expect anything up to 60 knots of wind. I could see the fear return to the eyes of my scared crew member and I knew she was now wishing she had decided to stay ashore.

Over the next 48 hours, the wind gradually increased. I made sure the watch leaders were disciplined when it came to reducing our sail plan and we always erred on the side of caution. To have a sail-tearing incident so soon into such a long race would definitely eliminate us from podium contention. We had a 60nm lead over *Hull & Humber* in second place and I felt sacrificing a bit of speed to make sure we didn't damage anything was a good trade-off. The wind kept building and the storm began to bare its teeth at the fleet. We were sailing very conservatively, with our mainsail at its smallest setting and our tiny storm jib up front. The rain was lashing down and the bilges quickly began to fill. The wind howled through the rigging and I declared that we would go into 'storm mode', where only the best helms would be allowed to steer, and we kept the number of crew on deck to a minimum.

To try to paint a picture of the conditions, imagine driving down a motorway doing 60mph (100km/h) in the middle of the night through the lashing rain. The windscreen wipers are on their fastest setting and still the visibility is poor. You can feel the car getting buffeted by the wind as it gusts up momentarily. Now imagine opening the sunroof, clipping yourself onto a strong fixture and then climbing out onto the roof. What you've just imagined is the same as the feeling of climbing out the companionway hatch onto the deck on *Spirit of Australia* during a North Pacific storm. It's dark, wet, cold and the wind whips the rain at your face with stinging force.

We were still racing, though. The conditions were bad, but that was no reason to slow down. We had the right amount of sail up and were sailing as fast as we could, within our limits. The problem was that we were very quickly being caught up by *Hull & Humber* in second place. In one sched, our lead was reduced from 60 to 45nm, the next one it was down to 28nm. By the midnight sched, they were just 13nm behind us and showed no sign of slowing down. I was stressing. We were getting creamed in the scheds and, if the trend continued, in another six hours they would have overtaken us. I expressed my worries to one of my core crew, JB, who replied straight away that we were doing the right thing. He said that if *Hull & Humber* kept pushing as hard as they were, then they'd definitely break something soon.

He was absolutely right. We were doing the right thing and we knew from bitter experience what happens when you overpower a boat in rough weather like this. *Hull & Humber* must have been sailing right on the limit, overpowered, but keeping it just under control, just like we were in the South Atlantic. And just like us, it was only a matter of time before something gave way.

It didn't take long for JB's prediction to be validated. Two hours later, the satellite phone rang. It was the race director, Joff, who cut straight to the chase.

It was worse than I expected.

Piers Dudin, the skipper of *Hull & Humber*, had been washed down the deck by an enormous wave. His leg had hit a steel stanchion and the massive force of the water pushing past him broke the tibia and fibula in his lower leg and pushed the tibia out through the skin. He had been taken below deck by his crew and sedated with morphine and several other strong painkillers. *Hull & Humber* was now essentially skipper-less.

We were the closest boat to *Hull & Humber*, so we were ordered to suspend racing and turn back at maximum speed to help them. It was also fortunate that Joan, the accident and emergency consultant, was on our boat. She could provide medical advice to the *Hull & Humber* crew over the VHF radio once we got closer. Joff was trying to figure out how to get him evacuated and how to deal with a new situation. A Clipper skipper had never been injured like this before. He would call me again soon with more details, but for the time being my orders were to get back to *Hull & Humber* as quickly as possible.

The line went dead.

*Shit!*

I briefed the crew, who were shocked and frightened by the news, but there was no question about our duty and no complaints about giving up our race. We had to help Piers get to safety, whatever it took, nothing else was important. With grim-faced determination, we turned *Spirit of Australia* around and began beating and thumping our way upwind, back towards *Hull & Humber*.

The news really began to sink in as I sat in the navigation station, braced against the jarring impacts as the boat crashed through the waves. This had never happened before in all seven previous Clipper races. Crew members had been injured and evacuated, but never a skipper. For all the responsibility and kudos that goes with the title, we are not invulnerable and our bones break just as easily as anybody else's.

What was going to happen once we got there? There was no way we could transfer somebody from one boat to the other, the sea was far too rough to get the boats close enough together. There was nothing we could do until the wind and waves abated.

We were only 400nm from Japan, so I imagined the Japanese coastguard would send a rescue ship to come and collect Piers. We were too far offshore for a helicopter rescue. It would have to be soon – each boat only had a small amount of morphine. Once it ran out, the excruciating pain Piers would experience from having a broken leg aboard a yacht being thrown about in a rough sea would be terrible.

*Poor bastard.*

Piers was out of the race. A serious break like that would require surgery and months of physiotherapy and rehabilitation before it would be fully load-bearing, much less ready to cope with the rigours of ocean racing again. My heart went out to him. I had always liked Piers and I knew he would be gutted to see his race finished. He had invested a huge amount of time and energy in his campaign. He had overcome so much in this race already – rescuing his man overboard in the South Atlantic and then rebounding after being T-boned on the start line in Cape Town by *Cork*. He deserved more than anybody to finish the race, so for him to now personally suffer and lose his campaign felt so unjust.

The satellite phone rang again. Joff told me that the Japanese coastguard were sending out one of their high-speed patrol ships to meet us and get Piers evacuated. He told me it was my job to transfer off

*Spirit of Australia* onto *Hull & Humber* and make sure Piers was evacuated safely.

We discussed the plan. Once the weather calmed down further, we would bring the two boats side by side, 20m (65ft) apart. *Hull & Humber* would throw a line over to us, I would tie myself onto it, jump in the water and they would pull me over. I would have a safety line going back to *Spirit of Australia*, in case I needed to go back.

The thought of the transfer sent a chill up my spine – me, the only professional sailor, strung up between two boats being driven by amateurs and with no backup if anything went wrong. If the two helmsmen brought the boats too close together, I could be crushed between two 32-ton hulls. If they widened the gap and didn't play out enough slack in the lines, I could be hamstrung between the two, powerless to do anything besides cut the lines with my knife and become a man overboard myself. It was a dangerous situation, but I knew I had to do it – anyway, there was no other option. Piers' safety depended on me. I had no idea how experienced the Japanese coastguard would be with medical evacuations from sailing yachts. If they botched it and Piers fell into the ocean strapped to a stretcher, then it was game over. I had to be there to make sure it was all done properly.

Joff and I then discussed the plan once Piers was evacuated. There was no easy option. Going back to Japan was dangerous. The next North Pacific storm was due to hit us within 48 hours, just as we would be crossing the Kuroshio Current. The opposing forces of the strong current and storm force wind would make the sea huge and confused, like the inside of a washing machine. Exactly the kind of conditions boats get rolled and dismasted in. Even enormous 50,000-ton container ships stay well clear of that area if there is a big storm looming.

It is not a place you would ever deliberately put a 68ft sailing yacht, unless there was no other option.

Luckily, we did have another option. One of my core crew, Bob Bell, was a qualified RYA Yachtmaster and very experienced round the world sailor. He had already completed one circumnavigation, as a crew member aboard *LG Flatron* in another round the world yacht race called the BT Global Challenge. At 63, Bob was the oldest person on board. He'd had a hip replacement prior to the race, but despite this he was fit and experienced, and the rest of the crew respected him.

Being a qualified Yachtmaster, Bob could 'legally' skipper the boat from an insurance perspective. The plan Joff and I discussed at length pivoted on this fact.

After a long discussion and much deliberation, we came up with the plan that I would remain on *Hull & Humber* after the evacuation and Bob would become the temporary skipper of *Spirit of Australia*. The two boats would sail in tandem from our present location, across the North Pacific to San Francisco. We would not be racing or pushing hard and our goal would be to get there safely with the two boats undamaged. Saying it, it sounded easy, but the reality was much harder to swallow. The North Pacific is an incredibly dangerous ocean and I knew we would see our share of violent weather. When those storms hit, the fact we weren't racing would be irrelevant. We would be sailing to survive.

With a lump in my throat, I told Joff I would talk to Bob about it and get back to him.

I sat there for a long time. Bob was on deck, unaware of the conversation I'd just had. I needed to think this through before speaking to him.

Was it fair on Bob to hand him all that responsibility? Not really.

Would he want it? No, but I thought he would reluctantly accept it if I asked him.

Would he be capable of managing the crew? Yes.

Would he be able to lead decisively in a crisis, like a dismasting or man overboard? … I had no idea.

My conversation with Bob was open and honest and, as I suspected, he reluctantly agreed to the plan. I would remain in overall control of the two boats, deciding the course and the sail plan. We had to stay within 15nm of each other, the maximum range of our VHF radio sets. Bob would act as a conduit for information – keeping me informed on the state of the crew and any problems on board *Spirit of Australia* and relaying my instructions to Mike and Gareth, the two watch leaders.

He only accepted on the grounds that he felt the crew was capable of the challenge. If there was one boat in the fleet with a crew independent and strong enough to cross the North Pacific by themselves, it was *Spirit of Australia*. I told Bob I had absolute trust in his judgement and I would only be a radio call away if he needed help or advice with anything.

I had wanted a crew that could function without me on board – now I was about to put them to the ultimate test. Our safe port was 4,000nm away, with some of the roughest sea in the world in between.

The more I thought about it, the more conflicted I became.

*Was I really going to do this?*

Bring two boats safely across the North Pacific. Just getting one boat across is an enormous challenge, two would be a nightmare.

How would I get on with the *Hull & Humber* crew? I didn't know them at all and had no idea of their skill level or how they ran their boat. Going straight into that unfamiliar environment and having to get them through the dangerous conditions ahead without knowing their strengths and weaknesses would be challenging. How would that crew accept a new, unfamiliar skipper? Piers was the focal point of their whole campaign and the shock of losing him would hit them hard. I would have to get them onside quickly and gain their trust. There would be no time for long discussions or team-building sessions; we would be in the thick of it almost straight away.

How would the *Spirit of Australia* crew get on without me? I knew they could sail the boat and would keep each other safe, but would the team break down without my presence? We had our share of strongly opinionated personalities on board and they needed to be kept in check from time to time. How would my frightened crew member cope? She was already scared about the conditions ahead, but without me on board she would be terrified.

I called Joff back and told him we would go ahead with the plan. The last thing I wanted to do was to leave *Spirit of Australia* and my crew, who I'd become very attached to, but my responsibility for the safety of the fleet as a whole took precedence. It was the hardest phone call I have ever made. Whatever happened to the crews of *Hull & Humber* and *Spirit of Australia* on this dangerous ocean crossing, I was now responsible and the consequences would stay with me for the rest of my life.

The most difficult briefing I have ever given followed soon after. The dedicated crew of *Spirit of Australia* began to swallow the enormity of the challenge ahead of them.

After several hours of bashing into the wind and waves, which were thankfully abating, we came into view of *Hull & Humber*. We waited another few hours for the wind and waves to decrease further and for the daylight to arrive. The Japanese coastguard ship was motoring at full speed towards our location, but they were still a few hours away. Joan was busy talking with the *Hull & Humber* crew, giving them medical advice and advising on which painkillers to administer. Piers had reached the maximum allowable dosage of morphine, but was still in pain. More worryingly, his open fracture was highly susceptible to infection and he needed to be taken into a sterile environment as soon as possible.

I had a final briefing with the whole crew up on deck. The sun was shining and the sea was calmer now – the time for me to transfer was fast approaching. The thought of getting off my own boat had never really occurred to me until this situation arose. I figured I would be with my crew for every race. Now that I was in a position where I had to leave, I realised how much I really didn't want to leave them. While I always tried to keep a certain command distance between myself and the crew, I had great affection for all of them and would miss their good company. We had shared so much already and I was proud of everything we had achieved together. Now they were going to face their biggest challenge, crossing the largest and roughest ocean of the race, without me on board. This was the ultimate test of their teamwork and I would see how well I'd trained them.

The lines were rigged for my transfer and I climbed into my drysuit. We pulled up alongside *Hull & Humber* and discussed over the VHF radio how we were going to transfer me over. I made sure both boats had their best helmsmen on the wheel. I said a final goodbye to the crew, who became quite emotional as I hugged each of them and told them to stay safe and look after each other.

A crew member on *Hull & Humber* threw a line over to us and I tied it into the buckle of my lifejacket, doing likewise with the backup line from *Spirit of Australia*.

*Deep breaths. Stay calm.*

*Am I really going to do this?*

*Come on, Brendan. It's now or never.*

*I'm going in.*

With a splash, I hit the water. My lifejacket was already inflated, so I sat quite comfortably with my head well above the water. The crew on *Hull & Humber* began to winch me over, with the crew on *Spirit of Australia* paying out slack in the safety line. I was winched right up to the side of *Hull & Humber*, then connected myself onto a line from the top of their mast, which they used to winch me up and onto their deck. It was a textbook transfer, done quickly and safely. Both crews deserved a pat on the back for that one. I untied my safety line and cast it back to *Spirit of Australia*. It looked strange to see my own boat from a distance – I'd never seen her from this perspective before. The crew were happy the transfer had gone so well and gave me a big thumbs-up.

*It's all down to you guys now.*

There I was. On a new boat with 18 unfamiliar faces looking at me. I introduced myself quickly, shook some hands and went below to check on Piers. He was in quite a state. He was drifting in and out of sleep with all the morphine in his system and when I came over to him, I wasn't sure he recognised me. He lifted a hand, which I grabbed and held on to. He asked where his mother was and mumbled a few other sentences before drifting back into the fog of anaesthesia. His leg was strapped up in an inflatable cast, which was transparent, so the gruesome injury below was clear to see. His sleeping bag and cushions supporting his leg were covered in blood; it looked like he had lost a lot in the last 24 hours. In a way, it was lucky he had broken his tibia and fibula – if he had landed differently and broken his femur in the same way, he could have severed one of his major arteries and bled to death before help could arrive. In any case, he was still in pain. The small waves we were motoring through gave the boat a gentle undulation. Even this small movement was enough to shift his leg slightly and send waves of pain up his body. There was nothing I could do to help him, his crew were doing everything to make sure he was as comfortable and pain-free as possible. I just had to make sure the Japanese coastguard evacuated him safely. Then I had to look after his crew, keep them safe and get them across the North Pacific for him. It was a position neither of us wanted to be in, but we just had to make the best of a very bad situation.

I stayed with him for the next few hours as we waited for the coastguard ship to arrive. His crew filled me in on what had happened. He was up on deck, having a cigarette by the helm, when they were hit by a larger than average wave and the boat was knocked over. Piers was thrown to the low side and his leg got caught around a steel stanchion. He knew straight away it was broken. He shuffled on his bottom over to the companionway hatch and matter-of-factly informed the crew that his leg was broken and he needed help to get down the ladder. Down below, he injected himself with morphine in the thigh and the crew took over from there, getting his oilskins off and putting the inflatable cast on. No shouting or dramatics, just a calm and measured approach to sustaining such a painful injury. This guy was hardcore.

After a few hours, the Japanese coastguard ship hove into view on the horizon. When it was close enough, the ship launched a smaller rescue boat, loaded with a team of helmet- and harness-clad coastguards who quickly sped over to us. Once on board, we took them below to see Piers. There were frantic commands and instructions being given in Japanese and they paid us no attention at all. They brought a collapsible stretcher with them and quickly moved Piers down onto it and strapped him in. They carried him up on deck and then, using a line from our mast, lowered him down into their small rescue boat. My final sight of Piers was as the boat turned to leave. He raised his head and looked back at us, gave us a big smile and a small wave, then let his head fall back.

*Safe journey, mate. Hope they can get your leg fixed.*

The rescue boat sped back to the coastguard ship and was craned up onto the deck. Already the ship was moving again, gathering speed back towards Japan. If they were lucky, they would arrive before the next storm hit. The rescue was carried out safely. The Japanese coastguards did a tremendous job and were clearly experienced with this kind of rescue.

I took stock of the *Hull & Humber* crew. Some of them seemed fine. Some of them looked like they were in shock. I could tell several of them had been crying. None of them had slept much since the accident and I knew some of them would crash soon, now the adrenalin of the evacuation was wearing off. I called a briefing on deck, with sweet tea and cake to boost their sugar levels. It was like being back at crew allocation again – expectant faces looking to me for reassurance and new leadership. I only had one shot at making a strong impression and setting out the plan of how the next month was going to run.

After everyone introduced themselves to me, I told them about myself and my sailing background. After reiterating the plan, I decided to try to address their anxieties straight away. I was not here with any kind of agenda. I felt bad about having to leave my crew without a skipper, but that didn't mean I was going to treat this crew any differently. I wasn't here to put my stamp on things either. This crew had their own routines, watch system, values and goals. I wasn't going to try to change any of that. I was the one who was going to have to 'fit in' with their way of doing things. To try to make changes and run this boat in the same way I ran *Spirit of Australia* would be too disruptive. We were heading into the teeth of some very nasty weather, so I needed the crew to quickly regain their confidence and that would only come from doing things the way they had practised for the last six months. I reserved the right to make changes if I thought they were necessary for safety, but my goal was for this team to stay true to itself and keep the identity Piers had worked so hard to create. They would also have to allow for me and my way of doing things. My style of leadership would be very different from Piers', as would the way I interacted with the crew. I couldn't change these things, so they would have to get used to them. I told them that there was a lot I could learn from observing this crew and seeing how they worked after six months with Piers. Likewise, there was a lot they could learn from me. I hoped that experiencing a different skipper and getting a different perspective would be enlightening for them.

Next, I talked about our vision of success. I asked them to imagine these two boats sailing together under the iconic Golden Gate Bridge in San Francisco. Nobody injured, no torn sails or damaged equipment, and both crews feeling confident to carry on with the rest of the race. There were going to be times when San Francisco seemed like an eternity away, but with persistence we would overcome this challenge and achieve something we could all be proud of.

As night fell, we got the two boats sailing again. I chatted with Bob over the VHF, discussing our course and the storm looming up behind us. We made the decision to head south-east, rather than north-east, avoiding the worst of the weather. Everything was running smoothly on *Spirit of Australia*, the crew were tucking into dinner, and it appeared to be business as usual. Bob called a team meeting over dinner, where he talked through that same vision of success with the crew and asked for their input on how they could best achieve it. He seemed to be stepping up to the job admirably and between him, Mike and Gareth, I felt *Spirit of Australia* was in very safe hands. I would have to keep supporting those three as the days and weeks went on, though doing it over a public VHF radio channel was going to be much harder than face to face.

Sitting in the navigation station on *Hull & Humber,* I scanned back through their log book to the night of the accident. I looked at the sail plan they were using and, as I suspected, it was much larger than our own on *Spirit of Australia*. No wonder they were catching us up so quickly. They were seriously overpowered and, from that precarious situation, all it took was a slightly larger than average wave to hit them and throw them off balance. Something was going to break and, unfortunately, this time it was a bone and not a part of the boat. I wondered how Piers would reflect on the whole situation when he regained his clarity of thought in a few days. Would he feel guilty for pushing the boat too hard, like I did? Probably. That feeling, coupled with the disappointment of losing his campaign, the loneliness of being in a foreign country with no support and the anxiety about how the fracture might affect his future career in competitive sailing, would surely put him in a dark place. I made sure everyone on *Hull & Humber* had an opportunity to write him an email from the boat's communications computer. He was very close to his crew, a popular and much loved leader. They would miss his company as much as his leadership.

*Would my crew miss my leadership the same way if something happened to me?*

It seemed they would.

From: Andy Rose, Spirit of Australia
Sent: 14 March 2010 10:54
To: Brendan Hall, Hull & Humber ops

Hi skip,

Just a quick note to say sorry for not saying goodbye properly yesterday. By the time I got my wake-up call you were already ready to go. I had a tear in my eye and found it all surprisingly emotional. We are all immensely proud of what you are doing and the fact you have put us in the position to be able to do what we are doing as well.

Take care mate

See you in Frisco
Andy

The first test of the two boats came 24 hours later when we experienced our second big North Pacific storm. Our south-easterly course had taken us away from the centre of the storm and the conditions we experienced were easier than those the rest of the fleet were enduring further north. I was worried that the rough weather would bring back memories of the night of Piers' injury and upset some of the more shocked *Hull & Humber* crew, who were still struggling with the new situation.

There were a few crew members who requested not to go on deck during the rough weather, which I agreed to. I had to put my philosophy of 'facing fears to overcome them' on the shelf. A fearful, frightened crew member on deck was a liability. They didn't think straight and often couldn't perform basic tasks because they wouldn't let go of something they were gripping on to for security. They couldn't be absolutely relied upon to perform their job in a time of crisis, which could compromise the safety of everyone on board. The stakes were too high, everyone on deck was responsible for the lives of their watch-mates and the team was only as strong as its weakest link. If a frightened crew member forgot to clip their safety tether to a strong point on the deck, something I had seen happen in the past, they could easily get thrown overboard in storm-force conditions, putting everyone on board in danger as we attempted a rescue. No, it was better that the scared ones stay down below. They could help in other ways – there were a lot of small repairs and stitching to be done on the sails and ropes, which would keep the frightened crew busy and also let them feel like they were contributing. Some of them felt embarrassed and guilty that they couldn't go up on deck like everyone else, because they were too frightened, so they threw themselves at the maintenance tasks I gave to them with energy and determination, working just as hard as the crew up on deck in the pelting rain and wind. This was a strong team, there was no doubt about it.

The storm abated the following day. Both boats had emerged undamaged and all crew uninjured. The wind was still strong and the residual swell meant we were sailing fast, but we were through the worst of it – until the next one, which I judged to be about five days away. Bob and the *Spirit of Australia* crew had sailed conservatively and safely, just as I knew they would. My trust in their abilities was not unfounded – they were the real deal now.

Working with the crew on *Hull & Humber*, I began to notice differences in their on-board ethos to our own on *Spirit of Australia*. The crew managed themselves in an incredibly egalitarian way. They weren't as performance-driven as my crew on *Spirit of Australia* – their goal was to make sure each individual crew member had the best experience from the race and got as much personal fulfilment from it as possible. For them, this meant every job on the boat was shared equally around the whole crew.

Each crew member took a turn at being a watch leader for three days, in rotation, so everybody got the chance to be a leader. Even the people who didn't particularly want to were expected to take their turn. The idea was that the rotation gave everybody a chance to be in charge, giving them a richer overall experience.

This was in contrast to the system we had on *Spirit of Australia*, where we had two set watch leaders, who would remain in that position until the end of the race or they decided to give it up. The *Hull & Humber* system was certainly fairer, but the effect this constant change had on their performance was staggering. When a manoeuvre was performed on *Spirit of Australia*, Mike or Gareth took charge, put people in their positions and coordinated the manoeuvre in a slick, fast, confident manner. The crew became used to their way of communicating, trusted their ability, and knew they would spot problems and fix them before the final call to execute the manoeuvre was given. Their consistent, confident leadership was the cornerstone of the crew's confidence. They both had great leadership qualities and played to their strengths.

I was sceptical about the system of watch leadership on *Hull & Humber*. People were given the position of responsibility because it was their turn, not necessarily because they were the most suitable or capable people for the job. When a manoeuvre needed to be performed, an inexperienced watch leader would often get confused about the sequence of events or the commands they were supposed to give. Their voice wavered and they looked nervous. The pressure of having to command others wasn't something they were used to and it showed. When the manoeuvre was executed, there were far more mistakes and a breakdown in communication resulted. The inexperienced watch leader wouldn't know what to do to fix a mistake, so somebody else would begin shouting commands. Sometimes, it was two or three people shouting. Things got confused, people became flustered, and the manoeuvre took longer and was less safe than I had seen on my own boat. After the manoeuvre, the inexperienced watch leader felt less confident, as they had been overridden by the shouting. The perceived fairness of making sure everybody had an equal opportunity came at the cost of high performance. This crew was not playing to its strengths in the same way my *Spirit of Australia* crew were and the difference was evident. But nobody on *Hull & Humber* seemed unhappy about the set-up. For them, this was the way it had always been done and they prided themselves on the fairness of their system.

It was an interesting thing to watch and observe. It made me think back to the fundamentals of leadership. What makes a leader? What makes a *good* leader? Can *anybody* be a leader?

Anybody *can* be a leader, and in theory anybody can be a good leader, but they need the right attitude, confidence, technical proficiency and experience. They need confidence in themselves to inspire confidence in the people following them. We are all brilliant amateur psychologists and can instinctively recognise the subtle changes in vocal tone and body language when somebody isn't confident in the orders they are giving. On *Spirit of Australia*, the confidence of the watch leaders had grown and grown over the last six months. They had made mistakes and learned from them. They had instructed their watches to perform manoeuvres in very dangerous situations and kept them safe. The crew, especially the new leggers joining in each stopover, immediately felt safe and comfortable under the leadership of Mike and Gareth. It was that base feeling of trust in their watch leaders that gave them the confidence to try new things, to be bold and perform at their best.

On *Hull & Humber*, that trust in the rotating watch leaders went up and down, depending on whose turn it was. If it were somebody experienced and confident, then the crew would work faster and safer. If it were somebody inexperienced, the trust evaporated, manoeuvres took longer and the watch leader's orders were overridden. I didn't want to interfere with the way the crew worked, but for the safety of the boat and the crew I decided to make a change. I called a crew meeting and told them of my decision and the reasons for it. We would stop the rotating watch leaders and I installed the two best and most competent leaders, Tom Salt and Mike Burton, into the position of permanent watch leaders. The crew trusted these two guys and I was confident they would work well with me as skipper. I was anticipating a strong resistance to my decision, but I was surprised to find that the crew as a whole were very happy to make this change from rotating to fixed watch leaders. I think that, on some level, they also felt a consistent leadership was going to be necessary for dealing with the dangerous trials ahead of us.

There were other changes the crew would have to get used to. It became clear that I spent a lot more time down below deck doing the navigation and resting than Piers did. He was on deck for most manoeuvres, supervising the action if not directing it himself. He worked himself incredibly hard and the crew told me he would occasionally crash out after keeping himself awake for days on end. This was his style – he liked being involved with everything and felt personally responsible for making sure everything on deck was being done correctly. He was directive when he needed to be and very supportive of his crew, though I got the feeling from them that there was not much responsibility given to them.

This was, in part, down to the rotating watch leaders. He didn't have that continuity of watch leaders that I had on *Spirit of Australia*, who he could absolutely rely upon to get things done without his supervision, so the burden remained firmly on his shoulders. I knew Piers came from a very successful background of singlehanded sailing, so he would be used to doing everything himself, because he had to. I wondered whether this singlehanded mentality had led to his strong feeling of personal responsibility for everything on board.

In any case, the crew were very surprised when I told them to perform a manoeuvre and I wouldn't be coming on deck to supervise. They could call me if there was a problem, but I trusted them to do it safely. They were even more surprised when I delegated the responsibility of making the sail-plan decisions. I stuck a note up on the wall saying which sail should be flying in what wind strengths, and let them make the decision on when to change them. I urged them always to err on the side of caution and inform me before they made a change, but that was all. I was quickly delegating responsibility off my shoulders and on to theirs. They were ready for it and the two new watch leaders rose to the challenge.

I had great respect for the crew of *Hull & Humber*, but I knew they could not have sailed themselves across the North Pacific, even if they did have a qualified Yachtmaster aboard. They relied too heavily on the skipper for guidance and initiative. The responsibility was concentrated in one place, not shared amongst the crew. They needed his presence on deck for guidance and reassurance and they relied on him telling them when to change the sail plan or perform manoeuvres. Now they were being forced to take responsibility themselves, in the way my *Spirit of Australia* crew had been doing since almost the beginning of the race. As I lay in my bunk I heard muffled comments from a few of the crew, accusing me of being lazy, selfish and disinterested because I wasn't up on deck to supervise every sail change and manoeuvre. They might not have appreciated it at the time, but I was taking those backward steps, slowly beginning to share responsibility with the crew, and it would make them a stronger and more capable team in the long run. My ethos remained the same – this crew would have to be able to sail the boat to a safe port if I suffered an accident like Piers did. They weren't at that stage yet, but I hoped that by the end of the crossing they would be.

My reasons for doing this weren't only for the development of the crew on board, but also because I was acutely aware of how I needed to keep myself as safe as possible. The words of my crew member from the Cape Town stopover came back to me – 'If we had a man overboard, I'd want you coming back for me, not us coming back for you.' I had to be even more cautious now my responsibility was doubled. I had command of two boats and two crews. If I was incapacitated or killed in a North Pacific storm, then this little convoy would be in big trouble, further from land than they had ever been before. I called Bob on *Spirit of*

*Australia*, told him my thoughts and asked him to avoid putting Joan, our A&E doctor, into positions where she was more likely to be hurt, like on the bow during a sail change. There was a good chance we would have to deal with more serious injuries on this leg and we needed her safe and sound, so she could use her expertise to help them.

The fleet raced on ahead of us. They were racing hard and eating up the miles. Luckily, there had been no further incidents or breakages since Piers' accident. The sailing for *Spirit of Australia* and *Hull & Humber* was more sedate. We kept a safe average speed and stayed further south in slightly lighter winds. It was a classic 'better safe than sorry' approach. Our next big storm was on the way and expected to hit us just after we crossed the International Date Line.

Crossing the International Date Line was a big milestone for us and in honour of the name of the invisible line where one day ends and another begins, we played our own version of the UK game show, International 'Blind Date' Line, between the two boats over the VHF radio. It was a fun evening and lifted spirits greatly. We saw the Date Line as the halfway point of our crossing and as we celebrated and set our watches back 24 hours, we hoped the second half of the North Pacific was easier and safer than the first half. Sadly, we didn't have to wait long to see this hope dashed.

The barometer was plummeting, the sure sign of a powerful weather system approaching. I had been brooding over the synoptic charts for days, looking at the low-pressure system that was coming up behind us. The four-letter abbreviation next to the centre of the low had been changing with every new weather map. At first it read GALE, then STRM (storm), and now it read HRCN (hurricane) and it sent a chill up my spine. A North Pacific hurricane – the words themselves have a dread-like quality to them. This would probably be the strongest wind and biggest sea any of us had ever seen. I read the description in my trusty nautical almanac for hurricane force conditions at sea.

Huge waves. Sea is completely white with foam and spray. Air is filled with driving spray, greatly reducing visibility.

The description it gives for land is more revealing.

> Very widespread damage to vegetation. Some windows may break; mobile homes and poorly constructed sheds and barns are damaged. Debris may be hurled about.

This was going to be the big one. It was too large and too close for us to avoid. This was going to be the ultimate test for every boat in the fleet. If any catastrophic incidents were going to occur, then they would occur here. The loads the hurricane force wind and massive seas would place on the ropes, winches, steering system and crews' bodies would be extreme. To say I was worried about the conditions fast approaching and how these two boats under my command would cope would be an epic understatement.

Selfishly, I wanted nothing more than to get back onto *Spirit of Australia*, reassure the crew, and stay with them through the worst of it. Like a protective parent, worried only about their own child, my scope of concern narrowed to my own loyal crew. They were my guys and I wanted to keep them safe above all else. I knew they were in good hands – Bob, Mike and Gareth were doing a great job and were all strong leaders, but how they would cope in an extreme crisis, like a dismasting or man overboard, I had no idea. If the worst happened, I *had* to be there to take command and sort the situation out, like I did in the South Atlantic.

But I couldn't leave. To get back onto my own boat would be to leave this crew on *Hull & Humber* in an even more dangerous position and I couldn't let that happen. It was impossible anyway, the waves outside were too big to attempt another transfer. The *Hull & Humber* crew needed me here, and I would do my very best to keep them safe, but I silently and guiltily wished I were back aboard *Spirit of Australia*, keeping them safe.

The freezing, hurricane force wind continued to build. We were screaming along with only our mainsail at its smallest setting and nothing else. We could have reduced our sail plan further, or taken all of our sails down completely, known as 'going bare poles', but my instinct was that we needed a little speed to stay safe. The waves were enormous, 9–12m (30–40ft) high, and were moving at 18 knots. If we were going too slowly, they would come crashing down on top of us. If we could keep our average speed around 10 knots then they should pass under us. That's the theory, anyway.

I had spent the afternoon making sure both boats were prepared for the night ahead. The wind was expected to peak around the early hours of the morning and the already large waves would continue to grow until that point. I had spoken at length with Bob about the conditions ahead and made sure he had briefed the crew. Both boats were in storm mode, with only two people on deck at any one time. There was a third, standing on the companionway ladder, looking out the hatch, to make sure the crew on deck were alright and to act as a conduit for information between myself and them. Only the best helmsmen were allowed to steer the boats in these conditions and they would quickly become tired. The steering wheel was heavy to turn and needed constant, assertive turning to keep the boat under control. For this reason, and the freezing temperature, we limited time on deck to 20 minutes.

Darkness descended on the seascape. The helmsmen on deck were now getting pounded with pelting rain and spume, whipped up by the wind. The boat began to lurch more violently as it surfed down the faces of the building waves. The wind continued to build, gusting up to 65 knots. The temperature up on deck was below zero, factoring for wind chill. Below deck it wasn't much warmer. The next helmsmen in the rotation were sitting nervously in the saloon of the boat, sopping wet and waiting for their turn to go up on deck. Periodically, the 'watchman' stationed on the ladder pulled aside the plastic hatch cover to call out to the two crew at the helm, letting the icy wind and rain come howling down into the boat, making us all inhale sharply. Every 20 minutes the helms would change, the bodies of the two who had just finished coming down to slump in the saloon with aching shoulders, biceps and wrists. Their fingers and toes were numb and faces flushed red with windburn. This storm was already taking its toll on the crew, but we hadn't seen the worst of it yet.

A short time later, we experienced our first North Pacific knock-down. A knock-down occurs when a wave hits a boat's flank and rolls it over onto its side. On a big knock-down the mast touches the water and the worst type is where the boat rolls over and the mast is pushed below the water, which usually results in instant dismasting. The weight in the keel means the boat will always bob upright again once the wave has passed, but the jolting impact of the knock-down can be enough to damage the boat and badly injure any crew who aren't braced for impact. The first one was relatively small compared to the ones we experienced later, but the unexpected suddenness and force of it scared the daylights out of us. The sound was a powerful thump, followed by a ringing reverberation as every fitting on the boat shuddered in protest.

To imagine a knock-down, take a look around you at the room you're in. Now, with the sound of a thunderclap, imagine the whole room violently tilted onto its side. Suddenly you're hanging in mid-air from the chair you're sitting in. Most likely, you have been thrown out of it and fallen to the wall, which has now become the floor. Everything not bolted down has been hurled sideways and broken. Seconds seem like minutes as the room slowly turns upright again. Now, go and switch off the lights, sit back down and wait for the next one. It could be ten seconds from now, ten minutes or ten hours, you have no idea. Welcome to life on a yacht in the middle of a North Pacific hurricane.

Before long, one of our heavy-weather helmsmen, Della, had been injured. Not from a knock-down or an impact, but simply from the exertion of turning the steering wheel. The wheel kicked back against her grip with a sudden jolt. She struggled against the overpowering force and pushed the wheel around with all her strength, painfully dislocating her shoulder and straining her ligaments in the process. The backup helm grabbed the wheel and Della came below, the pain in her shoulder getting worse and worse. There was nothing we could do for her – she would need physiotherapy on it in port, but for now she was put to bed with some powerful painkillers. She would be unable to helm or do anything strenuous for the rest of the crossing. She had done her best, putting her body on the line to stop the wheel from spinning out of control, and we would make sure she was as comfortable and pain-free as possible until we could get her proper treatment.

I was sitting in the navigation station, talking to Bob on *Spirit of Australia* about how the crew were coping with the conditions. They were doing well – they had the same minimal sail plan and helming rotation as we did and while they had also had a big knock-down, nobody was injured. I turned my head to look at the communications computer and saw a new email had just arrived, and the news it contained was definitely not good.

The yacht *Uniquely Singapore* had been knocked down. Badly.

Their skipper, Jim Dobie, was on deck at the time and had been washed overboard by the force of water.

In Jim's own words:

'I heard the wave then bang, I was dragged over the side and held under by the enormous pressure of the water. The boat righted itself and somehow I ended up back on deck. I immediately looked for Jon Hays as he was on the helm when it happened and I couldn't see him. Then I heard him shouting from over the stern and saw him climb back onto the aft deck.'

I let go the breath I didn't realise I was holding and continued reading.

'When I saw everyone was safe, I jumped on the wheel and it immediately became clear that steering was hard. A part of the wheel had buckled inward, catching on the quadrant, but with some force we are still able to steer. At that point I noticed the companionway hatch had completely gone.'

The heavy-duty stainless-steel steering wheel had buckled under the force of the water and the solid fibreglass companionway hatch cover, secured by thick steel railings, had torn off completely. The force of the water must have been phenomenal.

Without the hatch cover, *Uniquely Singapore* basically had an enormous hole in the deck. Another knock-down like that could see several tons of water get forced down inside the boat. They set about jury-rigging a new hatch cover and emptying the substantial amount of water that had filled the bilges. I was thankful they were all uninjured, though I know Jim would be feeling worried and possibly in shock after being washed overboard. He was lucky he wasn't injured at all. If his arm or leg had caught on one of the strong steel deck fittings, then he could be looking at an injury like Piers had.

I briefed the crew on the knock-down aboard *Uniquely Singapore*. They had taken all their sails down and were running under bare poles when it happened and were sailing as conservatively as possible. They were just in the wrong place at the wrong time. In the pitch darkness, the waves were impossible to see or avoid. It was just their bad luck to be hit by such a big one side-on. That wave had their name on it and it slammed them with terrifying force.

Were there two more out there with *Hull & Humber* and *Spirit of Australia*'s names on them? There was nothing we could do to avoid them; we just had to hope luck was on our side.

The minutes ticked by with agonising slowness. This was a feeling I had never experienced on a sailing yacht before, to be totally overwhelmed by the forces of nature. Suddenly, our rugged, sturdy, 32-ton yacht didn't feel such a substantial barrier between ourselves and the maelstrom surrounding us. We had the boat under control, but there was nothing more we could do to avoid the worst. We just had to drive straight and hope for the best.

There was a feeling forming in the pit of my stomach and, at that moment, I knew deep inside that this terrible night had more in store for us. The constant worry and stress had taken its toll on me and I was dead tired. I rested my head against the wall of the navigation station and closed my eyes, only to be jolted awake moments later as the satellite phone rang. Its ring was an easy, almost friendly warble, but I only knew that sound as a harbinger of very bad news. With a cold, wet, shaking hand, I reached for the receiver. It was Joff and the news was bad indeed.

*California* had set off their EPIRB. An EPIRB, short for Emergency

Position Indicating Radio Beacon, is an electronic device used by yachts and ships to indicate they are in life-threatening distress. They send a signal containing the vessel's position coordinates to orbiting satellites, which relay the signal to maritime emergency rescue services around the world. An EPIRB is only activated in the most dire emergencies, like if your vessel is sinking, you have a fire on board or you have a crew member who needs critical medical attention. The problem is that the EPIRB doesn't send any signal saying what the emergency is, just the position.

So *California* had set off their EPIRB, which alerted the UK coastguard, who immediately called Clipper. Joff tried calling *California* on their satellite phone – no answer. Nobody knew what had happened to them, just that they had a serious emergency and they were out of communication. A United States Coast Guard C130 search and rescue aircraft had taken off from Alaska and was screaming south to investigate. That was all we knew.

Our orders were to divert our course and head directly towards the location of *California*'s EPIRB, over 100nm from our present position. We would be given more information as it came to light. With a wish of good luck, Joff disconnected.

My worry and fear for the safety of these two crews, which was already at maximum, shot up a few more notches. *California* was in serious trouble and we could do nothing to help them.

*Hope for the best, prepare for the worst.*

The boat could have broken and sunk, the crew abandoning ship to liferafts. They could have been rolled and dismasted, with all their communication systems torn away by the force of the water. They could have a crew member dead or nearly dead with some grievous injury. The fact they had activated their EPIRB and could not be reached by radio or satellite phone led to deadly conclusions. There had never been a death on a Clipper race before – was this going to be the first?

With an impact like a punch to the stomach, a chilling thought came into my mind. What if something like this happened to *Spirit of Australia*, something really bad – like the boat breaking and beginning to sink or the mast being destroyed by a huge knock-down? There was nothing I could do to help them. They were only a mile away, but they might as well have been on the moon for all the help I could give them. In the event of a critical emergency, it could be my knowledge and seamanship that makes the difference between somebody being killed and staying alive, but I was powerless. There was no way I could transfer back over in these conditions. They were completely on their own and the elements around us were indifferent to them being without a professional skipper. I felt like a parent with their child on the operating table – filled with worry, but powerless to do anything about it.

*People die in conditions like this.*

The sour taste of bile came up my throat and I couldn't fight it back down. I rushed into the toilet and threw up into the bowl. Again and again, my body retched and my stomach emptied its contents. I had heard the phrase 'I was worried sick', usually said by a mother scolding their child, but now I knew the very real and very literal meaning of it.

*Hull & Humber* shook and rolled violently as it was struck by another massive North Pacific wave.

The crew were thrown sideways and pinned down by the force of the water cascading down the near-vertical deck. This was the biggest and most violent knock-down yet.

The hurricane was reaching its peak, the crews of both boats were frightened, and we were on our way to the rescue of *California* and her crew, whom I feared were in grave danger. We had taken a pounding and the hours to come were going to be some of the longest of our lives.

Over on *Spirit of Australia*, it was a similar story. The boat was having frequent knock-downs and although they hadn't suffered any injuries or severe damage yet, any wave could be the one with their number on it.

Outwardly, I was strong, calm and in control, but inside, I couldn't shake the thought that still gives me chills to this day.

*People die in conditions like this.*

*One of my crew could die tonight.*

They were *absolutely* on their own, a crew of amateur sailors of mixed ages and abilities, battling to keep our boat and each other safe and survive the storm.

Four hours later, we received another call from the race director, informing us that the signal from *California*'s EPIRB was moving. Quickly. To my utter relief, this meant the boat was still intact and underway. If they had abandoned ship to their life rafts, then the signal would stay in approximately the same place. That's one disaster ruled out.

As the night drew on, the conditions began to abate very slightly. The hurricane was passing over us and rapidly moving east. The wind was down from 70+ knots to around 50. Still fearsome conditions, but the worst was over and it was only going to reduce further from here. The waves were still huge, but the knock-downs became less frequent and then stopped altogether. We were still screaming along and making excellent mileage. As grey dawn arrived, the sense of relief on the faces of the crew was evident. We had survived it.

A few hours after daylight broke, we received word that the C130 plane had located *California*. They had been dismasted and were motoring in the direction of San Francisco. With consummate skill, they dropped a hand-held radio in a waterproof canister next to *California*, so they could talk to them. *California*'s skipper, Pete Rollason, informed the plane that their boat had been knocked down and rolled underwater by a massive wave, snapping the mast off. They were left with a 5m (16ft) stump of mast in the deck. They had cut away the top section of the mast and dumped it overboard.

The problem was that one of his crew, Clive, was injured during the knock-down. He was sitting below deck and had been flung across the saloon. He smacked his head against a ledge on the opposite side, gouging a ragged gash in his forehead. It was a bloody and gruesome injury and would require serious surgery to fix.

The US Coast Guard tasked a container ship, the *Nord Nightingale*, to come to *California*'s assistance. The plan was to evacuate Clive onto the ship, which was bound for America anyway and could get him there a lot faster. *Uniquely Singapore* and *Jamaica Lightning Bolt* were fast approaching *California*'s position and could assist them. It would be another 12 hours before we would be close enough to help.

With a fresh surge of determination to help their fellow sailors of *California*, the two crews of *Hull & Humber* and *Spirit of Australia* pushed on towards the stricken yacht. By the time we got there, Clive had been evacuated onto the *Nord Nightingale*. Another crew member on *California* was evacuated onto the ship – he was too frightened and shaken to remain on board, so with his bag and passport he jumped ship onto the rescue boat and requested safe passage to the US.

As we approached the position, the race office made the decision that, after the evacuation, *California* would join my little convoy, so *Uniquely Singapore* and *Jamaica Lightning Bolt* could continue racing. We were going slowly anyway and, with two boats, we could provide effective help if anything happened to them. The other reason was that we would need to provide them with enough diesel to motor the rest of the way to San Francisco, still more than 2,000nm away. The reasons made sense, but the thought of me now being responsible for three boats added a fresh burden onto my back.

When we arrived with *California*, we could see she was a mess. The crew had done a great job clearing the deck, but the scars down the side of the boat told the story. When the mast fell down, it was still attached by the thick wire rigging and ropes that run up inside it. It would have been hanging over the side, pointing downward into the water, rubbing and grinding along the side of the hull. The danger in that situation is that the motion of the waves can force the mast fittings through the skin of the hull and put a hole in the boat, which could lead to eventual sinking. Luckily, the skipper and crew cut the mast and rigging away and let it sink before it could do any such damage but, from the look of the scarred hull, it could have been a possibility if they had delayed.

I spoke to Pete, *California*'s skipper, and got the situation on board. During the knock-down, a huge amount of water had flooded down into the boat and into the navigation station, shorting out all electrical systems. He was speaking to me using the radio that the US Coast Guard had dropped in the waterproof canister. That was their only means of communication and it had a range of around a mile. The crew were pulling together, though they were very shocked and upset. They were still coming to grips with their new situation. I told Pete what the orders were from the race office, that he was to join our convoy and we would keep them safe, provide a communication link between their boat and the outside world, and give them the extra diesel they would need to get into San Francisco, still ten days away. I could hear the relief in his voice as he thanked us on behalf of the whole crew. They would get a lot of reassurance from knowing we were close by and would be there to back them up if anything else should happen. Though we were through the biggest of the storms, there were still more on the way and we weren't out of the woods yet. My biggest worry was that the engine on *California* would fail. Ten days of continuous hard running is a lot to ask of any engine and if a major component broke, something they couldn't fix at sea, they would be in big trouble.

Pete and I talked further about the plan for communications. We would set up our own radio watch, twice a day at set times, when we could talk over the radio and update each other. His hand-held radio was battery operated and they had no way of recharging it, so keeping communication to a minimum was critical. After wishing each other well, we fell into escort formation. *Hull & Humber* ahead, *California* in the middle and *Spirit of Australia* behind.

On board *Hull & Humber*, the crew's minds were turning over ideas of how they could help the *California* crew. Over two days, we put together a care package of cakes, treats, magazines, books and silly drawings and sent it over to them, using the US Coast Guard's trusty waterproof canister. *Spirit of Australia* did the same. We understood how the *California* crew were feeling and knew even small gestures of kindness and solidarity would be valuable to them. With all of their communication systems inoperative, the crew were starved of contact with friends and family back home, who were rightly very concerned.

We decided we would bridge this communications gap, the old-fashioned way. We organised for the emails of support for *California* from friends and family to come to *Hull & Humber* instead. Della, with her arm in a sling and still on powerful painkillers, sat at the navigation station for long hours every day, transcribing the emails onto paper, which we sent over to *California* in the canister. They would reply with their own notes, which Della patiently converted back into emails and sent the replies. It was a huge task and took her the best part of every day, but she was determined that the crew of *California* would have communication with the people that mattered most to them. It was a touching display of fleet solidarity and a lifeline for the crew of *California* and their families alike.

The diesel was a harder proposition, but we managed day after day to keep transferring our eight plastic containers of diesel over to them, by tying them together with a float on the end and dropping them in the ocean. *California* was behind us, waiting. They would slow down, hook the float, drag the whole lot up on deck and empty the contents into their tanks. Then they would motor ahead of us, drop the empty containers off, and we would pick them up and begin the process again. It was arduous work and the sickly smell of diesel down below made many crew feel seasick. By the end of the voyage, *Hull & Humber* and *Spirit of Australia* had transferred more than 1.5 tons of diesel to *California* using this method.

During all this time, the crews on *Spirit of Australia* and *Hull & Humber* were having their daily meetings. In them, Bob and I reiterated the new vision for success, which had become slightly modified to getting all three boats into San Francisco, safely, with no injuries and confidence high.

I noticed crew issues begin to creep in on both of our boats shortly after. The adrenalin of coming to *California*'s aid had worn off and many crew were now becoming frustrated with our new situation. The wind was still strong and we could be going very fast with more sail up, but we were limited to keeping pace with *California*, who could only make around 7 knots under engine. It actually became a struggle to keep the boat going slowly and we had to deliberately de-trim our sails to keep our speed low. While everyone understood their duty as sailors to help other yachts in distress, the enforced slowness of our new escort arrangement was testing their patience. Remember, we had been at sea for nearly a month by this point. The crews were cold, wet and exhausted. The stodgy, processed food had become repetitive and boring and the creature comforts of land, like hot showers and dry bedding, were a distant memory. The crew were bound to be irritable and getting grumpy – they're only human, after all.

On *Spirit of Australia* there was a downbeat mood, as the crew's main source of motivation, competitive racing, was no longer present. For a high-performance team to be missing its main motivation left a big void and the act of escorting *California* and giving them our diesel didn't fill that void entirely. There was nothing they could do to change the situation, so I urged Bob to discuss the issue during a daily meeting and for the crew to come up with some creative ways to keep spirits high.

The crew of *Hull & Humber* became bored – the sailing became an agonisingly slow grind. They missed racing and they missed Piers. He was a very different type of skipper to me and I could tell the crew would want nothing more than to have him back. They were anxious about the future of their campaign. Their new skipper had been announced, but none of them had met him and they were understandably concerned about how he might want to change things on board. On top of this, many of them had family flying out to meet them in San Francisco and now their reunion was delayed further, adding to the general feeling of frustration on board.

While this was going on, Piers had undergone several operations on his leg in hospital in Japan, where the surgeons inserted a titanium rod down his tibia and bolted it in place. He was making a good recovery and had been flown back to England, where his parents were looking after him. He sent the crew frequent emails and even went so far as booking a few nights' accommodation in San Francisco for some of the crew who he knew wouldn't be able to afford it themselves. Despite his physical distance from them, he was still very much the head of this little family and cared deeply about the well-being of his crew.

During the final 2,000nm, our convoy endured two more storms, with winds reaching 50 knots. We were well prepared and both storms passed without further incident. The rain was still lashing, but it felt slightly warmer than before. The 50-knot wind no longer seemed so intimidating; we had seen far worse. We kept our healthy sense of apprehension, but the crew all seemed more at ease in the rough weather and could afford no distraction from the critical task they had to perform – keeping a lookout for *California*.

We lost *California* a few times when the waves began to increase. With only her 5m (16ft) stump of a mast, she was impossible to see – unless we both crested a wave at the same moment, she was completely swallowed by the troughs. There would be times when we went without seeing her for five minutes, then just catch a glimpse of her stump as she crested a wave. After a few minutes, I began to get that slight panic, usually felt by a mother whose child has run off in a supermarket. To catch a glimpse of them again was sheer relief.

During the days, I spoke to Pete a few times, asking how he was feeling and coping with the situation. He was missing his wife and son dearly and had his own set of frustrations about being delayed, particularly as San Francisco was *California*'s home port. When he left Qingdao, I bet he had visions of sailing under the Golden Gate Bridge on a clear, breezy day with his spinnaker flying full and proud to take first place. Now it was looking like he was going to be escorted under the bridge, with no mast, in the middle of the night and days after the rest of the fleet had arrived.

*Yeah, I'd be pretty hacked off about that, too.*

The days and the miles ground on, slowly. It was a grey, drizzly afternoon when we crossed the race finish line, 15 miles off the American coast. We had a small celebration, though most of the off-watch decided it wasn't worth getting out of bed for. Our goal was no longer about crossing the line and finishing the race, it was about getting three boats safely into port and only once the mooring lines were made fast would we know we had achieved it. We still had to negotiate the busy shipping lanes going into San Francisco Bay, so there were more challenges ahead.

I was exhausted. Physically, mentally and especially emotionally. I felt tiredness down to my bones. It was like the accumulated exhaustion from my pre-race preparation, the lead-up, the training and then the last seven months of intense ocean racing all fell on me at once. The constant worry and stress of being responsible for more than one boat had been especially hard. I felt like I could sleep for a week. I was desperate to speak to my parents and Lois and offload my emotional baggage.

A few hours later, through the gathering darkness, we approached the iconic red Golden Gate Bridge. A small fleet of supporters in their boats came out to meet us and cheer *California* into port. Their crew were all on deck in their matching oilskins, looking like a confident team once more. They were down, but certainly not out. We let *California* motor on ahead: this was their show now. On *Hull & Humber*, the celebration was tearful as we passed under the bridge and sailed into the harbour. The sense of relief was palpable. The crew had come through the storms of the North Pacific Ocean with courage, great teamwork and self-belief, after losing Piers only a week into the race. They had been a great crew to work with and I was so proud of them. I knew I would have a soft spot in my heart for this crew, no matter what happened down the track.

The crew hugged each other in long, emotional embraces that symbolised the strength of the team and the heightened comradeship these past five weeks had forged. As the celebration died down and the crew began the tasks of taking the sails down and preparing the mooring lines, I stood at the stern of the boat, looking aft. In the distance, a small green light was coming through the darkness, passing under the central arch of that towering red bridge. It was *Spirit of Australia*. My boat, my crew. Tears of relief and pride welled up in my eyes and I didn't try to fight them back. They were finally safe.

This was the first time a Clipper yacht had ever been sailed across an ocean without a professional skipper on board. The crew had achieved something amazing by doing it. They also did it on the longest, toughest, hardest, meanest leg of this race. They were amateur sailors all of them, just ordinary people with ordinary jobs – doctors, accountants, managers, students, journalists. Now they were more than that, in each other's eyes and certainly in mine. They were a team who had endured the worst storm I had ever seen and kept themselves and each other safe. This was the moment I knew defined them as a team. I hoped they knew how proud I was of them all and I hoped they were proud of me for getting both boats here safely and helping *California* along the way.

They couldn't have done it without the training I had given them and the responsibility I had shared with them. Their achievement today was also my supreme achievement. I had set out to create a team that could sail a boat to a safe port without me, but they had surpassed any expectation and sailed across the largest ocean in the world, through the teeth of a hurricane without me on board. I thought about the team I had when we left Hull, seven months ago – excited and enthusiastic, but totally green and inexperienced in the art of ocean crossing. Now they were a battle-hardened unit, experienced, mature and proud. Not every crew on this race could have just done what they did – they were exceptional, even among their peers, and I was honoured to be their skipper.

What would they be saying to each other right now? I wondered.

The race office had organised a speedboat to come and collect me off *Hull & Humber* and take me back to *Spirit of Australia* before we docked in the marina. Leaving my step-crew behind was hard. I had become very fond of the characters on board over the last month and enjoyed their company and fun-loving attitude. One of the crew, Jeremy, made a speech on behalf of the crew, thanking me for stepping in and getting them safely across the North Pacific. They had learned a lot from me and I had learned a lot from them. I told them that this crossing was the hardest thing I had ever had to do and I only got through it with their support and persistence. It was a genuinely emotional moment and my cool skipper face disintegrated as they all gave me a final clap and sent me on my way with a cake of friendship, to take back to *Spirit of Australia*.

The speedboat came and pulled up alongside *Hull & Humber*. With a wave and a smile, I climbed down into the boat, which sped me away towards *Spirit of Australia* and the reunion I had been waiting a month for. As the speedboat skipped across the small waves of the bay, she emerged from the darkness, silhouetted against the backdrop of the city lights. The silhouettes of the crew standing on deck said it all. Even from a distance, their body language showed an overwhelming sense of relief and comradeship. As I approached the stern and climbed up onto the deck, helped up by Mike (who cheerfully noted that I could come back on board because I'd brought cake), the crew cheered. Barry the head banger, wearing his bicycle helmet, presented me with my trademark leather bush-hat, which I slipped on. *Damn, it was good to be home!* My scared crew member was smiling, relieved at arriving unhurt and proud to have persevered through her fear. I hugged every one of the crew in turn and told them how proud I was of what they had done, without me. This leg was the ultimate test of their teamwork, seamanship and ability to support each other. There was no question – they had exceeded all expectations.

I saved the biggest hug of all for Bob. The man was a legend. He was a great stand-in skipper, who took on a huge weight of responsibility he never asked for, all for the sake of the crew and their safety. There were tears in his eyes as we parted and the words of gratitude and thanks I had planned became choked in my throat.

Words couldn't describe it, anyway.

I cast my mind back to crew allocation day in Portsmouth, when I had all those expectant eyes upon me, nervously waiting for me to tell them how we were going to approach this race. If I had told them at that point that they would sail the North Pacific Ocean without me on board, they would have thought it was a cruel joke. Now, through my willingness to give them responsibility and the room to use it, they had conquered the hardest challenge of all. This was their greatest achievement as a crew and my biggest achievement as a skipper. That night, standing on the deck of *Spirit of Australia*, having just been reunited with my crew after the hardest month of my life, is one of my happiest and most cherished memories.

# LEADERSHIP LESSONS

### Share responsibility

Looking back at the race, the act of sharing responsibility was the single most important factor to the success of our teamwork.

The ability of my *Spirit of Australia* crew to cross the North Pacific without me on board was down to the seeds I sowed at the beginning of the race. As you have read in previous chapters, I began the delegation of responsibility very early on. My goal was to have a crew who could sail the boat to a safe port without me, but the fact that they sailed across the North Pacific, through the teeth of a hurricane, without me on board is a testament to the power and necessity of shared responsibility in a team environment.

I trusted my crew, entirely. This trust was not given easily – they earned it over the previous six months and had proved to me time and again how capable, persistent and resourceful they were. It was going to be their greatest challenge, but I felt they were ready and knew Bob and the two watch leaders would look after the rest of the crew. If there was any boat in the fleet that could do this, it was ours.

As a leader, reaching this point can be a long struggle, but it is my firm belief that reaching a stage where the team working for you can function without your presence is something all leaders should strive for. It takes a lot of persistence, support and training, but the added commitment, motivation, ownership and resistance to problems are inevitable outcomes of this approach.

It's also the sign of a mature team, and by association a mature leader.

# 12

# FULL CIRCLE

*It is not the mountain we conquer, but ourselves*

SIR EDMUND HILLARY

The stopover in San Francisco was a great opportunity for all of us to recharge our batteries after the Pacific crossing. I took myself away for a week – hired a car, drove up into the mountains in Nevada and went skiing. It gave me a chance to unwind and not think about boats or the race in any shape or form. The crew understood my need to get away and clear my head and got on with the tasks of sail repair, winch maintenance and food shopping for the next leg without me.

The race committee decided to award *Spirit of Australia* ten race points on redress. We were forced to stop racing for reasons beyond our control and were in first place at the time. Our average points per race up until that time was ten, so we thought the decision was fair. Inevitably, there were some other skippers who thought it was unfair, but the decision went unchallenged and we stayed in first position on the leader board.

As the next race approached, my thoughts turned to how I was going to reintegrate myself into the team. They were independent now and used to working without my guidance. After the Pacific crossing, their confidence was sky high. I knew my biggest challenges would be reasserting my presence as skipper and making sure the crew understood and acknowledged my authority and the value I brought to the team. My second challenge was going to be managing Bob and his transition from being skipper back to crew member. I was going to have to handle that one delicately and keep Bob firmly onside. There can only be one skipper on any boat.

I spoke to Bob soon after and we discussed the matter. He was more than happy to go back to his old position. He assured me he wouldn't try to undermine me or second-guess my decisions in front of the crew. I assured him that his opinion was always welcome and if he disagreed with me on anything, he was able to bring it up with me in private. I felt I could confide in Bob and I trusted him to give me honest feedback about my decisions. He had learned a lot himself on the last leg and it would be foolish of me not to utilise that knowledge for the benefit of our overall goal to win the race. I was relieved to hear Bob say these things – he had obviously been thinking about this issue as well, and wanted the transition back to racing mode to be as smooth as possible. There was talk around the fleet that *Spirit of Australia* would be off the pace after the Pacific. We had sailed the same distance as every other boat, but we weren't racing and the impression was that it would dull our racing edge. We had to prove that, if anything, the experience had made us stronger and more focused on competitive racing and achieving our overall goal.

I also discussed the issue of me taking back the role of skipper with the crew at our pre-race briefing. I was pleasantly surprised that I didn't even need to bring the issue up – the crew brought it up and vouched their support for me and welcomed me back. They recognised the value I brought to the boat, and after the last leg I think they had a deeper appreciation of the role I played. They could cross an ocean without me, but they couldn't win a race without me.

The next race was from San Francisco to Panama and this race is typically characterised by light winds – very light winds. On past races, boats have been known to drift in lazy circles for days in zero wind, under a baking hot Central American sun. This was going to be a very different type of race to the last two and the change was welcome. The stress of drifting in no wind sounded pretty tame compared to the stress of worrying if the next knock-down will dismast the boat. The major challenge was going to be keeping the personal problems to a minimum in those conditions. In our pre-race briefing, I reminded the crew of the challenges of light-wind sailing – how the uncomfortable conditions, the frustration and boredom can shorten people's fuses and make them more irritable. We had been through enough light air conditions to know how crew issues can have a major effect on the boat's performance and had heard from crew on other boats how much the crew morale deteriorated in the light conditions. If we wanted to win this race and reassert our presence as the top boat in the fleet, we couldn't afford to let personal issues fester and distract the team from the goal.

With great fanfare, the fleet slipped their lines from the Golden Gate Yacht Club and motored out into San Francisco Bay for the start of the race. It felt fantastic to be back on *Spirit of Australia*, back with my willing and supremely able crew. I glanced over at *Hull & Humber* and smiled. If we were going to come first, I wanted those guys to come second. *California* was racing hard, with their shiny new mast. It had taken those guys no time at all to get back on their feet and into full racing mode and I hoped this race would be a successful one for them – they deserved a bit of luck after the last leg.

It was a bright, blustery afternoon and the blast of the starting horn was crisp and clear. Sailing out of the bay and back under the Golden Gate Bridge was a spectacular sight. The North Pacific awaited us once more, though the weather forecast was looking positive. We should have three days of fast sailing south before we reached the windless area of ocean around Central America.

There was a scoring gate in this race, around 1,000nm from the start. We had been very successful with the scoring gates in past races and we had our hearts set on getting through this one in first place. With this short-term goal in mind, we charged south for three days, bunched closely with the rest of the fleet. Slowly at first, the wind began to ease. We changed up through our sail wardrobe as the wind decreased, swapping our smaller sails for the larger ones to keep the boat moving.

Sailing in light airs requires more skill and subtlety than sailing in big wind. The smallest tweak of the sails can have a big impact on boat speed. The helming requires a soft and sensitive touch, with the helmsman holding the wheel with just their fingertips. The concentration required to react to each individual zephyr and keep the boat creeping along takes its toll on the helmsmen, who need to be rotated more frequently to stay focused and fresh. Sir Robin Knox-Johnston, the legendary yachtsman, says: 'Any fool can sail a boat in strong wind. The skill of the sailor is getting the boat to move in light wind.' Well, we were certainly putting that notion to the test and little by little we pulled ahead of the fleet, crossing the scoring gate first and gaining a bonus three points.

*Spirit of Australia* was back with a vengeance.

The rest of the race to Panama was spent going incredibly slowly under a blisteringly hot sun. Sunburn and dehydration became dangers we had to guard against carefully. The crew were drinking 8 litres of water a day and smothering themselves in sunscreen every two hours to keep their skin protected. The boat stank of sweat and though showering was a refreshing chance to get clean, the feeling of cleanliness only lasted an hour before we stank again. Up on deck, the sun beat down and made the deck too hot to walk or sit on without first dousing it with seawater. They were thoroughly unpleasant conditions, though we still felt it was a nice change from the North Pacific.

The racing was intense, more so because it was being played out in super slow motion. A mile or two gained on another boat became a very significant margin, representing many hours of lead time at our present speed. With small gains becoming so crucial, we experimented with some very odd combinations of sails, trying absolutely anything to get the boat to move just a bit quicker. Through sheer trial and error, we found some never-before-tried sail combinations that gave us a small but significant boost. Our motivation for this was the famous quote by

Dennis Waitley, which I stuck to the companionway ladder where we would see it every time we went up on deck.

> *Success is almost totally dependent upon drive and persistence. The extra energy required to make another effort or try another approach is the secret of winning.*

The extra energy we invested every day in trying new sail combinations was what made the difference. Bit by bit, we edged ahead of the fleet.

Until we sailed smack into a wind hole that stretched across the horizon. For ten long hours we drifted in circles, actually moving backwards on the current. It was supremely frustrating for all of us. At our daily meeting, we accepted that we couldn't do anything to change our situation. In zero wind, it doesn't matter what you do with the sails, nothing will make the boat move. We talked about ways we could keep spirits high and guard our minds against the feeling of despondency that was hanging over the boat. Two of the crew, Andy and Sarah – our designated 'ministry of fun' – put on a Mexican fiesta, with silly costumes, Mexican jokes, fake moustaches and terrible faux-Mexican accents. It was a real spirit lifter and a welcome distraction.

When the wind filled in again, we were ready and waiting. Slowly at first, *Spirit of Australia* pushed her bow through the deep blue water and we were off again. The wind hole had cost us two places and we were down to third. It was a big setback. We had struggled for days to keep the lead position and now, through a stroke of meteorological bad luck, it had been taken from us. I reminded myself of another valuable South Atlantic lesson – brick walls are good, they remind you how much you want something. I wanted to win this race, now more than ever. This wasn't just any old race, it was *Spirit of Australia*'s big 'comeback' race and we had something to prove.

Our dogged, relentless persistence paid off in the end. Three days from the finish line, we retook the lead and narrowly held off *Qingdao* and *Jamaica Lightning Bolt* to snatch victory. We had done it! We were back and the fleet better know it! Three scoring gate points, plus ten for the race finish, giving us the maximum 13 points for the race. Jackpot! We were ecstatic. Achieving the maximum points for the race sent a clear message to the fleet. Nobody would doubt whether the Pacific had dulled our racing edge now. The secret of our success was not down to a brilliant tactical plan or having better sailors on board. Our winning formula was dogged persistence, overcoming brick walls, shared responsibility and daily communication. So long as we kept that formula the same and kept our performance focus, we were looking like very strong contenders for winning the whole round the world race.

After a day in sunny Panama City, the fleet was mustered and sent through the Panama Canal. This was something I had been looking forward to since the start of the race. The Panama Canal is an engineering marvel, taking ten years to build in the early 20th century, after a failed construction attempt by the French, which cost the lives of 22,000 workers. Motoring into those enormous locks and feeling them fill with water at an astronomical rate beneath the boat is mind-boggling. The speed is the most amazing thing, the equivalent of filling up a standard-size bathtub in five seconds. The whole passage through the canal was an absolute pleasure. It was like an excursion from the race and the crew enjoyed being on board together without the pressure of racing.

The race up to Jamaica from Panama was a 600nm sprint. There was no room for tactical manoeuvring due to the constant wind direction. It was a contest of boat speed, plain and simple. The team that trimmed their sails the best and kept their focus would slowly edge ahead of the rest. Our persistence was paying dividends again, especially at night when everyone was feeling sleepy. On other boats, things slowed down at night – the sail trim was checked less frequently and the helmsmen began to get distracted. Not so with us on board *Spirit of Australia*. We were aware of this general slowdown at night and every evening we had a talk about how important it was to keep our focus during the hours of darkness. We didn't make the boat go any faster, we just didn't slow down. After three days, we had a 5-mile lead to show for it.

The final part of the race was the most intense yacht racing I have ever done. We rounded the eastern end of Jamaica and sailed into a huge wind hole. We were parked up, doing zero knots. The fleet charged up behind us. *Hull & Humber* appeared on the horizon and over the next hour proceeded to sail past us, skirting the edge of the wind hole. Eventually the wind gave out on them as well and they parked up. Over the next six hours, the progress was painfully slow. When we got the boat moving at a steady 2 knots, it was a big achievement. We were within 100m of *Hull & Humber* for the rest of that short race – a slow-motion game of chess where both skippers were glued to their binoculars, keeping tabs on each other's every move. *Hull & Humber* decided to play the wind angles, meaning they sailed further than us, but built up more speed. We opted to take the shortest distance to the line, going much slower. Neither of us would know if we had won until we crossed the line.

The tension was unbearable. Despite my fondness for the *Hull & Humber* crew after our Pacific crossing, I was hoping they would make a mistake and give us the advantage. In the end, we narrowly beat them over the line, taking our second victory of the leg and another ten points for our leader board tally. The scene on deck was one we knew well. Cheering, hugging, congratulations. We had made a clean sweep of this leg from San Francisco, taking the maximum of 23 points.

We had desperately wanted to prove to the fleet that our racing instincts were still intact after the nightmare Pacific crossing.

I think we made our point and we were a big step closer to our overall goal of winning the round the world race.

I was thrilled by our result, but also secretly relieved. I had firmly reintegrated myself into the team and made sure the crew's trust and confidence in me was not misplaced. On the dockside, after the champagne had been sprayed and the photos taken, we had our usual team huddle on the foredeck of the boat. The feeling of joy at our decisive victory was plain to see on the smiling faces of the crew. I told them that the finish of the race – those six hours of slow but intense racing – was a seminal moment of my sailing career. We dug so deep and the persistence was evident in everything we did. Nobody gave up for a second, even when *Hull & Humber* destroyed our lead and overtook us with 11 miles to go. We clawed our way back and won the race, through skill and sheer grit and determination. We had earned this victory and deserved the rewards.

After an enjoyable break from racing in Jamaica and a great prize-giving ceremony, where *Spirit of Australia* took the two yellow winners' pennants, it was time to set off. The next race would take us north to New York. I had done all the usual weather research and had a good plan on how to tackle the weather systems on the race.

The race start in Jamaica was similar to the finish a week ago – a light wind drift-off taking hours and hours. By nightfall, we had cleared the windless area around the island and were racing north at full speed.

As we approached the island chain of the Bahamas, there was a big tactical choice to make. Which passage between the islands to take? It was like a game show with three doors to choose from. Sadly, I chose the wrong one on this occasion and we found ourselves floundering in a wind hole with our arch-rivals *Team Finland*. The rest of the fleet chose a different passage through the islands and sped away from us. There was nothing we could do but watch the scheds and see our position slip further and further away. We weren't too concerned, though. Our strategy for the remainder of the race was to focus only on staying ahead of our nearest rivals, who thankfully were right there with us in the wind hole.

The wind finally returned. We did everything we could to catch up with the front half of the fleet, but to no avail. Their lead was too big and the race wasn't long enough to catch them. We finished a creditable sixth place, our lowest position to date, but we had stayed ahead of *Team Finland*, so any disappointment was short-lived. We were in the end-game period now; we just had to protect our position.

From New York, the fleet raced north again to the town of Sydney in Canada's province of Nova Scotia. It was an 800nm sprint, similar to the race from Panama to Jamaica. The other similarity was the fact that it was my crew on *Spirit of Australia* and my step-crew on *Hull & Humber* battling to be first over the finish line. To complete the feeling of déjà vu, the wind gave out just as we approached the line and we squared off again in a light airs sailing rematch. This time, the crew of *Hull & Humber* triumphed and crossed the line ahead of us. I was happy with our second place and I was extremely pleased for the *Hull & Humber* crew. They had been through so much on this race already – having a man overboard in the South Atlantic, getting rammed on the start line in Cape Town and then losing Piers in the Pacific. It was about time they had some good luck, they deserved this win more than anyone. I heartily congratulated the crew and their skipper, Justin, on the dock when we arrived.

On the overall leader board, we nearly had the whole race wrapped up. Through our persistence and competitive attitude, we were 20 points ahead of second-placed *Team Finland* and provided we didn't finish in the bottom three places on the subsequent races, or break the boat, then our overall victory was more or less assured. We spoke about this as a crew and vowed that we would not let our lead go to our heads or make us slack off. We would focus on winning each individual race, treating each one as a fresh start on a level playing field. If we kept that narrow focus and raced our hardest, then the overall race win would take care of itself.

The next race, from Sydney to Cork on the south coast of Ireland, was our final ocean crossing of the whole race and it was shaping up to be another rough ride. We were warned of icebergs breaking off the glaciers in Greenland and drifting south. The race organisers sensibly added some extra marks to the course, keeping us well south of the danger area. The other concern was the area of sea directly east of Nova Scotia, called the Flemish Cap. This area is renowned for thick fog and was also the setting for the movie *The Perfect Storm*, in which a fishing boat gets destroyed by a colossal wave. The weather was brewing up a deep low-pressure system that we expected would propel us on a fast and furious ride across the North Atlantic.

This prediction was exactly what came to pass. The crossing of the North Atlantic was scheduled to take 14 days; we did it in ten. We were especially driven on this leg. If we crossed the finish line in fourth place or above, we would be in a mathematically unbeatable position for the rest of the race. We could wrap the round the world race up right here.

Halfway through the race, we were pushing hard and were in a solid mid-fleet position, locking horns with *Hull & Humber* once more. Unfortunately, the fitting that holds our spinnaker pole to the mast sheared off. Without this critically important fitting, we couldn't use our powerful spinnakers, letting *Hull & Humber* pull away from us. By the time we had a working jury-rig fix, 12 hours later, it was too late.

The first glimpse we saw of Ireland was the famous Fastnet rock with its iconic lighthouse. We were less than 10 miles from the finish line, pushing hard with our spinnaker up, when suddenly we got a big gust of wind, which made the boat violently slew towards the wind. The spinnaker was inches from the water, still powered up. We just had to hold on until…

BANG!

Our spinnaker exploded under the pressure, torn the whole way down one edge and across the middle.

*Dammit!*

We struggled to pull the sail down and stuff it below deck. Luckily we didn't lose any of it, so it was repairable. I felt sorry for our on-board sailmaker, Kirsty. She had worked so hard maintaining the sails around the world and was probably hoping her work was done for the race. Now it looked like she was going to be spending many more hours hunched over her sewing machine, rather than enjoying the delights of Ireland.

*Sorry, mate.*

We finished a creditable fifth place, narrowly missing out on wrapping up the whole race then and there. If we came last in both of the two remaining races and *Team Finland* came first, they would overtake and beat us. Statistically, it seemed unlikely as we had never finished lower than sixth place, but we weren't about to discount it altogether.

The reception in Cork was typically Irish – very warm and friendly. The local yacht club was awash with supporters and crews' family members. It was the first time many crew had seen their family since leaving Hull, nine months ago. There were tearful reunions aplenty.

For myself, I was looking forward to seeing Lois, who was flying over to Ireland the following day. I had not seen her since she visited me in Singapore. Five long months apart, with only emails and phone conversations in port to sustain our relationship. It had been tough on us. She was worried sick about me in the North Pacific and was just as relieved as I was when we arrived in San Francisco.

She never wavered in her support, always offering me a kind word and some extra motivation when she could tell I was getting tired. She was thousands of miles away, but I couldn't have done it without her. Absence makes the heart grow fonder and it was the thought of our reunion in Ireland that had spurred me on across the Atlantic. When we saw each other at the airport the following day, it was amazing. She looked more beautiful than I remembered and her warm kiss was a sweet indulgence for my chapped lips, which had only felt the touch of salt and wind for the last five months. In that moment, I knew I never wanted to be away from her for that long ever again.

Back in Cape Town, Lois gave me a postcard with a quote by Nelson Mandela on it. *The world is truly round and it seems to start and end with the ones we love.* I had set out at the start of the race with the spirit of adventure burning brightly inside me. Now, it was fading and was replaced with a pleasant yearning to be back in comfortable surroundings, enjoying the company of the woman I loved. I was glad the race was coming to an end. I was ready for it to be over now.

A week of close companionship, great food, long walks and sunshine later, it was time for the fleet to set off again.

The two final races were short and furious. The first was from Cork to Ijmuiden, a port in the Netherlands, close to the famous city of Amsterdam. We sailed up the busy English Channel, passing the familiar headlands we knew from training. It was like being back among old friends. We sailed past Start Point, Portland Bill, the Isle of Wight and the white cliffs of Dover, heading towards the point where we would cross our outbound track, from when we sailed down the Channel at the beginning of the race.

The moment we crossed that track, the round the world crew and I officially became circumnavigators. We had sailed 35,000nm over ten months. The things we had been through together would live with us for ever. It was a special moment and it meant we became part of a very small club of sailing circumnavigators. More people have climbed Mount Everest than have circumnavigated the world under sail.

We had a big celebration on board, toasting our achievement with some fine Scotch whisky. This was the moment we had dreamed about since before the race began. I cast my mind back to seeing the finish of the 07–08 race and my feeling of awe at the crews who had just completed their own circumnavigation. Now we had done it as well. It was the fulfilment of a lifelong dream for many of us and the emotion of the moment was only interrupted when we noticed *Qingdao* on the horizon behind us, gaining quickly. Celebration could wait, we were still racing and we were as driven as ever to win these final two races.

We were in a four-way battle as we approached the Dutch coast. *Spirit of Australia, California, Cape Breton Island* and *Hull & Humber* were driving as hard as we dared under our powerful heavyweight spinnakers. The wind was gusting up, causing us to broach and slew under the pressure of those enormous sails. We were on the edge and there was no holding back. We would never have dared to push this hard earlier in the race, but we knew the boats could be pushed hard with this sail configuration. A poor sail decision a few hours earlier, which was my fault, meant we were in fourth place and struggling to catch up. The crew were racing hard, with gritted teeth and fire in their eyes.

We were going to finish this race at full speed. It didn't matter to us that so long as we crossed the line in any position we would win the overall race, we wanted another podium finish and would be satisfied with nothing less.

Try as we might, we just didn't have the speed to catch the first three boats and we crossed the finish line in fourth place. It didn't take us long to overcome the sense of disappointment at our individual result. *Spirit of Australia* had just won the 09–10 Clipper Round the World Yacht Race. We were mathematically unassailable now! Our quest for overall victory was finished. This moment was the culmination of all our hard work, an accumulation of those moments when we dug a little deeper than our opponents, pushed a little harder, made the heavy sail changes and never gave up. Victory was ours now and nobody could take it away from us.

*Woohoo!* Spirit of Australia, *Number One!!*

It had been a long time coming – we had felt confident of our eventual victory since leaving Canada, but to have it finally confirmed and sealed was a momentous occasion.

When we arrived in the marina, there was an enormous celebration on the dockside. I was handed a bottle of champagne, which I joyously sprayed all over the crew before upending the remains into my mouth! This was our moment and privately, it was *my* moment. I had vowed two years ago that the 09–10 Clipper race was going to be mine.

Now it was.

I was ushered off for a few media interviews and the crew stayed on the boat, celebrating their achievement and revelling in the congratulations from the crews of the other boats. The party went on until the early hours and the numerous rum bottles and beer cans strewn around the deck in the morning were signs of a party that lived up to the occasion.

That night in Ijmuiden was a great celebration, but we were saving ourselves for the final race to Hull and the celebration at the end of the entire race.

The final race was a two-day sprint from Ijmuiden, across the bustling North Sea and into Hull, where a turnout of thousands would line the river to watch the action at the finish and welcome us all home. The race was a tactical one and even though our place atop the podium was assured, we pushed our hardest – this was the last time the crew of *Spirit of Australia* would sail together and we were going to finish with a bang.

The racing was fierce. This was the last time the skippers and crew would pit their skills against each other. The skilled and persistent *Spirit of Australia* crew trimmed our sails perfectly. Our focused helmsmen kept us dead on course and I was playing a tactical game of chess with the other skippers, trying to think two moves ahead. We raced with that same fire and zest we had shown all the way around the world, completely focused on finishing our adventure on a high note with another podium finish.

As with the previous race, we found ourselves in a heated battle with *Cape Breton Island* under heavyweight spinnakers. We were both on the edge, pushing those huge sails to their limit. The wind was strong and we were both charging along at over 12 knots, surfing the small swells at up to 20. Over the course of the race, we had given our spinnakers names, to reflect their personalities. Our tough, heavyweight spinnaker was named Rocky, after the boxer. He had served us well all the way around the world and survived all the punishment we gave him. He was originally crisp and white, but now he was a dull grey and stained blue in some places where he had been dragged under the boat in the Southern Ocean and covered in anti-foul paint. This race was to be his last.

With a screeching tear, Rocky exploded. The sail tore vertically down the main seam and was flogging violently in mid-air. We eased the halyard and dropped him to the deck. He was a sorry sight and would need a long repair by a professional sailmaker. We couldn't do anything for him now, so we bundled him downstairs and stuffed him in his bag. Rocky had finally been KO'd.

*Thanks for everything, champ.*

We pushed on with our smaller sails and by tactically hugging the English coastline, we kept ahead of *Cape Breton Island*, who were further offshore and driving hard with their spinnaker.

As we approached the finish line, in a solid third place, the mood on board was not what you might expect. It was quiet, almost sombre. This was the end. The end of the race, the end of an amazing adventure and the end of this team. The crew worked quietly and thoughtfully. It was right that we end the race this way, on the boat, doing what we do best. Privately, all of us were thinking forward to the reunions with loved ones that would take place tomorrow at the official race finish. For me, it was a mixture of relief and happiness that we had achieved our goal and I would soon be in the arms of my family and beloved Lois, but it was tinged with sadness that this very special team would soon scatter to the winds and the family I had been with for the last ten months would be gone.

As we crossed the line in the dead of night, the celebration was quiet and sincere. The overt cheering and fist pumping from previous race finishes were nowhere to be seen. The crew embraced each other in long, tight hugs, privately celebrating their achievement and their friendship. I stood at the stern of the boat and watched them, not joining in. The pride swelled up from deep inside and I just felt so happy to be alive and right there in that moment. From 40 expectant, nervous faces looking at me on crew allocation day to the crew who stood before me now, each of them transformed for the better as part of this amazing team. I had seen them grow, develop, laugh together, cry together, argue, share dreams, grow closer, perform and succeed together. It had been a great journey of sailing and also a great journey of understanding. In that moment, the vivid pictures of our adventures together flashed before my eyes and, wiping away a tear, I stepped forward and joined the embrace.

We remained outside the River Humber for the next few hours, waiting for the rest of the fleet to cross the finish line, congratulating each of them on the radio as they crossed.

Once the sun had risen and the fleet was mustered, we gathered together and put on a display race up the River Humber. There were no points on offer and the race was purely to entertain the 150,000-strong crowd that had gathered upon the riverbanks to watch us come home. The racing was intense – every skipper knew their families and the TV cameras of the world would be watching, so putting on a good show and crossing that line first was the goal we all had. We tacked our way up the river, the boats ducking and weaving around one another, the crews focused and handling the lines with consummate skill. We raced past the crowds, who cheered and waved flags. We sailed further up the river, around a racing buoy, then turned downwind and aimed for the finish line.

I decided we would put up our spinnaker and cross the line with it billowing in front of us. It was a lot of effort, but the crew worked quickly and we were the only boat to hoist its spinnaker. As we sailed back up the river, the cameras saw a truly awesome sight as we made a close pass of the riverbank, powering along under our most powerful sail. It was the final flourish to our race campaign and an example to the crowd of why we had won the race. While every team was pushing hard, we were prepared to go that little bit further. We crossed the line to the booming blast of the same cannon that had started the race ten months earlier. The colourful crowds gathered on the riverbank swelled and cheered.

It was over.

We didn't have time to celebrate. We were barrelling along at full speed towards a jetty and only had a small space to drop our spinnaker to avoid hitting it. With practised skill, the crew did a picture-perfect spinnaker drop, further impressing the cheering crowds.

The boats were called into the marina one at a time, from last to first place. As the race winners, we were called in last and the cheering of the crowd reached a crescendo as we slipped through the lock and into the marina. Thousands upon thousands of people were lining the dockside – I had never seen anything like it and they were all cheering for us.

I remembered again the inspiring sight of *New York* coming into the Liverpool marina, having won the last race. Now it was our turn to play that part. They were larger than life, now we were.

We turned the final corner of the marina and I parked the boat alongside the others. All the crews were gathered on the deck of their boats and all cheering and clapping us in. My step-crew on *Hull & Humber* were loudest of all. We had won the race and won the respect of the fleet, both equally valuable.

This was the moment I had waited for, dreamed about and been inspired towards for the last two years. Being here had taken more work than I had put into anything in my life previously. It was the culmination of an epic journey and it had changed me for the better in so many ways. I stood there, tall and proud, soaking it all up.

It was the greatest moment of my life.

One by one, the crews were invited up onto the stage to receive their prizes. The same stage we had stood on ten months ago and were introduced to the crowd, before we walked down to our boats to begin the race. The crowds of supporters cheered for their favourite team, with the home boat *Hull & Humber* receiving the biggest cheer.

We were the final team to go up. As our battle song 'Around the world' blared from the speakers, we piled onto the stage, dancing along to the tune. This was our moment in the spotlight. Simon and Andy lifted me up onto their shoulders and the others cheered. I let my restraint go, pumped my fists in the air, threw my head back and shouted! If this was going to be my five minutes of fame, then I'd better make the most of it.

When the cheering died down, the MC asked me if there was anything I would like to say to *my* crew and handed me the microphone. I turned to face the crew, my crew, paused a moment, and said, 'Guys, you have been a fantastic crew. You've been doggedly determined, with the ability to overcome any obstacle. I can't say enough good things about you and it has truly been my pleasure and my privilege to have been your skipper.' It wasn't rehearsed or said for effect. It was sincere, personal and came straight from the heart. I wanted to give each of them a hug right there on stage, but the MC pressed on.

Sir Robin Knox-Johnston presented me with our yellow winners' pennant. It wasn't an ornate thing, just a simple, dyed triangular pennant, about a metre long, with those venerated words: *Clipper Round the World Race 09–10 1st Place Overall* printed on it. I handed it to the crew, who held it up proudly for the crowd and cameras. They knew they had earned it and I knew they deserved it.

Finally, I was handed the crystal Clipper trophy, which I held aloft for the crowd.

For a moment the world moved in slow motion.

I looked to my left at my assembled crew, smiling, waving and cheering for the crowd. That familiar feeling of pride in them swelled within me once more.

I looked past the blooming camera flashbulbs at the massive cheering crowd of friends, family and supporters. My family and Lois were out there somewhere. How would they be feeling right now? Proud, I hoped.

I glanced upwards at the crystal trophy above my head and my smile became even bigger.

*It's yours now, mate. You deserve it.*

After a few more questions and a lot more photographs, we were led off the stage and the prize-giving ceremony came to an end.

Waiting beside the stage for us were our friends and families. Mum, Dad and my sister Joce were all there, as well as some of my extended family and even some friends and old workmates of mine from Australia. There was so much to say to them all, to thank them for their support and to tell them how much I had missed them. I hadn't seen my parents since leaving Geraldton and seeing them again was a very special moment. The look of pride in their eyes was only matched by the look of relief. Their only son was back on land, safe and healthy. I had so much to tell them, but that would have to wait for another time.

Lois was there as well, looking radiant and happy. She knew I was back for good now and a new chapter in our life together was about to start. She had shared the highs and lows of the adventure with me and knew how draining it had been. Our time apart had tested our relationship and put a lot of strain on both of us, but it was over now and we were stronger and closer because of it. I could tell by the way she kissed and held on to me that this day was the beginning of something new and exciting for us.

The crowds had dispersed and the crew had gone away with their families. We would see each other once more, the following morning, before saying our final goodbyes.

I was exhausted. I hadn't slept much since leaving the Netherlands and the emotion of the day had taken its toll. Lois took me back to our hotel room and we sat on the bed and had some room service, talking about the last ten months and what our plans for the immediate future would be. Life was looking pretty good for both of us, we decided.

# EPILOGUE

The following morning, my crew and I organised a final get-together on board *Spirit of Australia* for ourselves, friends and family. The crew were happy and all had a big spring in their step. They were certainly enjoying being back among their families as much as I was. It was the last time we would be on board together, and we knew it. There were going to be some hard goodbyes today. There were families chatting, kids running around the deck and smiles everywhere. I gave a short speech, thanking the families and supporters and reiterating my feelings of pride towards the crew.

Quite unexpectedly, I was presented with a gift from them. A large framed photograph of *Spirit of Australia* charging into Geraldton under full press of sail, taken head-on, with me standing at the stern shouting orders. All the crew had written me a personal message around the outside and signed it. It was a touching and heartfelt gift, which remains my most valued possession to this day.

Then it was time to say goodbye. Some were easy, some were hard. I hoped we would all stay in touch and maybe organise a reunion somewhere down the line, but I knew deep down that this was going to be the last time I saw many of them. The quiet words that were said during long, sometimes tearful embraces strengthened the already close bonds we all shared. One by one, the crew and their families departed.

The 44 life stories, which had become interwoven on that crew allocation day a year ago, were separating again, twisting off in their different directions. I wondered how their experiences of the race would shape their futures.

*How would they shape mine?*

I sat alone on the deck of *Spirit of Australia* and sipped at a cup of tea. The sun was shining and the water was still. I looked out across the marina and reflected on the last two years.

The race was over and *we* had won it. *I* had won it. *Me*, a round the world race winning skipper. It just seemed too surreal to be true, but I had plenty of time to let it sink in.

I thought back to the moment of my inspiration, seeing the 07–08 Clipper race winners *New York* sail triumphantly into port. From that moment on, my life had been dedicated to the single purpose of winning the 09–10 race. I had been through the highest highs and the lowest lows on the journey. I had been tested in ways I never expected and discovered a strength inside myself I never knew I had. It was the best thing I had done with my life, so far.

I thought back to my frantic preparations before the race – interviewing past race skippers, doing psychometric testing, looking critically at my leadership skills and vowing to improve them and become a winning skipper. It felt like a lifetime ago that we were bashing around the English Channel doing our training races and getting the boat ready for the race. These ten months of the race had been the hardest, longest and most intense months of my life. I'd felt the extremes of frustration, anger, fear, disappointment and despondency. There had been some very low moments on the race, but they were few compared to the high points. These ten months had also been the best of my life. The enjoyment of sailing, the thrill of close racing, the laughter and companionship of my crew and the elation of success were more vivid memories in my mind.

I had learned more in the last year than I had in the last 15 years of my life, about people, about myself, about sailing and about the world.

I learned that people have astounding potential and reserves of inner strength they are completely unaware of. It's only by putting themselves in hard, dangerous situations that they come to appreciate these things. Many of the crew, when we left Hull ten months before, were plagued with doubts about their ability to cope with the conditions. Most were probably wondering if this round the world race was really a good idea. Some of them told me stories about their parents or friends telling them not to do it, telling them that it's too dangerous or they wouldn't be able to cope with the pressure. Looking at the crew now, this confident, happy, successful team, those pre-race warnings seem profoundly misguided. Watching the transformation of my crew from the race start to this point, I now firmly believe that nobody else is the authority on our individual potential.

The race was a great study in personalities. Take 18 near-strangers with differing motivations and expectations. Stick them on a cramped, uncomfortable boat for a month with minimal outside contact. Then put them under significant pressure and drive them to perform. It sounds like a twisted reality TV show, but those were the conditions we had been living in and I think everyone had learned a lot from it. Success in the race relied on good teamwork and good teamwork relied on team harmony. There were the inevitable personality clashes, though fewer than you might expect. Through the pressures and trials of the race, we saw everybody on board at their very best and at their very worst. I'd seen a crew member perform touching acts of kindness and support, and then a few days later be in a vile, angry mood over some perceived slight against them. In the end, we had to learn to live with each other and accept the others for who they were, warts and all. There were disagreements, conflicts, arguments and frustrations between crew members but the very fact that we were on a boat and nobody could escape each other forced them to get along, for the sake of team harmony, if not their own. In doing this, I think we all learned to be less judgemental and more accepting of people.

I had learned a lot about myself as well. I was the skipper of the boat, but I was just a normal person like everyone else, with my own strengths and weaknesses, foibles and eccentricities. The crew had come to accept me for the leader I was, good at some things, not so good at others. I had stayed true to myself throughout the race and had recognised the times when I had been at my very best and at my very worst. In the end, I decided I could live with the picture.

The main thing I had proved to myself was that I can do anything if I put my mind to it and persist. From the finish of the previous race two years ago, where I watched the victorious *New York* crew lift the Clipper trophy, to now had been the two hardest years of my life. I had worked tirelessly and never given up on the goal and dream of winning the race myself. Now that dream had come true and the only reason was the fact that I worked hard and never gave up.

Now the race was over, I was going to have to decide where I wanted my life to go next. There were a lot of options out there and a lot of uncertainty, but I wasn't worried about it. So long as I approached the next thing with the same persistence as I approached this race, then I would make a success of that too. I took great inspiration from that quote by US President Calvin Coolidge, which I had printed out and stuck up on the wall of the boat's saloon.

'Nothing in the world can take the place of Persistence.
Talent will not; nothing is more common than unsuccessful men with talent.
Genius will not; unrewarded genius is almost a proverb.
Education will not; the world is full of educated derelicts.
Persistence and determination alone are omnipotent.
The slogan "Press On" has solved and always will solve the problems of the human race.'

Our victory in the race was proof to me of the fundamental, profound truth of this statement. If you have persistence, you can have anything. The rest is just detail. Knowing this has given me the confidence to not be so anxious about the future. Whatever I decide to do, I know I will succeed, because I will always persist.

The ocean is a great teacher of life lessons, for all the things written above would not be possible if we were not tested and pushed by its moods. I remember the calmness and serenity of a blood-orange sunrise over a mirror-smooth sea. I also remember the fury and anger of the waves in that North Pacific hurricane. The ocean takes no prisoners. It waits patiently and bides its time. Then, when we least expect it, it will reach up and take what it wants from us, usually violently, always successfully. Through this, it teaches us respect, and with respect comes humility.

No matter what its mood, the ocean is an implacably hostile place for a human being to be. Without a vessel, we couldn't survive more than a few hours. The yacht itself, with the supplies and the small community on board, is all we have to survive in this hostile world. It's a wonderful feeling of self-sufficiency and it breeds a community spirit that I feel is missing in most big cities. In my mind, the journey of preparing the boat, finding the supplies and then crossing from one piece of land to another is the ultimate human bonding experience, racing or not.

The world is an enormous place and sailing around it gives us a real sense of that size. Unlike aeroplane travel, which transports us very quickly from one static location to another, sailing really gives a sense of crossing the surface of a spherical planet, in orbit around a star in space. That profound feeling of curvature on the horizon and the connection with the elements around us is a reminder that this planet of ours is enormous and how lucky we are to be able to travel and see more of it than any of our ancestors.

I learned a lot about being a skipper. This race was a test of my leadership in every way possible. I didn't get it right all the time and I am not afraid to admit my shortcomings. On the whole, though, I think I did well. I had a happy and very high-performing crew, who had surpassed my every expectation. I gave them responsibility and room to grow. I motivated them and supported them. They were my family for a year and together we achieved something extraordinary.

The most powerful leadership lessons I took away from the race are now indelibly imprinted in my mind. These lessons have changed the way I look at leadership and how I aspire to become a better leader myself.

From my experience of the race, I would humbly submit that the first step to becoming a good leader is to *know yourself*. Look inside yourself and get to know your strengths and your weaknesses. Play to them. The next is to *communicate*. Keep your team updated as often as possible to maintain their motivation. A good leader needs to *be self-aware*. Remember, as a leader, your mood becomes their mood. Next, train and *delegate* as much responsibility as your team are able to handle, when they are ready. To reach their potential, the team must be able to manage without you. Finally, accept that *problems are inevitable*. It's how you deal with them that make you the leader you are.

The race had also taught me a lot about life. Learning the life stories of my crew and hearing them share their hopes, fears, beliefs and dreams with each other made me pause and reflect on my own core values and the way I want to live my life, which I've decided will be to enjoy life, to leave minimal trace on the environment, and generally to affect people's lives in a positive way.

I learned that only the difficult things in life truly bring satisfaction. Achievement is proportional to the struggle needed to get there.

I learned that brick walls are good. We will all hit them in our lives and, moreover, we need to hit them once in a while. They make us stop and think about how much we want what we're chasing. If we want it badly enough, we'll climb over and keep running.

Finally, and most importantly of all, I learned the absolute profound truth in the statement that *persistence and energy conquer all things*.

Fair winds and safe sailing.

Brendan Hall

# THE CREW OF *SPIRIT OF AUSTRALIA*

**Bob Bell**
Thanks for stepping up, you salty DHB, we are all in your debt.

**Mike Hanssen**
Thanks for being there from the very beginning. You are a legend, Hollywood.

**Steve Davis**
Thanks for keeping us forever entertained, Dr Sched.

**Gareth Rees**
Thanks for being the rock of the team.

**Andy Rose**
Thanks for making sure everyone was clipped on, B1!

**Pen Rance**
Thanks for putting your heart and soul into the team.

**Kirsty Whyte**
Thanks for never giving up when we tore our sails.

**John Beveridge**
Thanks for reaching all the things the rest of us couldn't.

**Ian King**
Thanks for Wednesday and keeping the boat systems working.

**Sandra Paulus**
Thanks for making the great videos we will show our grandchildren.

**Dawn Evans**
Thanks for all the poems.

**Josie Sanders**
Thanks for being so good-natured and not screaming all the time.

**Dai Williams**
Thanks for being the dark lord of the helm.

**Kelvin Cope**
Thanks for being the most fearless B1 in the business.

**Felicity Armitage**
Thanks for being 'on a boat', shorty.

**Lyndall Blakeway**
Thanks for your brilliant muffin recipe.

**Paul Meech**
Thanks for the chuckles, brother.

**Jeremy Dawson**
Thanks for getting through the hardest times we had.

**Louise Ward**
Thanks for the crash-gybe melon balls.

**Mike McGill**
Thanks for being the meanest, grizzliest coffee grinder in the southern hemisphere.

**Tania Dolinschek**
Thanks for teaching us about tall ship sailing.

**Mark Popham**
Thanks for taking us over the start line in Geraldton.

**Drew Armstrong**
Thanks for being your funny, irrepressible self.

**Janet Hoskings**
Thanks for packing all those spinnakers so well.

**John Ross**
Thanks for doing whatever needed doing, no matter the conditions.

**Rob Chapman**
Thanks for always tinkering.

**Sean Hefferon**
Thanks for your thoughts on life.

**Rick Palmer**
Thanks for flying the flag proudly.

**Peter Sprott**
Thanks for never giving up and for Victory foods.

**Will Hunt**
Thanks for getting through the worst bits.

**Gorjan Alagic**
Thanks for baking up a storm in the galley.

**Joan Clancy**
Thanks for sorting the medical emergency in the Pacific.

**Barry Howarth**
Thanks for bouncing back, head banger.

**Liz Simons**
Thanks for being a great organiser and light airs helm.

**Rob Collins**
Thanks for making the website and making Pete dye his hair.

**Sarah Boyle**
Thanks for your humour and funny voice.

**John Davies**
Thanks for staying safe in the rough weather.

**Nikki Peace**
Thanks for keeping the mood light and spirits high.

**Kirsten Leslie**
Thanks for looking after everyone.

**Wendy O'Donnell**
Thanks for bringing a lot of fun to the boat.

**Pele Wendt**
Thanks for doing some great filming.

**Lance Costello**
Thanks for your wise advice.

**Liz Hamer-Davies**
Thanks for the great stories and your laugh.

**Jaime Stevens**
Thanks for always laughing and keeping spirits up.

**Simon Jodrell**
Thanks for being energetic and buying everyone drinks.

# APPENDIX

## THE ENTIRE TEXT OF MY TEAM SPIRIT VISION

## THE TEAM SPIRIT VISION

I want this team to become an outstanding sailing team, an enthusiastic and energetic team, where everyone works their hardest, receives respect, strives to improve and is recognised publicly for their contribution.

There are five key elements to my vision:

### Communication

I want good communication to become the defining characteristic of this team. I will put in place systems to ensure communication is open, honest and moves in all directions.

Every day at sea, we will have a lunchtime meeting where the entire team gets together to discuss our progress, upcoming weather, share knowledge and can openly discuss any problems.

Briefings are a way of life for any successful team. We will have briefings before each race leg, so the team has a clear understanding of our strategy and we can reiterate our goals for the leg.

We will have a briefing before any manoeuvre takes place, so everyone is clear on their individual role and mistakes are minimised.

Debriefing is equally important to great communication. After each leg of the race, we will have a debriefing where we discuss our performance, what we did well and what we can improve on next time. We will do this as a team and on a one-to-one basis.

Communication needs to be loud and clear at all times when sailing. For example, when easing a halyard, shout 'halyard easing'. This is absolutely essential at night, and a good practice to get into for any manoeuvre during the day as well.

## Crew integration

Team SPIRIT is a team of 44 people of whom 18 are sailing at any one time. Everybody plays an important part in our team and the success we have will be as a result of the combined energy and support from everybody, whether you're sailing or ashore.

From talking to hundreds of people I have put through training, one of the most common anxieties I hear from leggers is that they feel they won't be included in the core team, or won't be given any roles of importance because of their (particularly later in the race) relative inexperience.

The importance of integrating the leggers into the sailing team, both socially and in their sailing role, as quickly and smoothly as possible is paramount. There will be no exclusion or elitism in Team SPIRIT.

The responsibility for effective integration into the sailing team belongs to the whole team.

I have prepared extensive training material to read and digest before coming on board. My goal is for our leggers to be on average 30% more clued up than those joining the other nine boats. Leggers need to do this pre-leg training to ensure the knowledge gap is minimised and they can quickly slip into at least one sailing role, after a few days of shadowing an expert in that role.

Equally, the experienced core crew and multiple-leggers on board need to invest heavily into coaching, encouraging and building the confidence of the new leggers. If we invest heavily in training and coaching over the first week of any leg, our potential for high performance dramatically increases. To this end, we will have a team prize for the two best trainers on every leg.

Once a legger has completed their leg, their work for the team isn't over. We will come up with a system whereby 'old' leggers stay in close contact with leggers yet to join the boat and pass on all their knowledge and give some coaching on a topic of choice. That knowledge will give confidence, calm anxieties and make sure our leggers come on board with a thorough understanding of the way the boat is run, on both a sailing and domestic level.

## Continuous improvement

I want everyone to be thinking about ways to do things better. In short, if you can see or think of a better way of doing something, then I want you to share it.

On every boat on the last race they came up with their own ways of doing a racing headsail change, gybing the spinnaker and numerous other things. I have taken what I consider to be the best methods from the last race to use as our starting point, but I expect these will evolve as our race progresses and we discover what method gives us the highest performance.

On the high-performing boats in the last race, they strived to improve everything they did. They timed their sail changes and reefing drills, then set about improving on those times. It wasn't just about saving a few minutes. It was a mindset and an attitude that came through in everything they did and it was reflected in their results. I want our team striving for continuous improvement as well.

## A culture of knowledge sharing

In an environment of free and open communication, a real culture of knowledge sharing can grow. Pre-race, I will be assigning everyone some kind of research task on various topics, from sleeping patterns and weather systems to safety equipment and nutrition.

We will have an online space where these reports can be shared and we can begin the open exchange of ideas.

On the race, not only will our daily meetings be a way of exchanging information, they will be a forum where we can discuss ideas, review our progress and share best practice. Again, certain experts will be called upon to present briefings on performance-related topics like advanced trim or a refresher on a piece of safety equipment.

At each stopover, we will have a detailed crew debrief where we can reflect on the leg, review our performance, learn from mistakes, capture the knowledge of our departing leggers and identify ways of improving and make preparations to put them into action on the next leg.

In short, I want us to create an open culture of knowledge sharing and creativity, where the whole team is keen to share their expertise, coach others and generate new ideas to enhance the safety and performance of our boat.

## Effective conflict management

Conflict is unavoidable on a race like this. Every boat has its problems and I expect ours will be no exception. What will make our boat exceptional is how we deal with that conflict.

Conflict isn't something to be shied away from. In fact, issue-based conflict can be a very positive thing. A debate (provided it stays civil) over the best way to hoist the spinnaker is a constructive thing, making everyone consider the issue, identifying all the alternatives and concluding upon the best practice.

Personal issues are trickier, but again, these should not be shied away from. I want our team to adopt the approach of 'lancing the boil'. I don't want anyone being afraid to bring up an issue with somebody (myself included) sooner, not later. The longer you leave a problem to fester in your own mind, the bigger it becomes, compounded by repetition and your own tiredness.

This is something we need to flesh out on one of our team-building sessions, but by race start we will have procedures in place for managing conflict in an effective manner. We will make a set of rules and a list of acceptable and unacceptable behaviours.

90% of the solution to any problem, though, is just communication, communication, communication.

So there you have it, my vision for our team. It's by no means an exhaustive list, but I want those five points – crew integration, continuous improvement, knowledge sharing, conflict management and above all COMMUNICATION – to be the foundation upon which everything we do is built.